"Keep fighting"

Winston

FIGHT FOR YOUR LIFE

WINSTON BENNETT

From Tragedy To Triumph

FIGHT FOR YOUR LIFE

TATE PUBLISHING & *Enterprises*

Published by Tate Publishing & Enterprises, LLC
127 E. Trade Center Terrace | Mustang, Oklahoma 73064 USA
1.888.361.9473 | www.tatepublishing.com

Tate Publishing is committed to excellence in the publishing industry. The company reflects the philosophy established by the founders, based on Psalm 68:11,
"The Lord gave the word and great was the company of those who published it."

Book design copyright © 2011 by Tate Publishing, LLC. All rights reserved.
Cover design by Blake Brasor
Interior design by Sarah Kirchen

Published in the United States of America

ISBN: 978-1-61739-666-3
1. Biography & Autobiography / General   2. Self-Help / General
11.02.11

ACKNOWLEDGMENT

To my deceased mother, Shirley Ann Bennett: I love you with all my heart I can never live up to your Godliness, your love, and your passion. You have shown me the meaning of life by introducing me to the one and only Lord and Savior Jesus Christ.

To my father, Winston George Bennett, Jr.: I appreciate your second to none work ethic and your endless pursuit of joy, and happiness. You are the reason that I have been able to see the world with this game of basketball. And you are the reason that I am coaching today. I love you.

To my wife Peggy Denise Bennett: no one has displayed Christ more than you with your endless forgiveness and love. Words can't begin to describe my love for you. You are my endless love.

To my children Leontay, Princess, Jasmine, Stephanie, and my granddaughter Kassidy: I love you. My hope for you is that you will obey God in all you do, and give him the praise that he deserves.

To my mother-in-law Doris Roberts: You never gave up on me. I love you very much.

To all my relatives: I love you with an everlasting love. Thank you for your love and support.

To coach Ron Lassley: thank you for giving me the fundamentals of the game of basketball.

To the late Jerry Romans: thank you for your development.

To the late Coach Mitchell Ghent: thank you.

To Coach Shedrick Jones: thank you.

To the late coach Lonnie Willoughby: thank you.

To Maurice Payne: thank you for all you did for me at Male High School, and beyond. I owe you everything for putting up with me.

To Coach Joe B. Hall and Lenard Hamilton: thank you for giving me the opportunity to attend the best university on the planet, the University of Kentucky.

To Coach Eddie Sutton: thank you for never giving in or giving up.

To coach Lenny Wilkens and the Cleveland Cavaliers organization: thank you for giving me an opportunity to play on the world stage, called the NBA.

To the Miami Heat organization: thank you.

To Coach Rick Pitino: thank you for giving me the opportunity to coach and mentor young people. Without your faith and confidence in me, I would never have been able to pursue my passion. My prayers are with you and your family.

To Derrick Ramsey and Kentucky State University: thanks for giving me the opportunity to coach young men who had the audacity to go out and win the SIAC Championship.

To Dr. Robert Imhoff and Mid-Continent University: thank you for giving me an opportunity when no one else would.

To Dr. William Mason: thank you for all your help.

To Dr. Larry Orange: thank you for your prayers and friendship.

To all my players, past and present: thank you for your perseverance and dedication to your craft.

To all my teammates from the very beginning: thank you.

To Bishop Michael E. Ford who has seen me at my best and worst, but never judged me: thank you.

To Pastor Anthony E. Walton: thank you for your endless prayers and counseling sessions.

To Tate Publishing: thank you for your faith and courage to bring this work from dream to reality.

To everyone who spoke a word of encouragement, or said a prayer on my behalf: thank you. The only reason why I am able to tell my story is because someone prayed for me, kept me on their mind, and took the time to pray for me.

TABLE OF CONTENTS

PART 2

FOREWORD

The fact that we are physical, spiritual, and emotional beings is pretty much a given. However, within the Church and among the general Christian population it is not understood that we are also "sexual beings." And, that sexual part of our essence was not a mistake or an aberration that resulted from our "fallen nature." God made us that way and consequently our "sexual health" is one of the most important elements of our whole being and natural existence. But, what happens when the sexual part of our being takes over our entire existence. That is called, "sexual addiction!" Now, before you put this book down and conclude that this is just another sad story about an out of control person who's unwilling to take responsibility for their destructive behavior, please read "the tragedy part" of Coach Bennett's story.

Winston Bennett's *Fight for Your Life~ From Tragedy to Triumph!* Is an honest and transparent must read story about the tragic aftermath of Coach Bennett's struggle to gain the ascendancy over some inner demons that have had devastating consequences on his career and family! This is a book about the path of destruction that sexual addiction caused in the life of an accomplished athlete and an aspiring coach. Winston was on the "fast track" to becoming an NBA head coach. But, his destructive and out of control behaviors has short circuited his high aspirations.

I know we tend to call everything an addiction when one engages in any repeated unfavorable behaviors that the "at large" society regards as being unacceptable. We do not talk about basketball and football fanatics as being addicted. We do not assess the insatiable quest for money or the workaholic as an addiction! In fact, our society tolerates certain textures of obsessiveness. But this is not the case with sexual addiction. When a person becomes obsessed with sexual thoughts, feelings or acting out behaviors that affect their health, job, relationships or other parts of their life, that person is said to be "sexually addicted!" In Coach Bennett's case, every phase of his professional and personal life have been negatively impacted by his past compulsive behavior. In this book you will read about a man who was Mr. Kentucky in basketball, a consensus collegiate All American, an NBA star, an assistant coach on a national championship team, and an assistant for the Boston Celtics to the legendary and future Hall of Fame coach, Rick Pitino.

Coach Bennett makes no excuses for his past negative behaviors. He does not use the "cloak of addiction" as a cover and escape from his accountability and lack of integrity during this active addictive phase of his life! He accepts the responsibility for the pain and suffering that his past actions have caused his family and his career. But, in this book, Coach Bennett emphasizes the fact that one current situation does not have to be their permanent destination. That, if there is a way into a situation, there has to be a way out! The "Triumph" part of this treatise focuses on the requisite personal and spiritual strategies necessary to triumph over the darkest side of our human nature. The overriding theme in the book is a will to fight to overcome anything that stands between you and your God given purpose.

No one becomes a true success without faith in God and faith in themselves. There must be a willingness to fight against the "human proclivities" which attempt to deny us our God-given date with destiny.

Winston has always had a "coaching call" on his life. Not just to instruct students in the "pick and roll," the "full court press," and the "two-three defenses" of basketball. But, he has a call to coach others who are vulnerable and susceptible to becoming entangled in such a lifestyle that he's overcoming. I say "overcoming," in the same sense that an alcoholic is never cured, but is said to be in various stages of recovery! Coach Bennett has fought to overcome a plethora of situations that could have robbed him of hope and kept him from his date with destiny. In his sustained recovery track, the basketball and life coach is still fighting to overcome his personal weaknesses! The coach wants people to know there is hope even in a hopeless situation, if they are willing to face their demons, acknowledge the unmanageability of their situation, and to make their recovery an "all consuming passion!" We all need to turn our situations over to a higher power! The forgiving and redemptive power of God is real. However, you must be willing to, "Fight for Your Life!"

—Bishop—Michael E. Ford Sr.

MY APOLOGIES

This book addresses some extremely sensitive issues, and writing it has been one of the most difficult tasks I've ever undertaken. In doing so, I have dug up anew old feelings of remorse, anger, embarrassment, and much, much more. It would be ludicrous to think of writing such a book for any other reason than to show forth the grace and mercy of God in my life. And without His grace and mercy I would not have been able to tell my story, one of tremendous pain, suffering, and personal loss.

As always, I'm aware that it's not enough to say I'm sorry to my family, my children, and all the women and their families whom I have hurt through the years. Every day I live with the agony of realizing that I betrayed the trust of many innocent people, especially my family. It's hard to stomach when people shun you in public because they heard you were a sex addict. Or when they refuse to let their children play with your children because your daddy is a womanizer. So a tremendous apology goes to my wife and children, whom I love dearly. While I will forever be indebted to my family, I will have to continue this race with patience. Of course the other apologies go to the women— women who were looking for love, looking for a friend, a confidant, or looking for a lover. What they found in me, I'm afraid, was little more than a deceiver and a self-centered opportunist.

Please accept the apologies I now offer in a most heartfelt way. I am terribly sorry for all the pain I have caused so many people and will work diligently to become a better me. For me, this is a monumental task and only the Lord Jesus Christ can help me to fulfill it, but He will. He has already done a great work in me, and what I am today is not because of anything that I have done, it has been His grace and mercy.

One of the things that I have learned through all of this is the inevitable consequences of our actions. Every action has a consequence—either good or bad. The consequences of having chosen a promiscuous life-style have come to me in many forms—from the loss of personal possessions and financial security, to the more important loss of reputation and respect. As the Bible says, "*A good name is rather to be chosen than great riches, loving favor rather than silver or gold" (Proverbs 22:1)*. Our name is all we have; someone said it takes a lifetime to build a reputation, and a few seconds to destroy. How right they were.

I was asked by a dear friend why I wanted to go back and drudge up all the horror that had caused me to lose my job, my reputation, and most everything else that I had worked so hard to achieve through many years. "It doesn't make sense," he said. "You are either crazy, or you're asking to be fired again." The truth is I really didn't want to come forward and clean out my closet, the Lord had dealt me this assignment, I have not taken it willingly and I don't expect that everyone will understand. I have made a lot of enemies; some men think I have given up the sacred greed of men, which is to have as many women as one can stand. But someone has to tell our young men that being with one girl is enough, that they don't need multiple sex partners, and that God meant for sex to be a beautiful fulfillment of His love between two married people.

Someone must tell our young ladies that they don't have to give in to every carnal desire to be with multiple men. God will give you the man He wants you to have in due time.

I know that revealing my past is risky, but if my past can help someone have a better future, then the revelation is well worth the risk.

PROLOGUE

I had arrived in the office of the Boston Celtics early that morning, as usual. As an assistant coach of one of the most respected NBA franchises, I was expected to be at the office no later than 6:00 a.m. That was no problem. I was on time that morning, and the other assistant coaches and I set about "breaking down film." For the layman, this was the chore of reviewing videos of games played by opponents and jotting down the plays they used so that we could defend against them. We had a lot to do to get ready for our upcoming games.

A little later, one of the other assistants called me to the phone. "It's Coach Pitino," he said, referring to Rick Pitino, the head coach of the Celtics, the man I had began working for back at the University of Kentucky, the man who had led Kentucky to the national championship in 1996. He was, by now, a legend, for he had successfully rebuilt sports programs at Boston College, Providence, the New York Knicks, and Kentucky. Now he was working to reposition the Celtics and bring them back to glory, and he had chosen me as one of his assistants for that task. How proud I was of that fact!

But I was now troubled by the fact that Coach Pitino was calling me. He never called just to say hello. We all had our assignments, and we were expected to do them. When the team next met, in practice or at an actual game, he would give us any additional assignments. But he never called...unless something was wrong. A lump formed in my throat as I picked up the receiver.

"Hello!" I said, my voice trembling a little.

"Winston," Coach began. "Are you alone in the room?"

"Yes," I answered, now surer than ever that this call was not a good omen. "What is it, coach?"

He didn't waste any time. "Have you been sleeping with a young lady on Brandeis campus?"

My heart fell. So he knew.

My mind raced. This was serious.

What was worse, not long before, Coach Pitino had warned me to stop my philandering? The very same thing had happened at Kentucky, and I had been called into his office there and given a very stern warning. I had survived that time, but this was even more serious. I could sense it somehow.

I paused a little longer while I tried to think of some way to get out of this, but nothing came to mind.

Why had I been so foolish? I wondered. *Why hadn't I been more careful? Why was I forever getting myself into such embarrassing situations?* I had never understood it, but it was the reality of my daily life.

What could I say now to the man who had believed in me and given me such a great opportunity? I found that I couldn't lie to Coach Pitino, so after a long pause, when nothing else came to me, I answered, "Yes, I have."

"Well," he said. "You've just jeopardized our contract to use the facilities of Brandeis University for our practice sessions, and I have no choice but to fire you."

I couldn't believe what I was hearing. In shock, I dropped the phone and ran from the room.

"What's wrong?" Coach Jim O'Brien asked as I passed, but I couldn't bear to tell my good friend that I had just been fired for sexual misconduct. He would know it soon enough—as would everyone else in the whole wide world. In the high-powered world of the NBA, everything was closely scrutinized by the media. My story would quickly heat up the wires.

My heart sank to my feet. I was finished, and I had brought it all upon myself. After only eight months on a job most anyone in my position would have killed for, I had just been fired, and I would have to leave the Celtics organization in disgrace.

In the seconds that followed, my whole life flashed before me. A poor kid from Louisville, Kentucky's, west end, I had clawed my way to the top, fighting hard through several local basketball leagues, and then through high school and college basketball, to become a potential first-round draft pick for the NBA.

As luck would have it, I had been injured early on in NBA play and had to play in Italy for a while before my NBA career could begin in earnest. But then I had been able to play three seasons for the Cleveland Cavaliers before again injuring my knee, an injury that eventually led to an early retirement.

I had been devastated by all of this because I had anticipated a long and fruitful NBA career, but again I refused to let life keep me down. I fought my way back and became a coach—first at the University of Kentucky, where the Wildcats went on to win the NCAA Championship, and now with the famous Boston Celtics. Could it be true that such a promising career was now finished? Could this really be happening?

My wife Peggy and I had both fallen in love with Boston. The city was absolutely gorgeous, with its breathtakingly beautiful harbor. It was somehow the place to be at the moment, the center of academia—with Harvard University, Massachusetts Institute of Technology, and Boston College right there, as well as others (including Brandeis).

Based on my Celtics salary, Peggy and I had only recently purchased a brand new home on the outskirts of Boston and moved our family there from Kentucky. We had been in the house such a short time that we still hadn't completely unpacked and the house still had that new house smell to it.

It was a dream come true. Situated on a hill with a wonderful view, it had five bedrooms, a living room, dining room, office, great room, and fully finished basement. We had loved it so and been so proud of it that we had invited my parents to come and visit us.

Now what? Surely we would lose the house, as well as our new cars. One of them was a black-on-black Mercedes and the other was a new white Ford Expedition. There was no way we could afford them now without the Celtics' salary.

But the house and the cars were only material things; they could be replaced. There were worse consequences to now face. What would I say to Peggy? How would I explain to her what I had done? And would she ever forgive me? She was a fine Christian lady who had forgiven me many times before. Now I would embarrass and hurt her all over again. Could our marriage survive another case of infidelity?

What would I say to my parents, who had sacrificed so much to see me get to where I was at that moment? They were fine Christians, as their parents had been before them. Dad's parents were even preachers. Now my public scandal would bring shame upon the whole family. My parents would be arriving that very day. How could I face them? What could I say?

But most of all, how could I face my God? He had given me many chances to do better, and I had let Him down again.

I had grown up in the church and had been saved as a teenager, but through the years I had seemed to drift in and out of my faith. I believed in God, and I'd never stopped believing in Him. And I wanted to serve Him. I attended church services, read the Bible, and fasted and prayed. Still, I found myself to be too weak to resist the sexual urges that came over me, and I had sinned against God in this way over and over again through the years.

I had often prayed about this problem and sought the prayers of others for it, even getting in prayer lines for deliverance. I had confessed to pastors and sought their help. I had studied the Word of God and tried to use it against my urges, many times vowing never to sin again, only to go right back to it—just like a dog to his vomit.

Each time I succumbed to my urges, they only seemed to get worse.

What was wrong with me? How had it come to this? And was there any hope for me, for my soul, for my marriage, for my career?

At the moment, everything I had worked so hard for seemed to be in ashes. But I was a fighter and had long known that for anything worthwhile, you have to fight, scratch, claw, whatever you have to do to succeed, but never ever give up. Now I would have to fight as never before, if I was to recover and go on to live a normal and productive life. One side of me was clearly positive and wanting to fight, but the other side was clearly opposed to fighting again. Over and over again I had failed at trying to overcome my urges for sexual pleasure. Why should I fight a fight that seemed to be fixed? If I was going to lose anyway, why not give in from the start? No, no, no, I will never ever give up no matter how many times I fail; victory is just around the corner from the next defeat.

PART I

UP, UP, UP...AND THEN DOWN, DOWN, DOWN

A MIRACLE CHILD

Born into a very religious family, I was, in a great sense, a miracle child. After my mother, Shirley Ann Bennett, miscarried her first child, she fell into a deep postpartum depression and despaired of ever having children at all. But she was a praying woman, and God heard her cry. Just three months after that miscarriage, Mom found that she was pregnant again—with me. Needless to say, she was overjoyed with this news.

My father, Winston George Bennett, Jr., was also extremely happy about it. When I was finally born, on February 9, 1965, at Jewish Hospital in Louisville, Kentucky, Dad regularly came to the hospital to visit. He wanted to see my mother, of course, but he spent most of his time watching me. He was *very* proud to have a son.

I was named after my father, who had been named after his father. I thus became Winston George Bennett, III.

Those were difficult times economically. My parents were so poor that they were living in a back room of his parents' home. Dad was making eighty dollars every two weeks, working at Louisville Builders and Supply, but he only worked during the summer. When winter came, he was laid off. That made life very difficult for the young Bennett's, and the family had to survive on food stamps.

Eventually Dad's work became steadier, and we were able to move into our first home (a rented place). It was located at 2819 West Walnut Street in Louisville (now Mohammed Ali Boulevard). I was still too young to remember much about that period of my life.

I do remember the next house we moved into. Located at 3753 Penway Avenue, it was a beautiful little Two-bedroom ranch house with a kitchen, bathroom, living room, and den. Like the famous television series, "The Jefferson's," it looked like the Bennett's were "moving on up," but instead of it being "to the Eastside," we were still on the west side of town. The west end of Louisville was where most of the people of color lived, but just like everywhere else, there were good places and not-so-good places. It was there that most of my adolescent years were passed, and since it was all I knew, I thought it was pretty good.

Our little cottage had its advantages and disadvantages. One of the advantages was there was a lot of love in our house. We did not have much, but one thing we did have was a genuine love for one another. No matter what we went through as a family, I could always remember my mother saying just keep God first and everything will work out all right. In retrospect, everything did work out, because God was keeping us no matter what audacious circumstances we faced.

One of the things I hated about the little house was that it was so infested with cockroaches. At night, when I got up to use the bathroom, I would always meet "the brown brothers," as I came to call them.

We had plenty of them. They would scamper across the floor, as if they had just seen a ghost, and no matter how many we would kill, more of their relatives would show up the next night. The use of Raid® and even a visit from the Orkin Man only seemed to make these creatures multiply more.

The other menace to my world on Penway Avenue was the mice. I hated them with a passion.

Because there were so many roaches and mice in that house, I got in the habit, as a boy, of sleeping with my shoes on. I absolutely never walked across any of the floors of the house without shoes. Looking back, I suppose I wore the shoes for two reasons. (1) I could defend myself better if I had shoes on, and (2) I was always ready to run if I needed to.

Habits die hard. To this day, even if I'm in my own house or in a nice hotel room, I always keep my shoes on (although not for sleeping).

Very early in life (at no more than seven or eight), I decided that I wanted a better life than my parents had. They had more than their parents, so their life wasn't considered to be all that bad, but I somehow had a deep desire to do more and to be more. Seeing my parents struggle was the root cause for my drive and determination to be successful. I could see very early in my life that I could achieve anything I wanted to achieve if I put God first in my life, and I wanted it bad enough to go after it with everything in me. I know a lot of people who want more for themselves, but are not willing to put forth the effort and the determination to make it happen. And then there are people that are doing everything they know how to do, and are still in there own estimation not successful. So what is the barometer of success? Each of us has what he or she feels is their own definition of success, but its God's definition that will ultimately be accomplished in our lives.

I later realized that my parents' lack was not all their fault. They had been raised in a church society where they were taught that if a person was in poverty, it was because it was the Lord's will. If a person was striving for wealth, he was probably a sinner. These beliefs stemmed from a narrow interpretation of biblical passages such as:

> Then Jesus said to His disciples, "I tell you the truth, it is hard for a rich man to enter the kingdom of heaven."
> Matthew 19:23 (NIV)

> "No one can serve two masters. Either he will hate the one and love the other, or he will be devoted to the one and despise the other. You cannot serve both God and Money."
> Matthew 6:24 (NIV)

This misinterpretation of the Bible caused entire generations not to stretch themselves, not to push to expand their education. I just do not believe the Lord has us here on this limitless earth and wants us to be paupers.

The Scripture says,

> Dear friend, I pray that you may enjoy good health and that all may go well with you, even as your soul is getting along well.
> 3 John 2 (NIV)

I know prosperity is not just material; it also deals with the prosperity of our soul and our spirit. A lot of times I get engrossed into more money, a bigger house, and a better car. Some days I feel invigorated when the prospects of achieving these things looks to be in my favor, but just as fast as I am upbeat and positive, my attitude can take a turn for the worse when there seems to be no way I can make my billionaire dreams a reality; those are the times I feel frustrated with life, depressed, stressed, with no way out of the rat race. I am sure you are familiar with the Rat Race, you know when the rat is running on the wheel that continues to go in a circle with no hope of changing, that seems to be the doom and despair that I face on a daily basis. That's not real prosperity; the prosperity the Master talks about is our soul and our spirit being in communion with Him. My generation came up under a new set of teachings. We began to hear that it was okay to strive for perfection in your education and in your career.

> The Scripture says, "A good man leaves an inheritance for his children's children, but a sinner's wealth is stored up for the righteous."
>
> Proverbs 13:22 (NIV)

Then the righteous had better know something about successful investment techniques. That would all come in time. Meanwhile, I at least had the potential for a better future.

After all, the Scripture says,

> But you are a chosen people, a royal priesthood, a holy nation, a people belonging to God, that you may declare the praises of him who called you out of darkness into his wonderful light.
>
> 1 Peter 2:9 (NIV)

I will admit there have been many times that I did not feel as though I was a part of a royal priesthood or a holy nation. How many of us really feel like a special people when we are down deep in the pit of sin? Sin has an appealing factor; if it were not so, Lot's wife would not have looked back when she was told not to, when the cities of Sodom and Gomorrah were being destroyed. Because of sin's addictive nature, she looked back and turned into a pillar of salt. Too often in my battle with unhealthy life choices, I have found myself looking back just like Lot's wife. I would look back to a life of lack and say I can't have more, no one in our family has ever had more; why should I think that I can, but then the Scripture would come to me that I can do all things through Christ that strengthens me. Christ became poor that we might become rich in Him. There is no lack in God; He has the cattle on a thousand hills. The earth is the Lord's and the fullness thereof.

Do you define your life by what you have or don't have? We live in a world that says you must have the biggest house, the nicest car, and the most beautiful spouse. These are all outward things that will pass away, the most important and eternal possession we can have is a relationship with our Savior. He will be the only one that we can turn to in crisis situations.

A "SCAREDY-CAT"

I was such a big "scaredy-cat" growing up. When a storm was coming at night, for example, I always got in bed with my parents and huddled between them for protection. Sometimes, when they didn't want me between them, I would get a blanket and sleep on the floor beside their bed. This must have been quite a nuisance when it interrupted their intimacy. At the time, I couldn't have realized it, but after my own daughter Stephanie began doing the same thing to my wife and I, I learned quickly just what a nuisance it could be.

During this period of my life, there was a television show that also scared me to death. It was called "Fright Night," and it was the spookiest show on TV. A man would appear out of the darkness, and in a deep, graveyard voice, would say, "Lock your doors! Shut your shades!" I would instantly jump up and run to make sure that all the doors in the house were dead bolted, and then I would hurry back and huddle down between Mom and Dad on the couch. For whatever reason I felt that mom and dad was my wall of protection from anything that threatened to hurt or harm me.

Mom tried to get me to have faith in God and not be afraid of anything, but that seemed like a difficult lesson to learn at the time.

Mom would always quote the Scripture,

> There is no fear in love. But perfect love drives out fear, because fear has to do with punishment. The one who fears is not made perfect in love.
>
> 1 John 4:18 (NIV)

She would say just keep loving and your fear will soon subside, just keep on loving. She would also quote the Scripture,

> We live by faith, and not by sight.
>
> 2 Corinthians 5:7 (NIV)

She would say, "What you see will change, it is temporal; but what you don't see, that is eternal, keep your mind on the eternal." All that sounded great, but I still feared the mice, the roaches, and anything else that forced to endanger my person. Of course in retrospect now, I see why mom had such a reverence for God. She knew that God could deliver from anything. He could deliver a marriage, He could deliver your finances, and He could protect you when you felt as though there was no protection. Now I see why she prayed with such fervency, I see why she reverenced the Lord so much. She use to say only what you do for Christ will last, I guess that's why she was constantly doing something to advance the kingdom. She cared little about earthly pleasures; she believed in the scripture that said,

> For where your treasure is, there your heart will be also.
>
> Matthew 6:21 (NIV)

She wanted her treasure to be in heaven and not on this earth.

I would often be awakened in the night by the sounds of Mom's pleas to God for the safety of our household, "I plead the blood of Jesus over my family, over my marriage, over our finances, the blood, the blood." She believed fervently in the power of prayer, and I don't ever remember a single morning when she didn't start her day in communion with God. She would either be praying, reading the Bible, or fasting—or all three. This left an indelible impression upon my young life.

My faith was not nearly as strong as Mom's. With all of her dedication, I wondered why God didn't do something to give her and Dad a better way of life. How could He sit in heaven and watch them struggle so? What kind of God was He anyway? I have learned over the years that God is a God of mercy and grace. He is also an all-knowing God. He knows exactly what we will do if He gave us untold wealth. For some of us, if we had the wealth of Bill Gates or Warren Buffett, God knows in our minds there would be no need for Him. Why would I need God if I had everything that I wanted? God sometimes allows us to struggle to keep us praying and fasting and calling on Him. God is a jealous God; He said I will have no other God before me, not money, not sex, not anything. I alone am God and beside Me there is no other. Still, no matter how great our struggle, Mom continued her prayers. In fact, the more we struggled, the longer she prayed. I wondered if God was hearing.

The point I see now looking back is that God does not always deliver us from our problems. Sometimes He allows our problems to persist; believe it or not, He sometimes allows bad things to happen to good people. Often what's bad to us is an opportunity for God to show off. Most of the time, it's not our problems that He changes; it is usually our attitude toward our problems. It was like the three Hebrew boys in the fiery furnace, who said, if our God does not deliver us, He is well able. Even if He does not change the situation, He is well able. If he does not deliver the way we think he should, His grace is still sufficient.

He is looking for glory out of our lives. How can He get the glory out of me is the question that I constantly ask myself. Often times, we look for the glory, how can I bring myself untold riches and fame, but God wants the glory. It's not that He can't give you riches and fame, He certainly can but He wants to be glorified as the one who gave you all that you have. He wants to make sure that whatever we have doesn't have us. Ultimately He wants us to know we are stewards, what He has given us to enjoy during our lifetimes, are gifts that we have for a very short moment. Enjoy what you have but know it's to be used wisely for His divine purpose.

Mom never had more children, so I remained an only child—which can be very challenging. I had no one to go to when things got rough, and early on I started to passionately rely on music as my closest friend. I would listen to the radio all day long. I enjoyed listening to a great variety of music—from Top-Twenty tunes, to R&B, disco, and hip-hop—and, of course, Gospel. Mom really didn't want me listening to anything *but* Gospel music. She'd been taught that to listen to secular music was a sin. But she didn't interfere when I listened to the other kinds of music.

I didn't only listen; I participated. Setting up old peanut butter canisters or coffee cans, I would beat on them as if they were my drums. I wanted a drum set so badly, but my parents thought I would make too much noise with it. And, of course, they were right.

My favorite artists during that time were Michael Jackson and the Jackson 5. I thought they were fantastic. I loved getting up on Saturday mornings to watch their cartoon. One day Mom bought me an old record player at the Goodwill store, and sometimes, when we would go shopping on Saturdays; Dad would buy me a Jackson 5 album to play on that old record player. Mom would never have bought me secular music, but Dad was a little more lenient in that regard. If mom bought me anything it would be one of the old gospel medleys, Andre Crouch's song (seven-time Grammy Award-winning gospel singer, songwriter, arranger, recording artist, record producer, and pastor) "Soon and Very Soon We are Going to See the King," or his song "The Blood Will Never Lose Its Power." I thought I would die a slow death listening to all this gospel music. Instead when I heard mom lurking and prowling in the hall as if she was the head of the FCC (Federal Communications Commission) about ready to make a grand entrance into my makeshift music studio, I secretly switched from Michael Jackson's, "Dance Machine," to one of moms gospel favorites. That way everyone was happy mom got her gospel and I got my "Thriller."

I remember the day Mom had enough money left over from bill paying and her other shopping at the Goodwill to buy me my first television, a twelve-inch black-and-white set that had been on sale at a mark down price. I couldn't wait to get it home. Having my very own television set was an awesome experience.

Mom knew where to find the greatest bargains, and so the Goodwill store was where we did most of our shopping, even for clothes. She would dress me like a model out of some fashion magazine for just a few dollars. She taught me to be thankful for whatever I had, no matter where it came from and no matter how little it cost. But that wasn't hard. Usually no one noticed that my clothes came from the Goodwill store. Mom had a way of making those psychedelic color schemes fit together and look good.

Do you have the latest and greatest IPod touch; do you have the latest clothing line, or the hot new line of Nike shoes? Our society is so trendy; you don't have to have the latest and greatest to be effective at what you do. Kids are bullied and mocked because they don't have the latest fashion. Adults are trapped into thinking that their lives revolve around getting the latest convertible Corvette. Things do change, trends and fashions change. We are solicited with a borage of persuasive advertising all geared to get us to buy the latest and greatest new gadgetry. It is all an attempt to get your money out of your pocket and into the pockets of the billion dollar companies that make the new products. If you can afford the latest and greatest new gadget that's one thing, but if you are living above your means, take stock, and quit it immediately. Your life will not be defined by your possessions. Your life will be defined for your love of Christ. This is easier said than done, as we all are fighting to have the best life we can have. Go after the good stuff if that is what you want, but know it's not what's important.

ALL MY FAVORITES

One of my favorite toys growing up was a big yellow Tonka truck. My parents always saved up and bought really special things at Christmas time. I would get on that truck and push it everywhere—inside and outside the house. Our gravel drive was perfect for the rough and rugged truck.

I also had a Texaco gasoline truck. You couldn't have a Tonka without a gasoline truck to refuel it. How else could I "hit the road?" I had such a passion for trucks in those days that one of my earliest dreams was to become a truck driver.

Another of my passing desires was to become a police officer. "One Adam 12" was my favorite police show, along with "Dragnet," "Starsky and Hutch," and "The Mod Squad." And what would our world have been like without "Batman and Robin," "Superman," and "Spiderman?" We surely would have been destroyed without them. And I mustn't forget my man "Speed Racer." He was relentless in his fight against crime. Although he wasn't a police officer, he was nevertheless protecting the world.

Like many, I also enjoyed "The Beverly Hillbillies." I thought it was simply awesome how Jed Clampett and his family had been poor for so many years and then had discovered oil on their property, and how this had totally changed their lives. Jed was wonderful. And Ellie Mae...well, I had dreams about her for many years. I guess in many ways I had hoped that we too would be the Clampetts in some respects. I had hoped that something miraculous would happen that would cause us to strike it rich. I had hoped that we could move into our own Beverly Hills mansion with no roaches or mice. I had hoped that by us striking it rich, there would be no arguing over the bills at the end of the week. I fantasized about being rich and all the things it could do for me and my family. It was like being on Fantasy Island with Mr. Roark and Tattoo. Anything was possible; it really felt sensational to image how it would be to not have a care in the world to travel anywhere in the world you wanted to go, to buy anything you wanted to have. The fantasy was great, but after all, it was just a fantasy.

In reality we were as far away from being the Clampetts as one could be. We were more like the 1970's television series "All in the Family" with famed character Archie Bunker and his family. It seemed as if Archie always had his negative comments about everything, he couldn't and wouldn't believe anything unless he saw it with his own eyes, and my dad was a lot like that.

We could have also been characterized as "The Honeymooners" (comedy television series made famous in the 1950's), when Jackie Gleason, who played Ralph Kramden, who was a bus driver, would always come home with some innovative way to rescue his family from the meager lifestyle they were living. He was the poster boy for the next get-rich-quick-scheme that never worked. His wife Alice attempted to warn him about being swayed by these run of the mill schemes but Ralph refused to listen. He was famous for telling his wife Alice, "One of these days...POW! Right in the kisser! One of these days Alice, straight to the Moon!" On those inevitable Fridays when my dad got paid and there was never enough money to go around I am sure he felt like Ralph Kramden,

"POW!!! Shirley (my mother's name) right in the kisser!!! Straight to the Moon."

"Lifestyles of the Rich and Famous" with Robin Leach was another of my favorite TV programs, champagne wishes and caviar dreams. I was always amazed to see how other people lived. Some of them seemed to have everything they could ever desire, while the rest of us struggled just to exist. *Why was this?* I wondered. In time, I would develop an opinion (more on this later).

Although I have always been a rather serious person, I got my share of laughs as a boy from "The Three Stooges"—Larry, Moe, and Curley. "Gilligan's Island" was also one of my favorite comedy shows. As a kid, I tried to imagine what it would be like to be stranded on an island with either Mary Ann or Ginger. It was not an unpleasant thought. And, I decided, I was hoping to one day have the bankroll of Thurston Howell, III. The fantasies of childhood gradually gave way to the realities of life in Louisville's west end.

The most powerful thing about being a kid is the power to image, dream, and pretend. When we become adults we forget the unlimited power of dreaming. Tony Robbins, the famous motivational speaker and author wrote a book called *Unlimited Power*. In his book he spoke with conviction and assurance that if we would start to believe in our own unlimited power nothing would be impossible to us. So there is a reason to keep fighting and to keep dreaming, you have unlimited power. No matter what tsunami has taken over your life, keep dreaming, no matter what losses you are facing, you are still here, the sun keeps rising and your dreams should keep you motivated to strive for more. If you are reading this book it's evident that you are here for a purpose, and there is still work to be done. There are still dreams that you have yet to dream, buildings that have yet to be built, and businesses that have yet to be started. So dream on my friend, dream on.

BASKETBALL BEGINNINGS

On my seventh birthday, I received the greatest gift ever—a Nerf basketball hoop, you know the kind with the little suction cups on the end that with a little spit stuck to the mirror. I had always been tall for my age, so I seemed like a natural match for basketball, and I gravitated toward the game at a very early age.

Dad helped me learn the game of basketball in a most unique way. This was no ordinary dad; my dad was 6'5," four hundred and fifty pounds of human flesh. This man was huge. Can you picture this giant going up against this 5'5," fifty-pound kid? At first, he would just shoot me some "leaners" while lying on his bed. He was a good shot because these leaners had to pass through a four-inch-space over his bedroom door. Dad was a prolific scorer from that position. He was like Jack "Goose" Givens, who scored forty-one points on Duke in the 1978 championship for the Kentucky Wildcats. He was like Darrell Griffith, whose silky smooth jump shot led the Louisville Cardinals to the National Championship in 1980. He was smooth and shot the sock effortlessly.

The ball we used for this makeshift game of basketball had been made of two socks rolled together. When Dad shot the sock ball, I tried to jump up and block him. Day after day, seven days a week, three hundred and sixty five days a year, I would attempt to block the sock. Year after hopeless year I would continue to stretch and reach to block those dreaded socks. It seemed like a feeble attempt. I wasn't good at blocking the socks to start. It took me years to improve my blocking percentage. What was the purpose of all this energy and effort, was my father trying to teach me something, was this the way to success, and is that what he was trying to teach me? No, he was not trying to teach me success, but he was trying to teach me to fail. Yes you heard it right; dad was teaching me the art of failing.

Day after day he would see me attempt to do something he knew I couldn't do, but yet he would keep shooting the sock as if I had the highest odds of blocking it. He knew something that I could not have possibly known. The way to success only comes through the gut-wrenching attempt at failing.

ABC television use to have a program called the wide world of sports. On this program, they use to show a clip of the thrill of victory and the agony of defeat. For the thrill of victory the network would show a successful skier gliding in the air as if he was an eagle with a perfectly safe landing, and then they would show the agony of defeat and how a skier goes burling off a cliff, breaking all sorts of bones in the process. Failure is just like the skier burling over the cliff. It's agonizing, it's dreadful, it's demoralizing, but it's also the only way to success.

It took many failed attempts before I finally learned to defend against my father. It was like we were already in Rupp Arena with over 23,000 fans cheering me on.

Now I had graduated from playing "bed ball" to full-court Nerf basketball inside my room. This was quite a progression, and I went about it very seriously. I had the whole ABA (American Basketball Association) League in there. (The ABA was similar to the NBA, but the ABA had "Dr. J" [Julius Irving] at the time.) The NBA wasn't yet as important for me because we had an ABA team in Louisville that Dad and I followed. They were the Kentucky Colonels with stars like "the A Train" (Artis Gilmore), Dan Issel, Louie Dampier, Rick Mount, and Walt Simons.

I attended one of the Kentucky Colonels games at Freedom Hall and was very excited to see professional basketball players in person. They were giants. I was tall for my age, but these guys were absolutely humongous.

While I was watching the game that night, I saw something fall from the ceiling of Freedom Hall. Whatever it was, it was causing a terrible commotion. Amazingly, it turned out to have been a man at high altitude sneaking across the catwalk, trying to sneak into the game. How he survived that thunderous fall I will never know. The people in the stands were motionless, not believing their eyes. After that rather dramatic start to my first professional game, I began to seriously watch college and pro basketball on television, and from them, to glean all that I could about the game.

Dad, who was a big sports fan, began to ask me when I was very young, "Can you see yourself playing college basketball some day? Can you see yourself playing in the NBA?" He seemed to know something very important that I needed to learn. He knew that, like the Scriptures said, without a vision the people perish.

I would always answer, "Yes, Dad, I can see it," even though I never knew if the dream of playing college or professional basketball would ever actually become a reality for me. As a matter of fact, I really didn't believe it could happen for me at this early age. My dad's comments of "can you see it," just seemed to be too far out, too lofty for me to believe. Even though I wasn't a total believer of my dad's "can you see it," the one thing that I saw very early on was an opportunity to use basketball to make my fantasies a reality. Maybe I really could become a Thurston Howell, III. Maybe it wasn't just a fantasy. I really began to think seriously about what I wanted to accomplish as a basketball player. I knew without a doubt that I wanted to be the best player I could, whatever it took. My parents had taught me the difference between fantasy and reality usually began with hard work. Anything worth having, they would say, is worth working for. My father would tell me if you really want to get good at something the first thing you must do is focus on it, get it in your mind, and then begin to learn the fundamentals. He would say once you have mastered the fundamentals, then you will have a chance at success.

Do you believe you can do extraordinary things, do you have someone in your life like my father asking you the question "can you see it?" If you don't that's ok I will be the one who will coach you to victory. I will be the one who believes that you can even when you think that you can't. You see we all need a coach in our lives that can push us to believe in the impossible. My dad was my coach, I will be your coach, you can do the impossible, you can dream the unthinkable, nothing is impossible for you, why because I believe in you.

Why did my dad seem like the perfect coach, why was he so definite about the power of "can you see it?" He was a believer of "can you see it" because as a youngster growing up he had a dream of "can you see it." He wanted to be a great football player. He grew up in a family of eight sibling's four brothers and four sisters. His upbringing was hard. He grew up in a house that revered God. His parents were always busy taking care of the family. Both his mother and father were often sick. His dad had an enlarged heart and after many years of working at the lumber yard, became stricken with cancer, his mother was chronically ill with high blood pressure, arthritis, and congestive heart failure.

One day a coach from my father's high school, Jeffersonville High, in Indiana took a real interest in him and wanted him to play football. This was the first time that anyone said my dad had the potential to be great at anything. This one person, this coach breathe new life into a lifeless young man. My dad was on cloud nine, he thought that he could accomplish anything after that. With every practice he gave his very best effort living a dream of wanting to be the best football player he could be. Practice after practice, game after game my dad would look in the stands hoping to see his father or mother supporting him. But there would be no one there to support my dad, no one there to yell "go get him son," "work hard son," "don't give up son," "you can do it."

My dad never heard those words from either his mother or father. His parents were either too busy taking care of his brothers and sisters, or too sick to do anything else but survive. By the end of my father's junior year in high school, things had gotten so bad at home that my father chose to quit the team, rather than follow his dream of being a great football player. My father chose to survive rather than follow some far-fetched dream. You see my father was the oldest boy; he had to be the mother and father for his eight siblings as his parents suffered through deadly sicknesses. There was no money coming in the house at this time, so my father got a job working on the highway crew. My father had no choice but to forfeit his dream of being a great football player. Because his past was so vividly sketched in his mind he made a vow to himself that if he ever had a child of his own, he would do all he could to support his dream. He didn't care what sacrifice he had to make, he would give up his own dream to help others live theirs. So "can you see it" was a dream my father had that he could not live out himself, but he could live it out through me pursuing my dream.

Do you have a dream? Can you see it? Let me help you, coach you. I will be your raving fan. I will be the one who will tell you, yes you can. Have you suffered through job loss, have you lost a love one, have you lost your ability to dream? Ok, dust yourself off and let's get back to dreaming.

MY EARLIEST FRIENDS

I had a limited number of friends during my early growing-up period. Luke Curry was my earliest best friend. He lived across the street in the sky blue and white house. Luke had a big brother named Keith and a little brother named Stevie. He also had a younger sister named Michelle. For many years, Luke and I would get together nearly every day to play ball.

Since our parents couldn't afford a real basketball hoop, we developed another substitute—the garbage can. We considered this to be an awesome advancement. There was nothing like it. It was as if we had our own regulation court. It was hard handling the ball on gravel, but that's probably the best way to learn to dribble the basketball. When you dribble on gravel, the ball never comes back up to your hand without many failed attempts, but it is through the failed attempts that you learn how to control your dribble.

As the years passed, our circle of friends grew and our playing partners increased. I always tried to make sure that everyone came to my place and played. That way, I had the home-court advantage. I also realized at an early age that it was better to have fans pulling for you than against you. Our fans were the trees, the birds, and my dog, Lady, a vicious German shepherd.

There was another reason I liked to play at home. Our rule was that wherever the game was played, the person who was at home was the chief referee. Generally speaking, this meant that all the calls went their way. So life on the road was tough. It's much the same today. We love the home-court advantage of having the local referees and the fans on our side, and we hope to get a better call at home than on the road—although this philosophy doesn't always hold true. As a child, I was a fierce competitor, only occasionally giving in and going across the road to play at Luke's house or somewhere else.

A tragic accident happened one day when some of my friends and I were playing at our home. The game was heated, and the ball was bouncing this way and that as each of us tried to score. One of our friends, Andre Yager, went too close to Lady's fence, and she jumped up and bit a big chunk of hair out of his scalp, it was a helter skelter moment. It was the most gruesome sight I had ever seen. Andre stood there screaming bloody murder, and Lady stood there with his hair in her mouth and blood dripping out from around it; it was as if Lady had conquered the enemy. She hated that bouncing ball. It was like she was the enemy of the opposing team. She wasn't letting any enemy play at her house.

After she had savagely bit him, Lady was satisfied and became sedate, calm, almost eerily so (because the dribbling of the ball, which had always annoyed her to no end, finally stopped). How that crazy dog hated the sound of a bouncing ball or a lawn mower! She would go completely berserk at either one. She somehow reminded me of the Malice at the Palace. This was a huge brawl that broke out between the Indiana Pacers and the Detroit Pistons of the NBA. It was November 19, 2004, when Diet Coke was thrown on then Pacers forward Ron Artest while he was laying on the scorer's table. Ron, like Lady, didn't take too much off of anyone so he angrily entered the crowd to demolish anyone who would stand in his way. Of course this was a violation of league policy for a player to leave the court and to go into the stands after a fan. Lady also violated policy when she jumped the fence and savagely bit Andre.

Andre had to be taken to the emergency room to be stitched up, and Lady had to be taken to the dog pound and put to sleep. That was a very difficult day for me. Lady had been my very best friend in the world, and suddenly she was taken from me. I felt very lonely and helpless for a while after she was gone. Lady's death was my first experience of trying to deal with the death of a loved one. It was clear that I had a lot to learn about life.

At that time in my life, I felt that I must never allow anything to get that close to me again, for fear of losing them. Being an only child, I had already felt that I was on an island of my own with no one to relate to. Lady was the one thing that I had that could relate to me. They say that a dog is a man's best friend. Lady certainly was mine. How was I to make it now without Lady? There would be no more casual conversations, no more having home-court advantage with Lady my number one fan, gone in the wind. Lady was not only my number one fan; she was also my security, she was my protector. She would not let anyone get close to me, that she did not know. Lady gave me confidence; before she came into my life, I always felt insufficient, mediocre, and average. I was never good enough. I was always a day late and a dollar short. This never mattered to Lady; all she saw was she had a friend that she had to protect. It was almost as if she could sense my insecurities, my fears, and my inhibitions.

Do you have a friend like Lady, someone who will stand by you when you can't stand for yourself? Friends are very important to have. True friends are hard to find. Choose your friends wisely, we are known by the company we keep. I know a friend who sticks closer than a brother. His name is Jesus.

THE TRIALS OF YOUTH

Things were going well for me in the neighborhood...until a bully we nicknamed Demon intruded. He got his nickname honestly, because he acted like a demon sometimes. If we were playing touch football in the street, sooner or later we could expect Demon to crash the game and insert himself into the line-up. He always had to be the quarterback. When he was on defense, he would push us down on the concrete and cause us to scar our knees. I had hoped at some point Mom or Dad would be looking out the window and would see how Demon would humiliate us kids, but they never did. Maybe they watched and thought we had better let him handle this one on his own. Whatever the case was, I thought to myself that life is a one-way street one that you have to cross yourself; don't expect the cavalry to come and rescue you because guess what, they ain't coming.

The scene reminded me of "Batman and Robin," or even the "Lone Ranger" and "Tonto," except in those episodes whenever "Robin" or "Tonto" would be in a jam, "Batman" would always come and rescue "Robin" or the "Lone Ranger" would always show up for "Tonto;" but where was my help? I learned later on that my help comes from the Lord. Are there times when it feels that the Lord is just not there for you? Do you feel all alone with no one to call on? He said I will be with you; I will never leave you or forsake you, just call on me. I can't say that God always showed up when I called, but I can say He was right on time, not my time, but His. Since the Lord has no timetable, He can show up when He wants. He is not bound by time as we are. He made time; we live in it, and He doesn't. He said, He would not bring anymore on me than I could bear, so if I was getting the beat down by a bully, it must have been something that God was trying to teach me, like how to take a licking and keep on ticking.

Every time Demon came down the street and saw me, he had to do something bad to me. He would take any little money I had (or anything else I had that he wanted). His bullying started me doing sit-ups and push-ups. Since there was no help coming, I thought I have got to start training my body, because one day I am going to stand up to the bully, boy how I wish we would have had P90X back then (P90x is a workout program that promises strength and performance). I could have sculpted my body to defend against the bully. I could not allow what I had to be taken away, especially to someone who did not deserve it. The Scriptures talk about the enemy as someone who comes to steal, kill, and to destroy. In a very real sense, as a youngster I thought this bully was trying to do the same thing, steal, kill, and destroy me. Instead of fighting the bully or the enemy, I would just give over to him.

As I look back over my life, there have been a lot of times were I had allowed the enemy, Satan, to rob me of my joy. I allowed him to steal my commitment to God, and I also allowed him to steal my confidence. It wasn't until I realized that Satan was the bully just like Demon, and the way you beat a bully is to stand up to him. It has taken me a long while to stand up to Satan, but now I make every attempt to stand, after having done all to stand, I stand. I stand on the scripture that tells me I can do all things through Christ who strengthens me, and another scripture says, "If God be for me, who can be against me?" And then my favorite is, if you resist Satan he will flee from you.

In time, Demon started calling me "Herman the Munster," because I was tall and skinny, and I wore "Buddies." "Buddies" were a type of tennis shoe, otherwise known as "concrete busters." If you did not wear Converse Chuck Taylors back then, you had on buddies.

There was nothing quite like a fresh pair of white Converse Chucks. Those were the shoes that Dr. J wore. Dr. J was Michael Jordan before there was a Michael Jordan, or Kobe Bryant, or LeBron James. Again I felt worthless, pointless, never measuring up to what society says I should have or what I should wear or what I should look like. I was too tall, the other kids would make fun of me, my clothes came from the Goodwill and I wore concrete busters. I was a misfit. I had no confidence, my self-esteem was lacking; because of Demon's constant taunts, I became self-conscious about how I looked and developed low self-esteem as I moved toward adolescence. Another thing that contributed to my self-consciousness was my sweaty palms. I was always embarrassed about holding someone's hand. Acne was also a big problem for me about that time. I had so many pimples that I felt like a thousand miles of bumpy road. And Demon made sure he didn't let me forget any of this.

The only positive thing Demon had going for him was the fact that he had two beautiful sisters. They were much older than I. Once in a while, I would get a glimpse of them being picked up by a boyfriend, and I dreamed of someday taking them out on a date. For now, I would have to settle for being the ugly duckling. I can see now that the enemy is constantly trying to steal our self-worth, and our identity to the royal priesthood. One of the ways he claims victory is if we believe the lie that we have no worth. We must counter-act that Accuser by telling him I am of a royal priesthood; I am the son of the King.

As if I needed something else for Demon and other kids to tease me about, they also began tormenting me about how much time I had to spend in church. Christ Temple Church in Louisville was the cornerstone of our family life, and I was expected to be in church several times a week.

Often I could be seen running through the neighborhood toward home trying to reach the house before the streetlights came on. The rule in our house was that if I didn't make it home before the streetlights came on, there would be a whipping waiting for me. The streetlights coming on meant that it was time to go to church, and I had better not make Mom late. I hated the fact I had to be at church so much. I would have rather been at home watching one of my favorite shows, or outside playing with friends, but no we had to go to church. I never could understand what the big deal was. The pastor seemed to be talking about the same thing from the same old book every time we went. He never talked about anything I wanted to discuss; it was always about some man named Jesus.

We actually went to church five times during the week. There was Tuesday night Bible class, Wednesday night prayer meeting, Friday night ministerial meeting, and Sunday school class and morning worship on Sunday mornings, and then we went back for the evening service. A lot of people in the neighborhood called us crazy because we went to church so much, and I periodically resented having to spend so much time there. We were unashamedly called "Jesus Freaks."

During those early years, Bishop Robert L. Little was our pastor. Bishop

Little was a very stern man, and I was afraid of him. I never wanted to do anything that would cause me to have to sit down in his office and face him one on one. That was a scary thought.

As a child, church was no place to be talking or otherwise making noise. On several occasions, I decided that I would have my own little service and not listen to the preacher—only to be confronted by the belt when I got home. After experiencing this a few times, I learned to listen.

So, church continued to be a staple of our lives, and, because of it, I continued to be the brunt of neighborhood jokes.

A note on bullying. Bullying has become an unwelcomed part of our society. If you have not encountered bullying at some part of your life the odds are you will soon. Bullying is particularly dangerous for teens and young adults. The bullying epidemic has pushed its way beyond the bounds of a kid taking another kids lunch money. Now, bullying has reached cyberspace. Bullying is being reenacted through emails, Facebook, and instant messaging. Randy Dotinga and E.J. Mundell of HealthDay wrote an article entitled "For Many Gay Youth, Bullying Exacts a Deadly Toll." In the article it speaks about recent deaths of young people who had taken their own life after being bullied for their beliefs. While I don't advocate the gay and lesbian lifestyle, it certainly doesn't give anyone the right to demean and crucify people for their wayward choices. On Friday October 8th, HealthDay news reported the sudden an impulsive act of suicide by three teens. On September 9th, 2010, Billy Lucas of Greenburg, Indiana, hanged himself after enduring constant bullying. Two weeks later, 13-year-old Asher Brown from suburban Houston shot himself soon after revealing he was gay. On September 22nd, 18- year-old Rutgers University freshman Tyler Clementi wrote a note that he was jumping off a bridge after finding out his intimate relationship with another young man was filmed and distributed on the internet. On September 27th, another 13-year-old, Seth Walsh of California, died after injuries sustained from hanging himself. He too had endured "relentless" bullying. I can't image losing a child over something as simple as bullying. If you as a young person endure the constant taunts of bullying reach out to a wise adult who can help silence the bullying. We as a society cannot continue to stand by and watch our young people lose their lives because of the insults, taunts, and endless ridicule of bully's, let's stop bullying now.

THE LEGACY OF GODLY PARENTS AND GRANDPARENTS

I cannot but thank God for the godly influences that helped to shape my life, particularly church and home, and I cannot over emphasize the influence my parents and grandparents had on me. As a child, of course, I couldn't yet appreciate this.

Mom was the disciplinarian in our household. I often tell people that she kept both Dad and me straight. She was definitely the glue that held us together. She was so fortified in the Word of God that she would never get rattled about anything. By that, I don't mean that she never got upset, or that she never suffered when she passed through hardships. What I mean is that no matter what she faced, she always bounced back. I like the title *Bounce Back,* which was also the title of Coach John Calipari's (Head Men's Basketball Coach for the Kentucky Wildcats) book. We are all looking for a bounce back. None of us go through life without some kind of trouble or challenge. Often times the challenge or weakness will defeat us until we learn we have the power to bounce back.

My mother seemed to have mastered the formula for bouncing back; she also loved to quote the scriptural truth:

> To them God has chosen to make known among the Gentiles the glorious riches of this mystery, which is Christ in you, the hope of glory.
>
> Colossians 1:27 (NIV)

But she didn't just quote the truth, *"Christ in you,"* she lived it out before us every day.

Even though I was Mom's only natural-born child, many young people at the church also called her "Mother." Mother's love of people and her unfailing devotion to God eventually led to her being appointed as assistant pastor at our church, after Michael E. Ford, Sr., became our pastor.

Pastor Ford took over the church after Bishop Little died, and when he did, he told Mom that he had noticed her commitment to God and wanted to make her one of his assistants. Now, after many years, she's still serving in that capacity. Recently, her debilitating rheumatoid arthritis has limited her mobility so that on some days she cannot even get out of bed, but she still fights to serve God and His people. She has been such a great example to all of us.

Mom inherited her faith from her mother, Josephine Lawless, who also learned to put her trust in God and never in man or money.

Mom left a legacy wherever she worked through the years. Among the places she worked were St. Joseph's Hospital (where some University of Louisville housing now stands), and a department store called Ben Snyder's, which was located in the former Big "A" shopping center. She also left a legacy around the community. I remember hearing the story of my mother leaving a lady a big bag of toys for her children when she learned that the lady had just gone through a divorce and had lost everything. I met that lady years later in a meeting with the NCAA Infractions Committee.

My maternal grandmother, Josephine Lawless, or "Mo Mo," as she loved to be called, prayed unwaveringly that Granddaddy Lawless would be saved. He was a very handsome man who loved his cigars and his worldly lifestyle. Because of it, he and my grandmother had been through a lot together, but they had, nevertheless, stayed committed to each other.

I will never forget the summer vacations we had when "Mo Mo" and Granddaddy would take our family to the Smokey Mountains or to Kentucky Lake. There was nothing quite like going on family vacation. While vacations were great, "Mo Mo" wanted one thing and one thing only, and that was for her husband to be saved (saved means to take on Christ's spirit). While it didn't happen overnight, before Granddaddy passed away, "Mo Mo's" prayers were answered. He found the Lord.

"Mo Mo" believed that nothing was more important than God and family. She died a few years ago, and while on her deathbed, she called me to her side. With a raspy voice that I could barely hear (although she was speaking with every ounce of energy she had left), she said, "Son, always keep God first—no matter what, and always stay with your family, and one day God's going to make you a nationally-known speaker." She also predicted that I would someday write a book.

I remember "Mo Mo" as a very upbeat person, who was always giving praise to God—no matter what she was going through at the moment. She always focused on the other person—never on herself. Even on her deathbed, she was concerned with her children and grandchildren and spoke of wanting to make it to church to speak to her Sunday school class one more time.

My father's parents where also God-fearing people. Both Grandfather Bennett and Grandmother Bennett were preachers. How they loved the Lord! Every Saturday, we would go to their house to see how they were doing. They didn't have much, but what they did have they were willing to share with others. We often had Sunday dinner at their house. It was a happy place where the volume was always turned up to the maximum. It was easy to see where Dad had gotten his lion's roar.

My parents were by no means perfect, and what happened most every Friday evening was a proof of that fact. Fridays were usually pretty rough days at the Bennett house.

On Fridays, dad would get paid, and then he would come home and give his check to Mom so that she could pay the bills. The problem was that there was never enough money to go around. Dad never understood why, at the end of Mom's inevitable dissertation about the bills, there never seemed to be any money left over for the things he had wanted to do. Usually this weekly discussion ended in an argument, in which I would always side with Mom.

Dad's a big man, standing about six feet, five inches tall, and weighing more than four hundred pounds. He could talk loud and not even know that he was roaring, on these days he reminded me of Ralph Kramden and Archie Bunker all rolled into one. Every Friday, I could expect to hear his roar about how much money he should have left after tithes had been paid and bills had been addressed.

Mom, who was diligent and exacting in accounting for every penny that came through the house, and had the insurmountable task of explaining to him that he actually had no money left over. She would usually leave these conversations feeling stepped on and unappreciated. She would retreat to the den to pray, and Dad would retreat into his "cave" with his TV and his ever-present gallon of water.

After witnessing many of these shouting episodes, I vowed that I would never talk loudly to my wife. I'm sad to say that I was not able to keep that promise. Although times were tough, I never saw either of my parents hit the other. They loved each other with an everlasting love—something it would take me many years to learn.

Dad was otherwise very affectionate with Mom, often hugging and kissing her in front of me. And, on many occasions, I could hear their bed squeaking and knew that they were making love to each other in their room.

In high school, Dad had been a successful football player, but his parents had never come to see him play. He vowed that if he ever had a child, he would stand by his side and support him in his endeavors, and he has always been true to that promise. When I was playing basketball in middle school and high school, Dad would often pile most of the team into the back of his Dodge pickup truck and take us to and from practices. He loved to be involved with the team. In doing that, he was somehow living out his own dream.

Dad was an extremely hard worker and worked at Louisville Builders and Supply Company for more than twenty years. I often wondered why, every day at four o'clock, when he got home from work, he would take a bath, get something to eat, and then go right to bed to rest a little while. I wondered why he didn't immediately break out the socks. Now that I'm grown and working myself, I understand the energy it takes to keep up with children.

All in all, it was a wonderful heritage, but it would take me years to appreciate that fact.

Parents, take the time to invest in your kids the way my parents invested in me. I know it's much harder to invest now a days with both parents working, and the odds are only one parent is playing the role of both parents. No matter what the case may be you have to find time to invest in your family. For some there family is there company, if that is the case you have to get beyond work life and enjoy your teammates. Nothing breeds team success like team chemistry. Get to know your teammates off the court, find out there likes and dislikes make an investment in friendships and relationships; it will be an investment that will pay a lifetime of dividends.

MY EARLY SCHOOLING

My kindergarten years were spent at Little Bo Peep on Oak Street. A cousin, Robin Hammond, also went there. It took me some time before I learned that she was my cousin. It was not the news I wanted to hear, because I thought she was the most beautiful girl I had ever met. My uncle Peter, only a few days older than me, also attended that same kindergarten.

I loved playtime at Little Bo Peep, because they had the best red blocks I had ever seen. Using them, I would build a fortress, which would inevitably be invaded and destroyed by either Uncle Peter or my neighbor and friend Luke. Interestingly enough, I had also built a fortress in my adult life, which included believing the lie that I could overcome my shortcomings by myself. No one gets to the Promised Land by themselves; it takes help, and lots of it. If you are trying to overcome your problems by yourself, you are doomed to failure. No man is an island in and unto himself, but every man is a part of the continent, meaning that we are all in this together. We all need each other.

One day, Luke and I decided to sneak off and go to the store while the rest of the class was busy playing outside. We thought we were grown up enough to accomplish it.

In order to get to the store, we had to cross Eighteenth Street, a busy intersection. We both made it across the street and to the store, but on the way back, we narrowly avoided disaster.

I went first, looking both ways and then scampering across the street. Luke was next. He looked both ways and thought he saw nothing coming, but by the time he reached the middle of the street, a car was upon him. It didn't actually hit him, but it was so close that we thought he had been hit. We both felt our lives flash before our eyes.

By the time we got back to school, our absence had been detected, and the teacher proceeded to spank our hands. I never knew what was worse—a butt whipping or a hand whipping. When our hands were whipped, it felt as if we had a thousand nettles sticking in them. They were on fire. But when we got such a whipping, it was usually because we needed it.

My early elementary years were spent at Cane Run Elementary School. There we had a teacher named Miss Pleasant, but she was anything but pleasant. I had heard tales of Miss Pleasant wearing some kid's behind out for getting out of line. She was the teacher you didn't want to meet in the hallway. She looked like she lived for the privilege of spanking little children.

Miss Pleasant had a look that said, "See me now, or see me later. But you're going to see me, and when you do, it won't be nice." She stood at least 6'2" and wasn't about to take any "stuff" from any of us. Amazingly, I never got a single spanking from Miss Pleasant during my grade school years.

My favorite games at school were basketball, kickball, and jacks. The competition for these games was fierce, and I hated to lose. If my team lost, I would ask for another game to redeem myself. I simply had to be the champion.

I also loved the food served in the grade school cafeteria; we even made a competition out of our meals at school, to see who had the best lunch. Mom would usually make me take my lunch, so I hardly ever got the chance to experience the delectable cafeteria meals. My lunch consisted of a bologna or peanut butter and jelly sandwich, while those who ate the school lunches were eating big bowls of chili with sweet rolls, obviously this was one game I wasn't winning.

Chili was my favorite with spaghetti. I lived to dunk my peanut butter sandwich into a big steamy bowl of chili.

I also spent part of my elementary years at Schaffner Elementary School. I remember having a recital at Schaffner in my sixth-grade year, in which I was to be the lead singer. This would be my big chance at stardom. I had been practicing all week, and I felt confident and prepared. But then, when I got up in front of the crowd of parents, I suddenly got stage fright and couldn't remember a thing. It was one of the most embarrassing moments in my young life, and one from which I thought I would never recover. Fortunately the music teacher bailed me out by singing a few verses for me. I thought for sure I would be the next Michael Jackson.

The activity I hated most in elementary school was square dancing, although Mr. Wiggington, our gym teacher, loved to make us do it. I felt as though he knew how much I wanted to play basketball, so he made us square dance instead—just because it got under my skin. Besides, I always had those sweaty hands, and the girls didn't like holding them.

The other thing I hated about school was report card time. I would always have the phrase "Winston talks too much in class" written on my card. (In many ways, this was unusual, because I was always a rather quiet person. Apparently I was trying to get attention at school.) It was never a pleasant thing to bring home such a report card to Mom. She would tell me, "Boy, you go to school to learn, not to socialize," and then she would commence to tanning my behind, often with Dad's belt, or she would have me go to the front yard to get a switch so that she could whip me with it. We had two gigantic trees in our front yard that seemed to sprout additional limbs just for this purpose.

Once I made the serious mistake of not coming to Mom when she called. When she started spanking me that time, I felt that my life was in God's hands. I decided to run and hide under the bed. This was the wrong move, because it infuriated her even more. I thought I would never live to tell about that spanking. I felt a little like the apostle Paul when he said he received forty stripes, save one. I felt like I had received forty lashes myself, save none. It was like Mom didn't believe in saving any stripes; she left her whole weaponry on my behind.

I survived, and in later years, learned to appreciate Mom's concern for my young life and its proper formation. She was trying to teach me many important lessons. My entire young life Mom had been persistent in teaching me the oracles of God. She would tell me never lie; it would take me straight to Hell. Never steal; it would take me straight to Hell. Never live your life for anything other than to please God or it would, you guessed it, take me straight to Hell, so a lot of what I did when I was younger, I did to experience Hell. Mom talked so much about it I thought I would do what she was telling me not to do just to see if what she was telling me was true. Well it didn't take long to realize, like the old saying, Mother knows best. If I would have just listened to Mom's sage advice, I could have saved myself a lot of heartache and tears. As I began to mature and take inventory of my life, I could see that everything was working out for my good. The fear of mice, and the Brown brothers, the bullies like Demon; all my fears were molding me into a fabric that relied on God, and not external forces. Even the passing of my German shepherd, Lady, taught me that the only trust and confidence I had, had to be in God and not things. While *things* are nice to have, they can't keep you when you get sick; while *things* are nice to have, they can't save you when your heart is in deep despair; while *things* are nice to have, they can't rescue you when your soul is crying for help; only the Master can do that.

THE FIRST
BASKETBALL LEAGUES

While at Schaffner, I met a classmate named Brian Lassley. His father called our house one day and asked if I would be interested in playing basketball in the Southwest YMCA League. Brian's uncle, Ron Lassley, would coach the team. Dad and I were tremendously excited about this, although neither of us knew where it might lead. As it turned out, I was the only African-American in the league, so I had the privilege of breaking the color barrier for the Southwest YMCA. I felt a little like Willie Mays and Hank Aaron must have felt when they attempted to break into a league that had been segregated for most of its tenure. I felt like Martin Luther King must have felt when he said I have a dream that blacks and whites would commune together.

Playing in this league was a great challenge. Our games were held every Saturday morning at Lassiter Middle School, and I would be so nervous before them that I would be shaking like a leaf, and my stomach would be filled with butterflies. I was the tallest player there, but that didn't matter. I knew nothing about organized basketball, having only played street ball.

In my inaugural season, I remember being in one of those close games where every possession was important. Our team name was the Indiana Zips, and we had a point guard named Curtis Watson. "Captain Curt," as I used to call him, was the little general of the team. He was fearless and fast, and wouldn't take any stuff from anybody; pound for pound, he was the toughest little guy in the league. He would always manage to elude a couple of defenders and throw me the ball in the paint (which was where I would stay throughout my career), and I could usually score a bucket or else get fouled. In this particular game, Curtis went through his legs and behind his back to totally confuse the defense and threw a nice crisp pass to me in the paint. I caught the ball, faked one way and turned the other, and I got fouled, with a chance to go to the foul line and win the game. I remember feeling my heart beating like it was about to explode out of my body. I stepped to the free-throw line shaking like a leaf, it was all on me now, and it was either put up or shut up. I remember going down, bending my knees, and following through on my shot, but the first shot clanked off the rim; well by now, I was feeling like I was going into cardiac arrest, as I only had one free throw left to tie the game. My breathing began to take a misdirection as I gasped for every breath; it was as if I was the only one in the world, standing at the line with the weight of the world on my shoulders. I went down in my knees and followed through on my shot. *Clank.* I had missed again. It was over, the game and my life was over.

The whole team was counting on me to make those free throws so that we might win, but it only finished in disappointment, letdown; a total disaster. As I reminisce over my life, there have been a lot of times were I have been at the free throw line of life with an opportunity to step to the line and make the free throw. Whenever I depend on myself, and think that I am the one, that I am the ruler and the master of my destiny, I miss the free throw, but when I can relax and trust in God whether I make or miss the free throw, then the shot has a great chance of going in. The big thing for me has been to realize I am not in control, God is in control. Yes, I have the responsibility of making the right choices and doing what is right. And yes, I have missed a lot of free throws because I chose to please me or my flesh instead of pleasing the Father. But now I am stepping to the line with confidence that He will lead, guide and direct me in shooting the free throws of life. Now I have confidence that every shot I take has a great chance of going in. But the real point of the matter if the shots don't go in, it's okay because it's all working out for my good.

I can never forget how terrible it felt to let my teammates down. From that point on, Dad would make me shoot a hundred free throws a day. He even entered me in free-throw shooting contests, and my free-throw shooting improved immensely.

I played in a number of other leagues after that. One of them was the Firefighters League. A kid named David French had been dominating the league until then. David was big and strong and looked more like a football player than a basketball player. He was good, and it was a challenge to beat him and his team.

I also played in the Doss Optimist League at Doss High School on Sundays. This was a very competitive league, and most of the guys in it were bigger, stronger, and more experienced than I was. I was still very thin, and was also still learning the game.

Todd Holt was one of the boys on my team. He was about my size, but he was a lot stronger. A couple of the other bigger boys I remember were Chip Watkins and Carry Duncan. They both went on to play for Coach Mudd at Doss High School.

One of the key determinates for my growth as a basketball player was playing against boys who were bigger, stronger and more mature than I was. This caused me to play harder just to compete, and also helped to hone my skills and build my confidence. I have noticed that one of the key determinates in my adult life has been the same way. It seems that God uses the same formula to get us to mature in Him. He seemed to allow us to be put in situations and circumstances that are too much for us to handle. He seems to put us in situations where we lose our most precious loved one, we lose a mate, we lose a child, we lose our house or car, we seem to constantly face situations of loss, but He says when it seems like you are losing, you are really gaining. He seems to give us loved ones only for a set time and season and then He takes them to be with Him when they're assignment is up. That's why He said, let your treasure be in heaven, store not up for yourselves riches that robbers can steal and take away, let your treasure be in heaven. Enjoy what you have while you have it because we only have people and things for a season, and seasons always change.

Change or innovation is constant. There used to be a saying that you can count on three things in life, death, taxes and the third is change. For companies change comes in the form of innovation. Not stagnating, always looking for better ways to improve your product. The same is true of families, organizations and teams; we have to constantly be on the cutting edge of change and innovation. Peter Drucker, the management guru, in his book *The Essential Drucker,* said "purposeful innovation starts with the analysis of opportunities." We must look for opportunities to get better in our families, in our companies, and our teams. Success is often hidden in the problems of change.

THAT DREADED
READING HOMEWORK

My joy on the court was often interrupted by Mom's insistence that I complete my homework. We had a number of rules at our house, but the main two were: (1) "You will always go to church," and (2) "There will be no extracurricular activities unless and until you finish your homework." Many times I could be found at the kitchen table after school, studying. Mom was such a stickler for education, she would be right there tutoring me.

My most difficult task was learning to read. When I was in the fifth and sixth grades, I was still reading on a third-grade level. I hated reading, but that would have to change as Mom began taking away my playtime to make me study. She always taught me that I could do whatever I put my mind to, so she believed I wasn't applying myself to read. She was probably right.

What a torment! There I was at the kitchen table doing homework, while my friends played ball in our yard. Mom liked it that way. She wanted me to see the other kids having a good time, while I was struggling to learn. She hoped this would motivate me. Mostly, it served to frustrate me further.

But we kept at it. I didn't have any other choice. When I wanted to give up, Mom wouldn't let me. She knew that learning to read could open up a whole new world for me. So she eventually hired a high school student who lived nearby, named Angie Cook. Angie began tutoring me in reading. Every day I began walking the green mile to Angie's house. I made it seemed like a death march. I hated it. I had no plans on becoming the next Shakespeare, who said, "to thine own self be true;" I was trying to be the next Dr. J. I would much rather have been playing hoops. But Angie (on Mom's orders) was relentless, she would tell me you don't have to be Shakespeare but you do have to learn to read. She would drill me over and over and over again. I eventually got the message—that it was better to do it right the first time. After much practice, my reading skills improved.

Of course, I could not appreciate it at the time, but this breakthrough in reading was one of the most powerful elements in deciding my future. If I had not learned to read, I certainly would not have been accepted into any college and would not even have finished high school. I could never have become a college-level basketball player, a NBA player, or a coach. Mom knew exactly what she was doing.

One of the biggest travesties I see as a college basketball coach today is the prostitution of athletes. Athletes should not be able to pass through school with no reading, writing, and arithmetic skills. No student athlete should be allowed to proceed to the college level without these fundamental skills. Allowing our student athletes to proceed through the education system without the proper foundation of education is a crime that should be punishable by imprisonment. Without these skills to aid our young people, we are crippling them for life.

MIDDLE SCHOOL

My middle-school years were spent at TMS (Traditional Middle School). "Traditional" schooling was a concept that stressed getting back to the basics of studying and doing homework. Mom absolutely loved this concept. It concerned her that students were not being required to do homework anymore, and she wondered just what was being taught in school. "Knowledge is power," she was fond of saying. "If you can combine what you learn at church with what you learn at school, you'll be successful."

Mom not only worked with me; she worked with the school. She was on the PTA board and attended all parent-teacher conferences. If there was anything going on at school, she was in on it. She was determined to support me academically, while my father was there for me athletically.

It was about this time that I started taking a serious interest in girls. Kim Coleman, who was short, but very attractive, was one of my earliest infatuations. Others would soon follow.

Mr. Eddy Lerding was my most-feared teacher in middle school. I hated diagramming sentences, and he loved to make us do it. It seems like only yesterday that I was sitting in his class struggling with those dreaded diagrams.

If it wasn't diagramming sentences, it was Greek Mythology. Mr. Lerding made us feel as if he were living in the wrong dispensation. He seemed to relate to Diana and Zeus better than he did to his students. I liken Mr. Lerding to my use of sex as a means of medicating my pain and escaping reality. It's easy to run to something that seems to be always there for you, but in reality is destroying you. Sex for me was just like Zeus, and Diana in Greek Mythology, they seem real when in reality they were a myth. Sex was the big lie, but to me it stood for truth. It helped me cope with the fears and anxiety that I constantly felt about life. Each year, I wondered if I would make it to the next year. My fear was that something would happen to me. I did not know what, but it was a constant fear that I would not live to see the next year. Every morning, you could wake up and read about a young person who had been killed, or was in a car accident. I figured this would be my plot in life.

My basketball coach was a totally different story; he lived life to the fullest. Coach Mitchell Ghent was a great guy; he was positive, always fun to be around. He seemed to have a zest for life, and he thought a lot of his players.

One of our best players was a boy named Peter Wentworth. Peter was big and strong, one of those boys you can look at and know that they'll play big-time football in college. He was a great athlete, but he was often injured.

I was doing well too. During my eighth-grade year, a photo appeared in the *Courier Journal,* our principal Louisville newspaper. It was labeled "The Up-and-Coming Blue Chippers." There I was sitting between Manuel Forest (who played high school basketball for Moore High School and college basketball for the University of Louisville), and Alphonso Miller (who played high school basketball for the Ballard Bruins and college basketball for the University of Vanderbilt). Manuel Forest was a "phenom" who averaged close to thirty points a game in high school and blocked every opposing shot. He was unstoppable and was thought to be a "can't-miss" college prospect. Unfortunately, he had to undergo a couple of major knee surgeries, and that seriously degraded his game in college. Alphonzo Miller, however, went on to have a fine career at Vanderbilt University. Also mentioned in the same article were phenoms like 7'2" inch Ralph Sampson from Harrisonburg, Virignia, 7'1" Sam Bowie from Lebanon, Pennsylvania, 6'8" Clark Kellogg from Cleveland, Ohio, and 6'9" Sidney Green of New York were all mentioned as can't miss top college recruits in 1979. I wondered what the future might hold for me.

LEARNING THE ART
OF FISHING

One of the most pleasurable things Dad and I did together through the years was to go fishing. He started me out fishing when I was very young, and we usually frequented one of three lakes that were within a half-hour's driving distance from home: Bill's Lake in New Albany, Indiana, Riggs Lake in Jefferson-town, and La Clara's Lake in Jefferson County. At each of these, we had to pay a small entrance fee, but we always had the hope of catching our limit of fish. Most times we didn't, but the fishing was still fun and relaxing.

I fell so in love with fishing that I could not wait for Dad to take me to the lake. The drive to the lakes was a short distance, but once we had set out for one of them, it seemed we would never get there. The anticipation was like the old Heinz Ketchup commercial that said, "Anticipation keeps making me wait."

Fishing, I found, also taught me many lessons that were useful for everyday life. I had to learn to leave my pole steady in the water, which meant I had to be patient. My dad would tell me if you are going to be a good fisherman, you have to be patient. You can't throw your line in and then pull it back in, in a few seconds the line must stay in the water until you get the big strike.

He also said make sure that you have bait on your hook; a fish is not going to bite a hook with no bait. If I did the right thing, I could be sure the big one would eventually come, and I could try to land him. There were always fish to catch—if I just knew what I was fishing for and what they would bite. Fishing was not too unlike living for God. My father would always tell me if you do what you are supposed to do, then God would do what he is suppose to do. Although I wasn't so sure about his observation, I continued to listen to his wisdom. By looking at my parent's life, I did not know if I would follow that advice or not. I knew that the Scriptures were true, but sometimes it seemed as if God didn't care whether a person was rich or poor. The poor he left poor and the rich stayed rich, and there was no changing the hand you were dealt or so it seemed.

We fished for carp and catfish in those early days, and I loved the fight they gave me. They truly knew how to fight for their lives, running and running some more, until they eventually grew tired. Then, I could reel them in without much of a fight.

Some carp surprised me though. I had them hooked and thought they were worn out, and I was just about ready to net them, when suddenly they gave life one more run and somehow escaped the hook in the process. I wanted to be like that. I wanted to be one of the ones who never gave up on life. I wanted to run for my life. I wanted to get everything the Lord had for me. But then I felt like there were times that the Lord had nothing for me. I felt as if I was in the lion's den, about ready to get eaten alive. I felt like the biblical character Joseph who had been sold in to slavery by his brothers and left for dead. But God. But God who is rich in mercy, who is able to deliver in any situation, showed up right on time and delivered me.

My biggest catch was a twenty-four-pound carp caught at Bill's Lake. I was very excited as I reeled him in. There's nothing quite like the thrill of catching "the big one." The most important thing about catching the big one is setting the hook. When the big one bends your pole, you have to jerk the pole to sit the hook in its mouth so the fish will not get away. In life, when we find out why we are here on this earth, we have got to sit the hook in life so life does not slip away without us getting all God has for us. I see a lot of people in life who refuse to sit the hook, either their fears or the need to please themselves have stolen their opportunity to sit the hook in life. When you know why you are here, sit the hook into your destiny and purpose so it does not get away. Don't be lured into the baby fish that leave you unsatisfied and feeling worthless, and unworthy. Go for the big boys, go for the big catch; that's were God dwells, in the big fish and in the deep waters.

I have some very humorous memories from these fishing trips. For instance, on one particular trip, Dad and I, Lenard Chandler (his best friend), and my uncle Kenny and his brother-in-law (also named Kenny) were at Rigg's Lake together. Uncle Kenny had just reeled in a big carp, and he was very excited. The fish had not been biting well that day (because it was hot and muggy outside, and, under those conditions, fish often seek deeper waters where it's cooler). After Uncle Kenny caught the carp, he got into a playful mood and began looking for someone in the group on whom he could play a practical joke.

It just so happened that the other Kenny had fallen asleep in the car with the windows rolled down, and that gave Uncle Kenny his opportunity. He took his catch and kissed it to the other Kenny's lips. When the rest of us saw what he was doing, we began laughing ourselves into hysteria, Kenny woke up, licked his lips and said, "Something smells and tastes fishy. What's going on?" At this, we all broke out laughing again, and he realized that he'd been the target of a prank by his brother-in-law.

But the other Kenny wasn't laughing. Getting out of the car in an apparent rage, he chased Uncle Kenny around the lake. As it turned out, it was all in fun.

On another fishing trip, we were at Bill's Lake with a whole host of friends. It was late, about midnight, when my friend Gary Hardin fell asleep. This time, another prankster named Kevin Johnson was on the scene. He took some lighter fluid and poured it all over Gary's boots. Then he took a match and lit it. When we all saw it, we began to shout, "Gary! Gary! Your boots are on fire!" He woke up in a panic and went straight for the water, jumping into the lake to douse the flames. We were all "fit to be tied." We laughed so hard our stomachs hurt. Fortunately, Gary was unharmed.

Yes, fishing was a great way to relax and have fun, and it taught me a lot about life. One important lesson that was loud and clear on these trips was, it's best to stay awake and be alert. If you are sleep you can't see opportunities when they present themselves. Be alert search for opportunities keep your eyes open. I don't care what the past has been for you, stay alert. Be in a constant state of belief. You lost your business so what, you will build a better business. You been through a nasty divorce okay it happens, let's get back in the game. Great victories happen to teams who stay in the game and keep fighting, keep scratching and clawing.

Donald Trump, the real estate magnate, has been a shining example of someone who went through tremendous financial loss but continued to stay in the game. Here is a man worth billions due to his art of making a deal. The Donald is now in to gaming, sports, and entertainment. Aside from the *Apprentice,* Trump and NBC are partners in the ownership and broadcast rights of three of the largest beauty competitions in the world. I am not saying you have to be the "Donald" to have skyscraper dreams, but I am saying you have to continue to seek opportunities, be alert and keep your eyes open.

THE HIGH SCHOOL YEARS

Because I had done well at Traditional Middle School, Mom decided to send me to another traditional school for my high school education. It was then known as Male Traditional School (now Louisville Male High School). It had been for many years an all-male school, but that changed before I got there. It was now a co-ed institution, but the name had remained Male.

I had been slated to attend Butler High School that year (because busing was beginning to be utilized to fully integrate the schools), but Mom wasn't having any part of it. Many families, both blacks and whites, were against the idea of busing. White families didn't want their children bused to the inner-city schools, and black families didn't want their children bused to the suburbs.

When busing was first instituted, tensions ran high for a while. One day Dad and I and Uncle Jerry, his brother, were headed toward Rigg's Lake to go fishing, when we spotted some men checking cars, yanking people out of them, and beating them, we immediately made a fast u-turn and headed back to the west end. On the way, we decided we didn't want this incident to spoil our fishing trip, so we headed out of town in another direction toward Bill's Lake.

Now, Mom was not about to see me bused to some other end of town. She chose my high school, and that was a fortunate fact. She sent me to Male Traditional High School. Male was not only recommended highly because it was a traditional school, which meant they believed in kids having homework, but it was also a basketball factory. The Bulldogs were known for turning out basketball legends every year. It was a great honor for me to attend a school so rich in academic and sports tradition. Darrell Griffith, who attended Male in the early 1970s, was the school's all-time leading scorer. Bobby Turner was also a part of that rich tradition. Wade Houston, father of former NBA star Allan Houston, was the coach at Male during the Griffith and Turner era.

"Griff" was the first player I ever saw do a 360 dunk in a game. He was a crowd pleaser, and I wanted to play just like him. Although that didn't prove possible, since we were so different. "Griff had a 48-inch vertical leap, I had about a 28-inch vertical leap, I wasn't going to be doing any 360-degree dunks anytime soon. "Griff was also a long distance shooter, leading the NBA in three point percentage when he played; I was an inside player playing near the rim.

I remember seeing "Griff" on the news, after he had been drafted by the Utah Jazz. He had gone out and bought his parents a maroon Cadillac. I thought to myself, *Lord, I would surely like to do that for my parents some day.*

My first two years at Male, Lonnie Willoughby was our coach. He was about 6'7"inches tall; he was a very intense coach who loved to win. I could remember, as a middle school student, having seen Coach Willoughby in action when I had come to visit Male High School and watch a practice. He had guys like Ray Zuberer who averaged 17.8 points per game and Rick Avare (who later became the business partner to Rick Pitino) who averaged 14.4 points per game diving on the floor after loose balls and going after blood.

My first two years at Male playing for Coach Lonnie Willoughby were trying times. We were a team that was young and inexperienced. We had lost two great players the year before to graduation in Ray Zuberer and Rick Avare. We were now being lead by Ronnie Sims, the smooth shooting guard. We also had Donald "Action" Jackson. Donald was a guy with a lot of talent but only showed flashes of brilliance; he would tease you with things he could do on the court. We also had our big man in the middle, Lanier Hobbs. Lanier was a big man that could step out and shoot the median-range jump shot. Joe Ross was our very athletic guard. Then of course we had the general, Steve Sergeant, our point guard who was in charge of running the show for our team. Steve was an excellent playmaker, with a nice shooting touch. He got a lot of assists by throwing the ball to me, and he made me a better player—for which I thank him.

Steve sacrificed a lot of his game for the good of the team. Most kids today are not willing to do that. Everybody wants the headlines, the fame, and the glory. Steve just wanted to win. We had epic battles against Moore High School who had the prodigy Manuel Forest, Ballard who had Alphonso Miller, Central High School had Detrick Chandler and Neil Robinson, St. Xavier had Tyrone Harbin, and Manual had Chris West, Doniel Fitzgerald, and Stanley Jackson. The top teams in the seventh region year in and year out were Moore High School, Central High School, Manuel High School, Ballard High School, and Jeffersontown High School. The seventh region has always been loaded. After playing two years under Coach Willoughby, he retired.

Maurice Payne was called in to coach us my junior and senior years. His friends called him "Mouse." Coach Payne came over from Thomas Jefferson High School, where he had been very successful, and he brought with him one of the best players in the state, Bryant Woodford.

"Wolf," as I called him, was a lefty with a deadeye shooting touch. He would also get rebounds and take the ball off the dribble coast to coast and score on an opponent at the other end. He was a relentless worker, never tiring. He could run all day long.

Yes, it was a privilege to be playing at Male Traditional High School.

About this time, another interest began to compete with basketball for my attention.

MY FIRST SEXUAL ENCOUNTER

I had my first sexual experience when I was just fifteen years old and a freshman in high school. The girl involved was a senior at Butler High School, and we had met and talked at sporting events. A star basketball player on the Butler girls' team, she had recently won a scholarship to play at the University of Louisville the following season.

She was sexually active and somehow our conversation led to the fact that we found each other attractive. She agreed to come to our house one day while my parents were at work so that we could have sex together.

Now that she was here, I wasn't sure how I felt. I seemed to be a mix of raging emotions—good and bad alike.

As a developing teenager, I had begun having thoughts of sex quite some time before this, and it had grown stronger and stronger with the passing of time. The fact that boys around the neighborhood and at school talked incessantly about sex didn't help me.

But, at the same time, I knew what the Bible said about these things. It had been drilled into me, along with the fact that

I should wait until marriage to have sex. We had been taught scriptural passages such as:

> Flee sexual immorality. All other sins a man commits are outside his body, but he who sins sexually sins against his own body. Do you not know that your body is a temple of the Holy Spirit, who is in you, whom you have received from God? You are not your own; you were bought at a price. Therefore honor God with your body.
>
> 1 Corinthians 6:18–20 (NIV)

I had a big decision to make.

Perhaps more importantly, a year or so before this, I had responded to an invitation given at the altar of our church after a message of salvation was delivered. There at the altar, I repented of my sins and invited Jesus into my heart. We called this being "saved." It signified a change of heart and life. We were very fond of the passage:

> Therefore, if anyone is in Christ, he is a new creation; the old has gone, the new has come!
>
> 2 Corinthians 5:17 (NIV)

Is your body any different? No, the passage is talking about the new heart and spirit you have to serve God, where previously you had no power against the enemy so you served him passionately, without reservation.

The scripture says,

> "I will give you a new heart and put a new spirit in you; I will remove from you your heart of stone and give you a heart of flesh."
>
> Ezekiel 36:26 (NIV)

This passage talks about taking our old heart of the flesh, that is only concerned with fleshly matters and giving us a new heart that is concerned with spiritual matters.

The scriptures also say,

> "This is the covenant I will make with the house of Israel after that time," declares the Lord. "I will put my law in their minds and write it on their minds and write it on their hearts. I will be their God, and they will be my people.
>
> Jeremiah 31:33 (NIV)

I believed fully in this promise of being a "new creation," and had confessed before all that "old things [had] passed away" and that "all things [had] become new," but when it came to sex, I found that it wasn't all that cut and dry. "New creation" or not, my body craved sex. This temptation was strong. I realize now that just because you are a new creature in Christ does not mean that the desire for the old lifestyle goes away all at once.

If I had known that my attraction to sex would become an obsession that would grow until it haunted my mind and spirit every moment of every day, I surely would have thought twice about performing the first sexual act that day. But I couldn't know all that. All I could think about was how pleasurable it would be at that moment.

For me, having sex seemed every bit as great an adventure as going to another planet. How could I pass up this opportunity? How could I have known that sex would promise me adventure, yet the adventure would turn into horror; how could I have known that it promised control, yet it controlled me; how could I have known it promised fulfillment, yet fulfillment is the least of its accomplishments. It masks itself in the pleasure principle when it only gives pain, anguish, and emptiness. Sex is a failed promise, an empty plea; the only fulfillment this life has to offer is a love affair with Jesus Christ.

But would God strike me dead for sexual promiscuity? I decided that I could go to church and repent, as I had seen others do. They seemed to receive forgiveness. Surely I could too.

In reality, my decision had already been made before the girl arrived that day. I had tried the case like a knowledgeable defense attorney going to trial, and my raging hormones were outweighing the voice of reason. This was a combination of the voice of my mother, the voice of my pastor, and the voice of my own conscience. The voices to do the right thing had put up a grand fight, but in the end, my hormones had overruled them. And now, as my mind raced and my heart pounded, there seemed to be no turning back. I couldn't just tell the girl that I changed my mind and send her home. No, I had to man up and go through with this. Or, so I reasoned conveniently.

She lay comfortably down on the bed as if she had been here before, and said to me in her most provocative and seductive tone, "Winston, can you please go get the rubber out of my bag." I had no idea what a "rubber" was, so I looked incessantly through her bag for the longest time, only to return and tell her, "I didn't see any 'rubber." She almost instantly got up and retrieved the prophylactic she wanted me to use, and we proceeded to consummate the act.

Later, I couldn't even remember whether or not this first sexual encounter had been a particularly exciting or satisfying experience or not. I did know that I felt guilty and ashamed and defeated. I had known what was right, but I had chosen what was wrong.

That evening, I tried to avoid Mom. She had a sixth sense and always seemed to know when I was doing something I shouldn't have been doing. On this occasion, I was able to elude her detection.

That Sunday, when the opportunity was given for those who wanted to go to the altar to pray, I got up hurriedly from my seat and went, as if I had been waiting anxiously for this very moment. Altar workers passed among us and asked each one of us what we needed God to do for us, and then they prayed with us. I had to say that I had sinned against God by having sex with a girl and that I needed God's forgiveness.

Making that confession was so embarrassing for me, but I had to do it. I simply could not lie to the servants of the Lord. They prayed for me, telling me that the important thing was that I never commit this sin again. I felt so bad that I was ready to make the commitment to never have sex again, or at least not until I was married.

But, whether the experience had been enjoyable or not, it served to stir my appetite. If I had been tempted before, it had been nothing compared to the temptation that came to me now. Day and night, my mind was flooded with it, and it consumed my thoughts. That first sexual experience was just the beginning of many sexual escapades that summer.

This hardly seemed possible for such a shy and retiring boy, but as I grew older, I began to outgrow the shyness and self-doubt of my childhood. Girls started noticing me. This was something totally new to me, and I began to gravitate toward this very welcome attention. Before this welcomed attention I would always hear the old jingle "Winston tastes good like a cigarette should, from anyone who heard my name was Winston. Now the girls were saying Winston tastes good for another reason and it wasn't basketball. Another element in this change was the fact that I was making a name for myself on the basketball court. This further ingratiated me with the girls even more.

All of a sudden I was going from being Mr. Potato Head with no girls, to Eddie Murphy in the 1988 movie "Coming to America" with the pick of the litter. I felt like the prince of Zamunda, I could have Baskin Robbins 31 flavors. I was trying all the flavors, and different nationalities I could get my hands on. Oh what a feeling to be king.

Before long, I began seriously dating a girl named Jill. Jill played for the Lady Bulldogs. We were serious enough about each other that we both wore the number twenty-four on our uniforms. We would often get into trouble at school for kissing behind the lockers.

Sergeant Tinsley, the ROTC teacher, was always lurking to see whom he could report for the infraction known as PDA (public display of affection), he was like a black panther waiting in the woods ready to bounce on his prey. Once Sergeant Tinsley had apprehended you, he would march you right up to the principal's office just like it was a court martial proceeding. He seemed so fulfilled to catch anybody in the act, it was as if he despised any display of affection, I wondered if he knew what it felt like.

Mr. Boone was the principal then, and Mr. Pairy was his assistant. Mr. Boone, who was white, would discipline the white students, and Mr. Pairy, who was black, would discipline the blacks. We would get the paddle for being caught disobeying the school's PDA policy. I got it often.

Other than school, the only time I could see Jill in private was on the weekends. Mom wouldn't allow me to go to a girl's house during the week. But when the weekend came, I made up for lost time.

Usually Jill and I would sit in her mother's living room and hold and kiss each other. The holding and kissing got pretty intense, and I wanted more, but Jill would never cross that line with me. She told me later that Mom was in the habit of calling her parents and saying that we should never get serious. She believed in the scripture that talks about being equally yoked. My mother always said, "A believer should not be unequally yoked with an unbeliever, it could cause additional problems in your relationship and your spiritual life."

My relationship with Jill ended when she found that I was not willing to be dedicated to just one girl—especially one who had put limitations of no sex on our relationship. I began having sex with other girls, and Jill found out about it. This lack of dedication and discipline would plague me for many years to come. I wanted to taste all that life had to offer—regardless of the consequences.

At the same time, I had a burning desire to please God and to do His will. This contradiction left me constantly defeated and demoralized.

One day Mom was putting away some clean clothes in my dresser, when she came upon a condom in one of the drawers. She was horrified; she screamed as if someone had just broken in the house. Petrified of what my response might be, she confronted me about it as soon as I got home. Crying hysterically, she asked me why I had done a thing like this. Didn't I know that I would bring a curse upon myself and upon the entire family? "After all you've been taught the difference between right and wrong, how could you do this?" she demanded.

I mumbled some vague excuse that all of my friends were doing it and that it was what young people do. But the whole episode left me very despondent. Now my mother knew. And of course God knew. He knew everything. Was Mom right? Would I now be cursed? Would I also bring a curse upon my family? And why couldn't I stop?

Since I clearly wasn't a "new creation," maybe my salvation experience hadn't been real. Maybe God had never heard my prayers of repentance. My actions left me with a lot of doubts about my salvation experience.

HIGH SCHOOL BUDDIES

About this time, I started hanging around with two older boys, Lanier Hobbs and Gary Hardin. They were both from church, and Mom knew their parents, so even though they were older than I was, she thought they were okay. (Lanier came from a family of seven children, and Gary came from a family of fifteen.) It wasn't often that Mom would permit me to spend the night at a friend's house, but Lanier Hobbs was the exception.

Lanier had a way with the ladies so I was always happy to hang out with him. I remember he used to date a girl named Karen, and I began tagging along to date her sister Debbie. It infuriated me then, when Lanier began going to see Karen without me. Apparently it was cramping his style to hang out with someone several years younger.

Gary Hardin was different. He didn't mind me hanging around him at all. At one point, in fact, he actually moved in with us—because of his difficult home life.

It was amazing that Gary and I were friends. Aside from the age difference, we didn't always see eye to eye on things. For one thing, Gary was a talker, and I wasn't. I hated it when he talked so much.

Another problem was that I had developed a temper with a short fuse, and it didn't take much to set me off. One time, Gary and I were arguing so heatedly that I threatened to hit him in the head with a Heinz ketchup bottle. Another time, I walked into the house, and he drowned me with a cup of water. I waited until I thought he had forgotten the incident, and then I mixed salt and pepper in a glass and threw it all over him. His eyes were burning like fire and he was furious.

But, although Gary and I had our battles, we were actually like brothers in many ways. He was the big brother I never had. Gary had a wonderful personality, was very congenial, and never met a person he didn't like. As a result, he never allowed me to upset him for very long.

It was at this stage in my life that Dad was able to afford a basketball hoop for the yard. There, Gary and I would play from morning until night—provided we had our schoolwork done and there was no church. Gary was a fierce competitor, and he refused to lose. If I beat him, he would badger me until I consented to play him again. "What? Are you scared I'll beat you?" He taunted. My competitive drive must have come from having to play Gary over and over and over again.

At his full growth, Gary was about 6'3" inches tall and had huge hands like "Dr. J." His arms and hands reached down to his knees when he was standing straight up.

Hanging with boys who were older than I didn't help my growing obsession with girls, and this fueled the constant battle within my soul.

A DEEPENING
ATTRACTION TO GIRLS

This struggle with conflicting feelings did not abate. I was always very conscious of the fact that I was blatantly disobeying God's laws as I had been taught them, but the Scriptures were the furthest thing from my mind when I was practicing sex. The feeling this act gave me just seemed to be too good to be denied.

How could anyone be celibate? I wondered. *This is the greatest feeling known to man, and God is telling me to wait until marriage? He must be crazy.* With that thought, my life spun further out of control. In time, of course, I would learn that He wasn't crazy at all, but at the moment, that was my thought.

When I was in the eleventh grade, I met another captivating girl at school. Her name was Lois. Gary had met Lois first and asked me to take him to her house one day so that he could visit. By then, I could drive legally and had my first car. It was a green and black Chevrolet Impala. Somehow, Dad had squirreled away a few dollars here and there until he had saved the several-hundred-dollar price tag for the car. Then he helped me trick it out with running boards on the side with night-lights on them, and he also bought me some fancy rims for the car. I thought I was "stylin"—big time.

When I took Gary over to Lois's house, she seemed more interested in me than she was in him. In fact, we seemed to hit it off right from the start. Lois was a classy girl from a wonderful family. With three older brothers, she was the only girl in the family. Both her mother and father were teachers, so Lois was very intelligent. I liked what I saw in that family—in every way. The thing that really impressed me was the unity they seemed to enjoy.

Lois and I started seeing a lot of each other and grew close very quickly. I looked forward to going over to her house every Sunday after church, and I could depend on the fact that her mother would cook a fabulous meal. After dinner, I would always ask if I could wash dishes, but neither of her parents would think of it. They always washed the dishes together.

By this time, I had become much more sexually active, and I was constantly burning with lust. As a consequence, Lois and I would often find ourselves alone in their basement, in a passionate embrace. Lois was actually a girl that I thought I could marry. Her family left such an indelible impression on me.

While thinking about the pleasures of sin, for a season I was also thinking that God would surely kill me or have some other catastrophic calamity come against me. I could never feel totally at ease with having sex, knowing I had been taught to trust in God's word for my life. For people who have never been taught the oracles of God, it's no problem having sex outside of marriage, because they don't see anything wrong with it; but when you have been taught differently, it's a big problem. Suddenly, sex was beginning to dominate my life. On some level, that concerned me. I thought long and hard about what it meant for my future and what I should do about it. But all I knew was that it felt gratifying and pleasurable at the moment, and that drove me to risk everything to do it again and again. I was obsessed with what I conceived as "my need" and could think of little else.

ON-THE-COURT PROBLEMS

There were very few problems between Coach Payne and I, but this all changed. One day when we were getting ready for a big tournament, Coach wanted us all to get in our running time, and I hated to run sprints. "Get there, gentlemen," he would say, and he had us run sixteen sprints across the court.

This phrase "get there" could also mean that we were being punished for some lax behavior and the punishment was the same, running more sprints. I came to hate that phrase "get there" with a passion. Coach Payne seemed to personify a young General McArthur, a young General Patton, or some other great war general with his authoritative commands.

Coach Payne would personalize it. "Hit the lines, Winston."

"Winston, can you see that line? Touch it and become acquainted with it." And he expected immediate and full compliance.

This day, I decided that I was in too much pain and that I just couldn't take it anymore, and I headed straight for the door. Coach Payne didn't say anything; he just let me go. After all he got his name honestly; he knew how to distribute pain.

Dad was usually at every practice, but, for some reason, he hadn't gotten there this time. As I was driving home that day, I was thinking to myself, *how am I going to explain this to Dad?* I decided that I wouldn't say anything...until it became absolutely necessary.

I went back to practice the next day, but Coach was not happy with me. "You've let your teammates down," he said, "by running out on them when things got too tough. I can't say what this will mean for the future, but for now, you won't be playing in the tournament." This was a very heavy blow. Coach Payne was clearly not one who gave into a star's every whim, and he was trying to teach me a lesson. The lesson was harsh, and it came through loud and clear: no one does what he wants to do and then expects a payday or in this case a play day. When you play hard in practice, you get rewarded by playing in the games. No practice, no games. That was Coach Payne's philosophy, and he was sticking to it.

We were to leave for the tournament in Ashland, Kentucky, the next day. How could I tell my parents that I would not be playing? Again, I decided that I wouldn't tell them, hoping that Coach Payne would somehow change his mind at the last minute and use me.

It didn't happen. When the starting players names were called on the opening night of the tournament, my name was not among them. As I sat on the bench and the game began, I tried my best not to look up into the stands to see my parents reaction to this turn of events. Maybe they would think that Coach Payne was up to something crazy.

(As an aside, one of the other teams in that tournament was North Hardin, and their star was Robbie Valentine. Robbie went on to have a good career at the University of Louisville.)

Our team lost that first-round matchup, and I was left to explain to my parents on the way home why I hadn't played in the game.

Dad "went ballistic" when he heard that I had walked out because I didn't want to do sprints. "You will never quit again," he said angrily, "because I didn't raise no quitter," and he pushed me to improve myself and be more cooperative with my coach.

Coach Payne was a great coach; he never got the credit he deserved. Coaching the Male Bulldogs was somewhat like coaching on the college level. The only way to get proper credit was to win it all. Every year, there was a great amount of pressure placed on the coaches to achieve. If a coach was not getting to the state tournament and winning on that level, he was considered to be an underachiever. But, believe me, Coach Payne was no underachiever.

He conditioned us to be tough. Once, after we had played against Butler High School (with their two stars, Neil Robinson, a playground legend, and Roger Porterfield, who could jump seemingly clear out of the gym), I discovered that I had suffered a broken toe. I hadn't realized it during the game, and we won anyway.

In the playoffs, I was able to score forty points against Kevin Wall's old high school team from Camden, New Jersey. They thought they would come in and pound us, but we pounded them instead.

The final game of my senior year was against the Ballard Bruins. Ballard had Terry Stuart (a great shooter), Adam Cheeks, and "Big John" White. We had been picked to win the regional and go all the way to the state tournament, and we thought we could do it.

The game was very tight throughout, but as the end neared, we were trailing by one point. You could feel the tension in the gym as it was anyone's game at this point. Fans on both sides were in a tizzy, it was a nail bitter, back and forth, Ballard would score then we would score, it had all come down to one final shot. In the final seconds of the game, Coach Payne called a time out and drew up a play for me to win the game. When the horn sounded, we went out and threw the ball in play. I caught the ball at the top of the key; I could almost hear the song "We Are the Champions" playing in my head. While squeezing the ball as if it were an orange ready to be peeled, I gave my defender John White a head fake took one dribble and fired the shot heard around the world. I got off a shot that could have won it for us. But, in doing so, I made a fatal mistake. Instead of going to the basket (where I was strong), I opted for taking a jump shot, and this was not my shot. I missed, and my mistake cost us the right to go to the state tournament.

It simply isn't possible to describe the gripping pain, disappointment, and anguish you feel after a loss. Suddenly, my whole world was turned upside down. We had fully expected to play in the state tournament, which was held in Rupp Arena in Lexington, Kentucky, home of the Kentucky Wildcats, but now our season was over.

Every time something like this happened, my thoughts ran wild. All I could think of was this was a punishment for my sins. If I had been faithful to God it would not have happened this way. This cycle of defeat often left me feeling the lowest of the low.

As with any perceived lie, I was thinking that God was just standing in heaven with a sledgehammer waiting for me to mess up. I didn't realize that God is love. He wants only the best for His people.

The scripture says,

The Lord your God is with you, he is mighty to save. He will take great delight in you, he will quiet you with his love, he will rejoice over you with singing.

Zephaniah 3:17 (NIV)

This scripture had a positive effect on my counter-attack against the enemy. I would promise God over and over again, that I would live a holy life and not give in to the temptations that had been defeating me. I would go to church and request prayer and repent of my sins. And my newfound resolve would last for a few days or even a week, but usually not much longer. Inevitably my passions would get the best of me again, and again. I would often plunge into a cycle of despair. I constantly believed the lie that was presented to me, that sex would give me lasting fulfillment. Sex would medicate the pain of low self-esteem or the fear of never being good enough. Sex would do for me what nothing else could. It was all a big lie.

FROM AN ALL-STAR MVP TO KENTUCKY WILDCAT

There was one positive thing that came out of our loss to the Ballard Bruins that year. I was chosen to play in the McDonald's All-Star game in Atlanta. Only the very best high school players from across the country participated in the McDonald's All-Star game. In 1983, the players chosen for the McDonald's All-Star game were Tommy Amaker, who went on to play for Duke University (currently the head coach at Harvard University); Freddy Banks, who went to UNLV; James Blackmon, who played at the University of Kentucky (currently high school coach in Fort Wayne, Indiana, and has won the high school championship); Mark Cline, who played at Wake Forest University; Dallas Comegys, who played at DePaul University; Tom Curry, who played at Marshall University; Bruce Dalrymple, who played at Georgia Tech; Frank Ford, who played at Auburn; Corey Gaines, who played at Loyola Marymount (currently head coach for the Phoenix Mercury of the WNBA); Keith Gatlin, who played at Maryland; Melvin Howard, who played at Georgia State; Antoine Joubert, who played at Michigan; Martin Nessley, who played at Duke; Dave Popson, who played at North Carolina; Tom Sheehay, who played at Virginia; Kenny Smith (currently TNT NBA basketball analyst), who played at North Carolina; Kevin Smith, who played at Minnesota; Mike Smith, who played at Brigham Young University; Barry Sumpter, who played at Austin Peay; Daryl Thomas, who played at Indiana; Reggie Williams, who played at Georgetown University; Ricky Winslow, who played at Houston; Joe Wolf, who played at North Carolina; and DeWayne "the Pearl" Washington, who played at Syracuse and was probably the most notable out of the bunch.

The "Pearl" was a magician with the ball in his hands. He got his nickname from the famed guard Earl "the Pearl" Monroe who played with the New York Knicks from 1971 to 1980. I was placed on the West squad, and Reggie Williams and the "Pearl" was a couple of my opponents on the East squad. Although the game was close my team won the hotly contested game, and I shared the Most Valuable Player Award with DeWayne "Pearl" Washington. What an honor it was to be named one of the best players in the nation and then to go out and prove it by winning the game and being the MVP.

I also played in the Capital Classic All-Star game in Washington, D.C., and there again I won the MVP Award.

Before a third All-Star game that I participated in, this one the classic Indiana/Kentucky All-star game, I was awarded the Mr. Basketball Trophy for the state of Kentucky (which meant that I had been crowned the best player in the state). This selection was made by the coaches, based on my scoring and rebounding averages. After that, I began to get calls from many colleges around the country asking me to consider playing for their school. I chose a few of my favorites and paid them a visit.

The University of Louisville was on my favorites list. It was a natural because Louisville was my hometown, and besides I had been a Louisville Cardinal Ball boy in the seventh and eighth grades. I knew all about its great basketball history. Robbie Valentine, the former Louisville basketball star, tells the story of my recruitment to Louisville. "Winston had come to the University of Louisville for a visit and all seemed to be going well. I was the host for Winston and took him to some campus parties on a Saturday night. Late, about 3 a.m. in the morning, after I had dropped Winston back at the dorms, we saw a caravan of big blue fans roll up to the dorms to whisk Winston away. The next morning, we woke up and had a meeting with Coach Denny Crum. Coach Crum asked where is Winston, we were panic stricken to tell him we saw the Big Blue faithful roll up at about 3 a.m. in the morning and carried him off in the clear dark night. The Big Blue Nation had come and carted him off to Lexington."

I also visited Georgetown University in Washington, D.C., where the legendary John Thompson was coaching. He had Patrick Ewing and was trying to sign Reggie Williams. "Big John" Thompson was clearly one of the hottest coaches around at the time, and I liked the idea of playing for him. In fact, I liked everything about Georgetown.

I also visited the University of Kentucky at Lexington. It was another of my favorites. I had attended a number of their home games—although Lexington was an hour and a half drive from our home.

Before I was able to make my final decision, I was also visited by Coach Bobby Knight of Indiana. He was "a piece of work," very brash and confident. He was a successful coach, having won two national championships (he later went on to win another championship while I was at Kentucky). Coach Knight asked me to consider playing for Indiana, but I didn't like his intimidating style of coaching, so I decided against it.

Coach "Wimp" Sanderson of Alabama also came to our house to see me. He said he would make me a star and place my name on a marquee in lights. I was flattered, but Alabama just wasn't for me.

After I had visited several universities, Coach Payne suggested that we spend a night in some quiet hotel, away from phone calls and other influences, so that I could have time to think and make my final decision. I wholeheartedly agreed as the recruiting battle between Louisville and Kentucky got to a fever pitch.

The next day, Coach asked me, "Well, Winston, what have you decided?" He had a brother who graduated from UK and he was hoping that I would choose it.

"I'm going to the University of Louisville," I said, with as straight a face as I could muster. Then, having paused a few seconds for effect, I said, "No, Coach, I'm just kidding. I've decided to attend the University of Kentucky." Coach Payne showed no reaction one way or the other, but I could imagine what he was thinking.

Kentucky had been my choice from the start, although it was very unusual for an African-American kid from Louisville to attend the University of Kentucky. That had not happened for many years, since the infamous Tom Payne.

The legendary coach of Kentucky, Adolph Rupp, was said to be a racist, and Payne had been his only black player. Now "prejudice" was the reason I heard most often when my friends said that I should not go to Kentucky. In fact, my decision caused a stir around Louisville. Black players from Louisville just did not go to the University of Kentucky.

But I was not unduly concerned. "The Adolph Rupp era is over," I told those who tried to discourage me. "He's dead. It's a new day."

"Yes," the answer came back invariably, "but his spirit lives on."

After I had made my decision, it caused some friction in Louisville. When we played the Camden, New Jersey, team, some of their players had chosen to attend the University of Louisville, while I had committed to play for the University of Kentucky. I was called a Benedict Arnold for betraying Louisville and going to Kentucky. Coach Denny Crum and all the University of Louisville fans were in the stands that night, hoping to see the visiting team crush us. They left the gym in frustration and disappointment that night as the Male Bulldogs crushed the visiting team from Camden, and I had my best night ever with over forty points.

My parents were never concerned about protocol, and they had encouraged me early on to go to Lexington and check out the program at UK for myself. If that university was the best for me, I should go there—regardless of the past. I liked what I saw at UK. My parents had always told me believe little of what was said, half of what is seen, and all of what you trust in your heart.

One of the things that encouraged me most about accepting the UK offer was receiving personal notes from UK basketball players saying that they hoped I would join them. Such notes came from greats like Sam Bowie, Melvin Turpin, Kenny Walker, Dirk Minnifield, and Charles Hurt. That made a huge impression on a kid who used to play basketball in a garbage can.

Another thing that persuaded me to pick Kentucky was their wonderful recruiting advantage, called the Wildcat Lodge. When I was first taken inside the lodge, my eyes bulged with wonder. Here I was, a poor boy from Louisville, accustomed to a two-bedroom house, and this place looked to me like the Taj Mahal.

The lodge was large and elegant. There was shag carpeting on the floors and antique telephones and a big-screen TV in every room. I had never seen such opulence in all my life. This place was far from the mice and the brown brothers that I was exposed to at the little house on Penway. This was a castle; this was like being at Disney World where all your fantasies come true.

The players who lived in the lodge also had a personal cook to prepare their meals, so they never had to eat in the school cafeteria. Whatever each individual player wanted was served to him made-to-order. "Who in his right mind would pass up all this?" I wondered.

If that hadn't been enough to convince me, I was then taken to Rupp Arena. With seats for 23,000 Big Blue Maniacs, the place was gigantic. I couldn't imagine what it was like to play in front of such a large crowd, but I was told that there was a capacity crowd at every home game. This fan support at UK weighed very heavy in my decision-making. Louisville also had strong fan support, but the fan support at Kentucky was absolutely astounding.

COACH JOE B. HALL

Coach Joe B. Hall was really the person who tipped the scales in Kentucky's direction. Coach Hall was the coach at Kentucky from 1972 to 1985. His only misfortune during his coaching career was following the legendary Adolph Rupp. In 1978, Coach Hall led the Wildcats to their fifth NCAA Men's Division I Basketball Championship. He was named the National Coach of the Year in 1978 and SEC Coach of the Year on four different occasions. His record at UK was 297–100 and 373–156 over his entire career. He is a Hall of Famer in my book.

I was also impressed with Coach Hall's top-gun recruiter, Leonard Hamilton (who is now Head Coach at Florida State University). Coach Hamilton, as it turned out, was the one to whom all the black players on the team would go when there was a problem.

Once, when we were on the road playing in Utah, for instance, I was itching like crazy and had no idea what the problem was. I called Coach Hamilton and told him about it.

He asked, "Have you been sleeping around?"

When I admitted that I had, he said, "You've got 'the crabs.'"

"The crabs?" I asked. "What's that?"

He explained and said that he would go out and get some medication for me to use. He also told me to take off all my clothes and wash them in hot water and to strip the bed and wash the bed linens. Eventually, I able to rid myself of that horrible itching.

This ordeal left me so terrified that I promised God that I would never again engage in premarital sex. And I didn't...for a little while. Then it started all over again.

It was almost as if I was willing to risk anything just for the high that sex gives.

Coach Hamilton would invite all the black players to his house for steaks, and he became the coach we related to. This was no disrespect to Coach Hall. It was just that an assistant coach could do things with the players that a head coach couldn't. The assistant has a chance to befriend the players without being perceived as the enemy. The head coach is often looked upon as the enemy, or worse, because he supplies the discipline and correction to the team.

Both of these coaches made me want to serve under them.

The final element in my decision to study and play at the University of Kentucky was prayer. I sought God's will in the matter and was sure that I had made the right decision.

Still, when my incorporation into the team eventually became reality that fall, it was like a dream. I couldn't believe it. I was a University of Kentucky Wildcat, and I loved every moment of it. It was the Mecca of college basketball, there was none bigger or better than Kentucky basketball. It was the Sistine Chapel of the sporting world; it was the college version of the New York Yankees.

If I had been interested in girls in high school, that problem was only compounded exponentially now that I was playing for the worlds most noted university. Not only was Kentucky known for its basketball, but it was also known for its beautiful women. College campuses were a breeding ground for sexual escapades.

Being away from home for the first time in my life, and freed from the constraints of my parents and pastor, I took my freedom to do what I wanted to the max. I was like a pig wallowing in slop.

THE KENTUCKY STAFF

It's impossible to talk about Kentucky basketball without mentioning Cawood Ledford, the voice of Kentucky basketball for more than four decades. Cawood reminded me a lot of Red Auerbach (former Boston Celtic coach and general manager) in the sense that they both experienced mastery in their field and they both had a trade mark. Cawood's unforgettable trade mark was his ever present pack of cigarettes and Red's trade mark was always his victory cigars. There was no one who called a game quite like Cawood. It has been said that Cawood prevented a lot of premature pregnancies during his time in Kentucky, because the state was always celibate while he was broadcasting a Kentucky game.

Another legend in the Wildcat family was Mr. Wildcat himself—Bill Keighley. Mr. Keighley had been the equipment guy for the big blue for ages. There was no one quite like Bill. He seemingly had been around Kentucky basketball since the beginning of time, and he could tell you stories that would make your head swim. Bill was the stabilizer for me. When I was down or depressed, I could always talk to "Mr. Bill." Mr. Bill could be Santa Claus when you needed or he could be scrooge. Since he was the best equipment guy ever, he would never let you get more than one Kentucky shirt as a player, that shirt had to last you the whole year. He would always tell you make sure you penned your laundry bag or your practice gear would come up missing. No shoes, only a couple of pair per year; that's it, unless you were one of the stars, then he might give you an extra pair. He simply did not believe in waste, that was Mr. Bill: no nonsense, all business.

Our trainer Walt McCombs was also a guy for the ages. Whenever you came to Walt with an injury there was only one remedy that he knew to prescribe, "Hey reach over there and put some ice on it," he would say. If Walt was the doctor at every hospital around the country there would be no injuries, he would just tell you, "You will be okay suck it up and put some ice on it."

Marta McMackin was also a fixture in the Wildcat organization. (She has since retired, but had been through several coaching changes. After Joe B. Hall, there was Eddie Sutton, Rick Pitino, Coach Tubby Smith, and Billy Gillispie.) She was one of those people who knew what to do and what not to do, and she became a close friend whom I respected and could go to in tough times.

Coach Hall was the leader of the ship for my first two years of college. He was one of the first coaches on the college level to start incorporating heavy weightlifting into the conditioning program. I didn't mind the weightlifting; it was the running that I hated with a passion. We would run from the coliseum to the track, about a mile. But that wasn't the bad part. It was the on-track running that made me think of quitting. I felt a lot like Forrest Gump must have felt; when he was just told to run, just keep running. Run Forrest run. I wasn't feeling like life was a box of chocolates at this time in my career.

We would warm up with stretching, a few fifty-yard dashes and some hundred-yard dashes. But, again, this was just the warm-up. The granddaddy of all our exercises was always the two-hundred-and-twenty-yard dash. I will never forget the day we were required to run sixteen of these dashes during practice. I thought I would die. My heart felt as if it was ready to explode. I could hear my body asking me, "Why? What have I done to deserve this?"

James Blackmon and Ed Davender had to carry me off the track that day. I told them I couldn't feel my legs. I began to wonder why I was there anyway. I hadn't signed for any track scholarship.

I began to hate Pat Echeberry, the weightlifting and conditioning coach. He was from some foreign land, and I wouldn't have minded right then if he had gone back to where he came from. His famous words were "No pain, no gain fellows, no pain, no gain." He was infamous at distributing pain.

But after running, we were not yet finished. There was a big hill we had to climb to get from the track to the weight room. I was out of it that particular day, and there was no way I could walk up that hill. It suddenly seemed like I was Edmund Hillary scaling the peak of Mt. Everest. Such workouts tested us to our limits and stretched us beyond belief, but eventually they would begin to pay off.

THE KENTUCKY PLAYERS

Coach Hall was a big man's coach. He had the "Twin Towers"—Sam Bowie and Melvin Turpin—and "Sky," Kenny "Sky" Walker. Turpin and Bowie worked together extremely well. Turpin was the power player, and Bowie loved to roam around on the perimeter. Walker was the perfect complement to the two of them. He got the rebounds the other two missed.

Melvin Turpin was a very talented six-foot-ten inch player who came to the University of Kentucky from Bryan Station High School in Lexington. "Turp" had a deadly fifteen-foot jump shot. He was one of the few big men during this time that could play both inside and outside.

Off the court, "Turp" had his problems. One of them was his eating habits. Many called him "Dinner Bell Mel." When he had come to Kentucky, he was as skinny as a rail, and when he left he was huge. Coach Hall had a plan for putting weight on him, and it worked to perfection. The only problem was after they started him eating, they couldn't stop him.

"Mel" would have his girlfriend sneak him Whoppers and fries by the bagful through his window after hours. There were numerous sightings of him out after curfew at the local McDonalds; one of the workers said Mel would come in and say, "This is a stick up. I want all of your Big Mac's with special sauce, lettuce, cheese, and pickles all on a sesame seed bun on the double." This situation got so bad that Coach Hall had to appoint a manager to stay in Melvin's room with him. But "Big Mel" was one of those guys who didn't really care. He was a happy-go-lucky fellow—no matter what he was doing. He was going to have a good time.

One day, Mel walked into practice with a strange limp. It almost looked like he had to go to the bathroom, but he couldn't sit down. He told us that he had accidentally sat down on a knife in his car. We later learned that his girlfriend had stabbed him in the rear for playing around with another girl. "Mel" always had some soap opera going on. One thing you could count on from Big Mel he was going to enjoy life to the fullest (Big Mel passed away on July 8, 2010, at 49 years of age we will miss him dearly).

"Big Sam" Bowie was even more of a ladies' man. All the girls loved him because he was smooth and very articulate, and knew how to relate to people. He also loved horses and horse racing and could often be found at Red Mile Track. Although he will always be remembered by basketball fans as the player who was drafted before Michael Jordan, Sam's career was limited because of injuries. I will never forget Big Sam.

I remember in my first practice at Kentucky, big Sam hit me with a sharp elbow, Sam was not the most aggressive player in the world, he was just a good guy, but in this particular practice, he caught me with a powerful forearm shiver right in the choppers. Well I was not one for intimidation techniques, especially since I was a freshman and Sam was a senior, I could understand if he was letting me know I was no longer in high school. But I was not taking any bullying, no sir, I came right back at him swinging. I was known for being aggressive and taking no prisoners, if we had to spar a few sessions that was fine with me. The sparing didn't last long before players and coaches stepped in to break it up. I remember Coach Hall coming over and telling me to apologize to big Sam. I thought to myself, *are you crazy, this big over grown 7'0" footer just cold cocked me and you talking about apologizing, no way, absolutely not. If anybody should apologize it should be the big fella.* Of course, I did eventually apologize, and Sam and I went on to become great teammates.

Kenny "Sky" Walker was another super talent standing about 6'8 inches tall, he was the highest jumper I ever saw. He could do every kind of dunk imaginable. When you saw him play, there could be no doubt in your mind that he would be great.

Kenny was also the most giving person I ever knew. He would give you the shirt off of his back. He drove an old white Oldsmobile that seemed to stretch a block long, but that fact never seemed to bother Kenny. He loved that car, especially for its eight-track player. He would drive down the street with his Marvin Gaye on, and everyone knew he was coming.

Kenny believed that he would one day be able to drive whatever he wanted, and he was right. He went on to play in the NBA with the New York Knicks. Kenny also went on to become the NBA dunk champion while playing with the Knicks.

James Blackmon, from Marion, Indiana, also seemed to be one of the high risers on the team. He had been a high school All-American, averaging more than thirty points a game, and was a gifted offensive player, because he was cat quick and knew how to score points. But, for some unknown reason, James never fit into Coach Hall's system. He would have been a sure pick for the NBA, but he never got that far because college play never panned out for him.

James and I were roommates and were very close...until I spoiled the relationship. We were two very different people with two very different outlooks on life. For one thing, he was outgoing, and I was quiet and kept to myself. But we had been good friends, until the day I arrived back at our room in the Wildcat Lodge and found James and his girlfriend in a passionate embrace after curfew.

I was already upset because we had just lost a big game, and I told James, "You'd better get her out of here."

"She's not going anywhere," he replied, "and why don't you get out so she can put her clothes back on?"

At that point, I grabbed him and began punching him in the face. Later, I couldn't believe that I'd acted so rashly. The next morning, James reported me to the coaching staff, and the coaches split us up.

Later, James confronted me. "Why did you do it?" he asked. The only thing I could say was the obvious—that I had been upset at the time, and the girl should not have been in our room after curfew. I was sorry it had happened, but our friendship was never the same after that. I will always regret this spontaneous act of rage, because James was like the brother I never had.

But I'll never forget the cold and blistery winter weekend James let me use his Trans Am to go home and visit my parents. I had a wonderful time in Louisville, but that Sunday, when I had to drive an hour and half back to Lexington, there was snow everywhere, and Highway 64 was covered with a sheet of ice.

To complicate things, I was in a hurry, trying to make it back to Wildcat Lodge before curfew. Suddenly I hit a sheet of ice, and the car did a three-hundred-and-sixty-degree turn. The next thing I knew, I was sitting in the median strip of the highway.

This particular median strip was at least four or five feet lower than the roadway. It was a ravine, or deep ditch, and there was no way I could get the car out of it. This was before the advent of cell phones; it was late at night, and there were no gas stations for miles around. So I was wondering what I should do.

I tried desperately to drive the car out of the ravine, but it would not move, and I began to panic. How many times had I seen a man or woman on the side of the road and thought in my mind, "I should stop and see if they need some assistance," but I never did. Now I wished I had helped someone else, so that maybe the Lord would send someone to my rescue. The few cars out that night were not stopping. They just passed me on by throwing snow and ice in my face as they went.

Mom had always told me, "When you need help, call on Jesus, and He will be there." But would the Lord hear me? I had never stopped believing in Him, but I had sinned against Him so many times now I could no longer count.

But I had no other alternative, and so I began to pray with everything in me. "Oh Jesus, please help me. Here I am with no help in sight. Lord, I need You to do something miraculous. It's late at night, and no one is stopping to help me. Please help me."

After the prayer, I decided to try one last time to drive the sports car out of the ditch, and I was amazed, I couldn't believe my eyes as the car began climbing the ravine and moving out of the ditch as if it had been a four-wheel-drive all terrain vehicle.

I couldn't believe it. The previous times I had tried, the car had just kept sliding back into the ditch. As I went on my way to Lexington that night, I praised and worshiped God, knowing that He had just performed a miracle for me. I was ecstatic to return James's car that night in one piece.

Roger Harden and Dicky Beal were the point guards on our team that year. Roger was a smart guard who knew how to use his court savvy instincts to lead a team, while Dicky was a speed demon, he was in high gear the whole game, he would push that basketball up and down the court as if the KKK was chasing him. He was one of the fastest players I had ever seen with the basketball in his hands. Well aside from the little 5'5 inch Leroy

Bird. Bird was a little guy who was quick as a cat, he was one of those players that always gets under your skin; if you happen to put the basketball down around him, he would take it; he was a thief with the basketball.

Jim Master was our zone buster. He never saw a shot he didn't like, and he was a great shooter. He would wipe his socks at the free-throw line, like Kyle Macy—who had come before him.

Tom Heitz was one of our big guys who rarely got a lot of playing time because he had future NBA players ahead of him like Bowie and Turpin. The thing I liked about Tom was no matter what the situation, he would give you his all. Even though he knew he probably wouldn't play in the games, he made every practice his game time. He felt like his contribution to the team was to beat on Bowie and Turpin everyday in practice.

Bret Bearup was another big body with a lot of talent. He was about 6'9", and could jump and shoot the ball well. Bret was also the jokester on the team. He was always doing something to agitate Coach Hall. One time he put a dead chicken in a girl's mailbox; the girl saw the chicken and about had a heart attack. He also defecated in a cardboard box and then put the box under the bed of his roommate Troy McKinley. Troy smelled the unusual out house aroma in his room and knew that there was something strange brewing, but he couldn't figure out where the smell was coming from. It took him weeks before he realized that he had been snookered by the jokester himself, Bret Bearup.

In spite of his practical joking, Bret was a smart guy. Although basketball never really worked out for him at Kentucky, he went on to law school and is now a very successful front office person for the Denver Nuggets of the NBA. He was a master at relationships and staying in touch with people.

Troy McKinley was another deadeye shooter, who we called sweetness, because his jumper was so sweet going through the hoop. He and Bret were always getting in trouble together. Usually Troy was the innocent bystander, but since we're known by the company we keep, he was thought to be just as guilty as Bret.

Bret managed to embarrass me a couple of times. Once, after a game, he saw that I had some "game slippage" on my white uniform shorts. ("Game slippage" is a term used by athletes for excrement stains left when, in straining to make the necessary moves; you accidentally excrete some body wastes.) At the end of the game, we had taken off our uniforms and thrown them into a big pile. Being the prankster he was, Bret noticed something very peculiar on my shorts, it was game slippage. Bret was not the person you wanted to see any game slippage because he would let everyone know about it. So he picked up my shorts and handed them around for all the other players to inspect. Suddenly, I had become the "Stain Master" and the name stuck.

On another occasion, I was misquoted in an article for *Sports Illustrated* magazine, and Bret picked up the quote and repeated it over and over again. I had been talking about a certain number of points and rebounds being a "milestone" in my career, but the *Sports Illustrated* reporter wrote that I had said it would be a "rhinestone" in my career. Bret rode me for a long while with those words. Every time he saw me, he would start singing the old country song by Glen Campbell "Like a rhinestone cowboy."

While I'm on this subject, I made the champion of dumb statements once, and he never let me forget it. A reporter asked me if I had undergone any other major surgery other than on my knee, and I answered, "I've never had major knee surgery on any other part of my body." I can never live that one down because it's now part of a book of the dumbest quotes ever. Although I am generally a serious person, sometimes you have to take time to laugh at yourself.

As mischievous as Bret Bearup was, he was a good friend. He was instrumental in introducing me to the world of speaking. We would go out and speak to high schools and churches. Our talks were mostly motivational and related to recruiting players for Kentucky basketball. Bret was big on doing public appearances like that and thus giving something back to kids and the community.

All in all, Kentucky was a great team to play for.

FRESHMAN SEASON

My first season with the Cats was the memorable 1983–84 season. First of all, it was a once in a lifetime experience to play for the most storied program in college basketball history. The University of Kentucky as of this writing is the most winning team in the history of college basketball, in both all-time wins and all-time winning percentage with an all-time record of 2023–638–1 (.760). Kentucky also leads the NCAA in NCAA tournament appearances with 50, and ranks second to UCLA in NCAA championships with seven, and second to University of North Carolina in NCAA tournament wins with ninety-eight. Could this be real? Little kid whose dad said "Can You See It" as a child and now I am with the greatest college team in the history of sports. Dreams do come true; never despise the day of small beginnings.

For the start of my freshman year, we were ranked number one in the nation, led by our pair of twin towers, Sam Bowie and Melvin Turpin. We also had the super sophomore Kenny "Sky" Walker. On the backs of these three players, we routed most teams. We started the season with an exhibition game with the

Netherlands. I know the Netherlands never knew what hit them as we demolished them 73–55.

We went on to play our archrival in the state, the University of Louisville, in what was to be called the Dream Game. Louisville was rated number six in the nation at the time under Coach Denny Crum, and we were still the top team in the nation. Playing the home rival was always special for me. It was like I would go to another stratosphere thinking about playing against guys I would play against in the summer back in Louisville. Charles Jones, Wiley Brown, the McCray brothers Scooter and Rodney, Lancaster Gordon and others. They were a very talented team as usual, but we had a little too much firepower. We beat the Cardinals 65–44. This game always had special meaning for me and my father, as we are the biggest Kentucky fans. It allowed us another summer of bragging rights.

It seemed that we faced every rival we could this particular year; next up was Coach Bob Knight and his Indiana Hoosiers. Of course Steve Alford (currently the head coach at the University of New Mexico) was the heady point guard for the Hoosiers. You could always count on the Hoosiers playing aggressive and playing smart. But again we had too much for the Hoosiers; we beat them 59–54 in Rupp Arena.

Our next big opponent was the Kansas Jayhawks. The Jayhawks were always tough to beat in Lawrence. By this time, we had fallen from our number one ranking to number two in the nation. It didn't matter; we were on a mission; we dismantled the Jayhawks 72–50 in Lawrence.

Wyoming and Brigham Young were our next two victims in the old UKIT tournament. This was a tournament that Kentucky used to have in Rupp just before the Christmas holiday cheer. We gave the fans a lot to cheer about as we sent both teams back west with a loss.

Cincinnati was next on the list of beat downs, and true to form; we gave them what they knew was coming and that was a loss.

One of the bigger games on our schedule was the University of Illinois. This was a huge game for us. Illinois was very good. They had great inside and outside play with Doug Altenberger, Bruce Douglas, and Efrem Winters. It was a blistery cold night in Champaign, with snow up to your knees; we actually got snowed in after the game. This was a close one, but we out lasted Illinois 56–54, when James Blackmon tipped in a miss shot that gave us the win.

Next on the list were Gene Keady and the Purdue Boiler-makers. No problem we blew them right out of the gym 86–67.

After playing the nonconference schedule, we raced into the conference with confidence. We knew that no one could beat us unless we were just having an off night and even then it would still be tough. We went 15–4 in the conference with losses to Auburn who featured Chuck Person and the infamous Charles Barkley (the round mound of rebound), Florida, Alabama, and Tennessee. The losses were good for us; it showed that just because we were Kentucky did not mean we could win without giving our very best effort. We would need this lesson as we chased a conference title and a NCAA title.

In the SEC Tournament, we were playing with a chip on our shoulders. The pressure had been on us thick to win a championship. We all wanted to do it for our fans and for Coach Hall. Coach Hall had suffered a lot of grief because he had not brought a NCAA Championship to Kentucky since 1978, were most schools would have been content with the championship in 1978, not at Kentucky. There is absolutely no room to sit back and read your press clippings, if you think you are going to sit in your rocking chair and take it easy at Kentucky, think again.

The Big Blue Nation wants to know what have you done for me lately. If you have not won numerous championships, then we have to think seriously about your coaching career at Kentucky.

With the pressure on, we swept through the SEC Tournament, destroying anyone who would stand in our way. Georgia and Vern Fleming were first; we took them out to the woodshed and gave them a good ole fashioned spanking 92–79. We then gave Bobby Lee Hurt, the great center for Alabama, a loss; this was a close game. Alabama and their infamous Coach Wimp Sanderson had beaten us earlier in the year at their place and still felt like they had something to prove; we were able to outlast them 48–46 in a low-scoring game.

The one game I will never forget was the SEC championship game against Auburn. Auburn had the Round Mound of Rebound, Charles Barkley; Barkley was only about 6'4 inches over 300 lbs, but he played like he was 7'0" tall. He played with a lot of heart. Kentucky fans often said that Barkley would absolutely man handle our center Big Mel Turpin. Well in the championship of the SEC Tournament, the big bully got man handled by the "Big Dipper" Mel Turpin. Both guys had spent a little too much time at the nearest McDonald's, but on this given night, Big Mel got the better of Charles Barkley. Charles went on to become one of the fifty best players in NBA basketball history. After the game Sir Charles, as he was sometimes referred, sat in the middle of the floor crying like a baby. The scene was priceless. It was a Kodak moment.

While winning the SEC Championship was one of the main steps on our ladder of success, it was not the only one; the next step would be our biggest, going to the NCAA Tournament.

We would go on to play in Birmingham, Alabama, in the Mideast Regional. Of course we knew we had a once in a lifetime opportunity to play in the NCAA. We were in it to win it. There would be no glory if we did not march through the tournament on our way to a final four. So that's just what we did. Our first opponent was Brigham Young we dominated this unworthy opponent, we got this game over quick fast and in hurry, 93–68.

Our next opponent was more formidable it was the Louisville Cardinals; we would be playing them in the Semifinals in Rupp Arena. It seemed that the deck was stacked in our favor. You don't get an opportunity too often to play a NCAA tournament game in your own backyard, and for me there was added benefit, it was the Cardinals my hometown team, we had to win this one. It seemed as if the stars had all aligned themselves for us to win the tournament. Although it wasn't that simple, Milt Wagner and Lancaster Gordon would have something to say about this game. As it turned out, the game was close and what a climatic finish. We were able to outlast the Cardinals 72–67. Oh how sweet it is to beat the Louisville Cardinals in a NCAA tournament game. Again, the size of the twin towers Bowie and Turpin made the difference.

We were moving right along as planned when we ran into another familiar foe, the Fighting Illini. We had played Illinois earlier in the year and had barely escaped with our life. This would be another doozy of a game. This was the regional finals in Rupp, the fans was crazy, mostly the Big Blue Nation. Bowie and Turpin were at their best; the twin towers were a little too much for Efrem Winters and the Fighting Illini, we beat them 54–51 in a nail biter. We were headed to the Final Four. There was not a lot of commotion because this was the plan all alone. The pressure to win the NCAA Championship could be cut with a knife, it was that thick. We were expected to be in Seattle. Our fans had punched their tickets for the Final Four in the beginning of the year. It was a done deal that we would be there.

In the book *Good to Great,* Jim Collins compares why some companies make it to greatness while others languish in mediocrity. One of the observations he made was the good companies get the right people on the bus in the right seats. When you have the right people on the bus in the right seats the bus drives smoothly without delay, but when you have the wrong people on the bus the ride is tumultuous. It was obvious to me we had the right people on the bus: Bowie, Turpin, and Walker were leading the bus right to the Final Four.

PLAYING IN THE FINAL FOUR

One of the highlights of my college career was playing in the Final Four as a freshman in Seattle, Washington. It was an unbelievable experience to make it that far as a freshman. When you grow up as a youngster, you dream of one day playing for the best school and making it to the championship round. I had worked so hard to be the best that I could be even though I still felt like my best wasn't good enough. I never felt strong enough or fast enough, I could not shoot the ball well enough, and could not handle the ball well enough. I never thought I deserved to be on the best team in college basketball. But yet I had made it despite my deficiencies.

While traveling on the airplane from Lexington, Kentucky to Seattle, Washington, I am sure each player had his own memory of what life had been for him up until that point. For me, I thought about all the times my dad asked me the question, "Winston, can you see yourself being there one day?" Sometimes the vision looked blurry; it didn't look real. It was foggy, almost out of reach. When you start at six years old preparing for a dream, you began to think that the payoff will never come. One of the hardest things in life to contend with is the reality that our dreams may never be fulfilled, at least not the way we think.

The plane ride to Washington was glorious. My childhood fantasies were being played out on a very real stage. As I gazed out my window, I could see the glory of God's creation. It was amazing how small everything else looks when you are 33,000 feet in the air. All my problems seem to pale in comparison to where I was now. I was a little kid who grew up with a dream of being the best, and here I was about to play in a Final Four.

As I stepped off the plane with my teammates, I remember wanting to kiss the ground knowing that this would signify our yellow brick road to a championship. If you remember, the Yellow Brick road was Dorothy's path home in the Wizard of Oz. I figured if it worked for Dorothy, it could work for us too. As we boarded the bus, I could feel the anticipation of a championship. We were chaperoned through downtown Seattle with police escorts, sirens blazing to their highest level as we weaved through traffic as if we were the President of the United States coming to town to enact war. Our arrival in the arena was pure mayhem; we were overcome with a deluge of media, television, radio, and reporters everywhere flashing cameras, with spotlights making us feel like we were instant millionaires. It was like being in the Super Bowl. I had witnessed scenes like this on television, but never in person. The scene was deafening. I began to realize that some coaches and players play and coach all their lives and never witness firsthand the atmosphere of a Final Four. It's one thing to watch a Final Four on television, but it's a whole different thing to be a part of the action. It reminded me of that old saying: actions speak louder than words. The crowds were emphatic and jubilant. They wanted a piece of the Final Four participants; it was like we were the Beatles. We were in concert, and everyone wanted to see us play.

One of the most difficult things to do in a Final Four is to maintain focus. The Final Four is like one big party. There are ticket requests to contend with; friends and family want to see you and spend time with you. If you do not maintain your focus, and remember that you are there for a purpose, the whole mission can be aborted in a hurry. Even if the tournament was half a world away from Kentucky, the ticket requests were endless. Our being at the Final Four was not a surprise to us or our fans; we were supposed to be there. But being there was not enough; we were supposed to win. Pressure is a beautiful thing; it will either cause you to run faster and jump higher, or it will cause you to fold your tent and go home. I wondered what we would do. Our fans were in Seattle in full effect; just like everywhere else we went, we took Rupp Arena with us. Kentucky had the best traveling fans of any school in the nation. That's one of the reasons they are called the "Big Blue Nation."

Our coaching staff felt it was important to stick to as much of a normal routine as possible. Of course that's easier said than done. It's the Final Four with hundreds of thousands of people in the Superdome. Even with all the hoopla, we stuck to our usual routine of watching film the night before the big game. We knew all about our opponent, the Georgetown Hoyas. It was actually an even greater moment for me, because I had seriously considered Georgetown during my recruiting process. We knew the key to the game would be to handle their aggressive play, and their pressure defense. We also knew we would have to contain Patrick Ewing, their All-America center.

The night before the big game is crazy. So many things go through your head. Most great athletes tell you they will try to visualize the outcome of the game in their head the night before. I am a strong believer of visualization. The very fact that I was in a Final Four stemmed from a vision my dad had fifteen years earlier, called "Can You See It." I believe you have to see it in your mind's eye before you can have it. What is it that you see? You shall have what you see.

Well the big day finally arrived; it was game day, the Final Four. Just the same as every other game we had this season: we had our usual pregame meal, full of carbs, and protein, pancakes, fish, and chicken. Usually on game day, there was very little talking, particularly on the bus headed over to the game. Those were moments of introspection. It was an opportunity to think about your responsibility during the game.

Just like in every other game I have played in I was as nervous as could be, the butterflies were definitely flapping their wings profusely. It was the perfect time for last-minute visualization, and most importantly for me, prayer.

In Game One, it was the Kentucky Wildcats vs. the Georgetown Hoyas, and in Game Two, it was the Virginia Cavaliers vs. the Houston Cougars. This was big-time basketball—the clash of the titans. This was the year of the big men.

We had our Twin Towers Bowie and Turpin, but Georgetown had All-America center Patrick Ewing and his able-bodied sidekick, Michael Graham. Georgetown's coach was not called "Big John" for nothing. He was about 6'9" inches, three hundred and fifty pounds, and all of his players took on his aggressive mentality.

Other than Patrick Ewing, Michael Graham, David Wingate, and Reggie Williams were probably the most revered out of the Georgetown lineup. Michael Graham was the supposed intimidator, he had his head shaved bald before it was fashionable, and he did it to add to his thug like image. He also had a growl that could make a dog whimper.

Playing Georgetown was roughhouse basketball, but I didn't mind their style. This was right up my alley. I had a little roughhouse ball in me anyway. Since Georgetown was one of the schools I had visited coming out of high school, I knew all about the Hoyas and their intimidating style of play. I was not against getting into a melee or two myself.

But our Final Four appearance against Georgetown University turned out to be a nightmarish experience. We had played a masterful game the first half, getting the ball to Bowie and Turpin. We had been down by twelve points in the first half only to comeback feverishly to take a seven-point lead at half time. We had everything working in our favor; Patrick Ewing had three fouls and the Hoyas would have major problems beating us if we could put Patrick on the bench in the second half. Unbeknownst to every Kentucky fan in the Big Blue Nation, it seemed that someone had put an invisible lid on our basket at half time. We couldn't seem to throw the ball in the ocean. Jim Masters would take a shot, and the ball would bounce off the rim; Bowie and Turpin would make a move inside, and it would bounce off the rim. We shot a miserable 3 for 33 in the second half. It was the biggest game of our careers. What a time to shoot only eleven percent from the field! Surely Georgetown's excellent defense had something to do with it. Whatever the case, like the movie, we were "Sleepless in Seattle" that night. It was as if we had stayed up, and stayed out all night, the night before the game.

True enough, it's very difficult to sleep the night before a big game, but this was ridiculous. The night before the game, we were all in our rooms thinking about the big game, and how we would win, losing never entered our mind. I could not have prognosticated this outcome in a million years. Just as fast as it began, it was over; we had treated the Big Blue Nation to our most dismal play of the year, a 40–53 loss to the Hoyas.

Just as quick as the dream came into reality, it was gone in a puff of smoke. All the endless drills, all the sprints, all the made baskets were finished in one forty-minute game. The hopes, dreams, and aspirations, gone with the shots of missed baskets. Failed attempts at success, failed hopes and dreams. Everything hinging on a shot that may never go in, a defensive stop that may never happen, life is short; the only championship to be won is the one that God has already mastered, and that is this game of life.

Virginia and Houston met in the second-round match-up. Virginia had 7'3" Ralph Samson, and Houston had "The Dream," Akeem Olajuwon. If we could have only made it to the championship, we had already played the Houston Cougars in Rupp Arena earlier in the year and had beaten them 74–67. Houston would go on to win the game against Virginia and Ralph Sampson, and Akeem would go on to become one of the best centers in NBA history.

The championship game of the 1984 NCAA Tournament was between the Georgetown Hoyas and the Houston Cougars. Georgetown proved to be the better of the two teams; the Hoyas just had too much balance. They were more than just Patrick Ewing. They were a team. From that championship team, Patrick Ewing, David Wingate, and Reggie Williams all went on to have excellent NBA careers. Patrick Ewing, along with Akeem Olajuwon, went on to become two of the top fifty NBA players of all time.

I would never again have an opportunity to play in the Final Four, but I couldn't know that yet. For now, all I knew was that my first season had come to a close; we had finished the season 29–5 with a berth to the Final Four. The pain of losing in the Final Four was brutal, but I thought to myself with three more years remaining that maybe I would get another chance. For our seniors Bowie, Turpin, Masters and the rest, this was it. Their college days were over; it was time to face the real world. For at least two of our seniors, the real world would turn them into instant millionaires by the way of the NBA; for the rest, business careers would begin. As for me, I was looking forward to summer.

I had heard discussions among the team members about the summer "activities." Each year, when the players were freed from the restraints of lodge life and the constant surveillance they were under there, they took jobs for the summer and rented apartments where they could do what they wanted. To me, that sounded too good to pass up, and I decided to join them. Needless to say, the summers spent in Lexington were not good for my spiritual health.

MY SOPHOMORE
SEASON AT UK

In my sophomore season at UK, Kenny Walker was our leader that year. He was unbelievable, leading us in scoring, field-goal percentage, free-throw accuracy, rebounding, and blocked shots. Kenny averaged more than twenty-two points a game, making him the only Wildcat to average double figures that year. Most teams knew they had to stop "Sky" if they wanted to beat us. But how to stop him was the question. Kenny wore an "S" on his chest, for Superman, he could leap buildings in a single bound. How do you stop someone who is unstoppable?

Our first game of the season was an exhibition game against China in Rupp Arena. The China men were good, but were extremely overmatched when it came to speed and agility. We tried to run them to death. We beat them 94–69.

Our next opponent was Toledo of Ohio, who was also a less than formidable opponent; we beat them 63–54. Our next four games were all losses; three out of the four teams were top ten in the nation. Purdue was the only team during this stretch that was not in the top ten. Purdue beat us 56–66 at their place. Our next opponent, Southern Methodist, also beat us. I remember getting into a melee with one of the players with Southern Methodist; it was one of their big guys, named Larry Davis. He would elbow me as I went through the lane to post; his elbows seemed as sharp as kinsu knives, I took that for about two good shots, the third time he did it we got face-to-face, up close and personal. I knew if I lost my temper, I would be thrown out of the game. So I figured I had to get him back but not in the conventional way. So as we got face to face, I took the liberty of giving him a ferocious, Doberman-like bite on his nose. You know the kind of bite that Mike Tyson the former heavy weight champ gave Evander Holyfield when he bit his ear off viciously. I did it so quick that the referee knew I did something, but he couldn't quite figure out what it was that I did. Surprisingly I did not get thrown out of the game, and the SMU player got the message: no more forearm shivers.

This moment also reminded of an incident that happened in Taipei, Taiwan. I was a part of the Junior Olympic team in 1984. The team featured notable names like Karl Malone (one of 50 greatest players in NBA history); Brad Daugherty, who played at North Carolina; Olden Polynice, who played at Virginia; and Mark Allery, who played at North Carolina. We were in a hotly contested game with Italy. Italy had one foreign player on its team, from the States. This particular player was Italy's top gun, he was the guy that took most of the shots, and he was their Michael Jordan. I was on the bench at the time, taking note of everything that transpired during the game. I noticed that every time Mark Allery would run across the lane to post up, the Italian foreign player would hit him with a forearm shiver that made the fans in the stands cringe. He hit Mark so hard I felt the pain on the bench. It was a Mike Tyson knockout punch. Our coach at the time was Lute Olsen, the former legend who coached the Arizona Wildcats. After about the third forearm shiver I bolted from the bench unconsciously and attacked the Italian player while his back was turned, just as he turned to face me. It was too late. *Wham.* I knocked him out with a blind side forearm shiver of my own. Just as fast as I scurried to the court, I vanished speedily back to the bench. I was like Casper the friendly ghost, now you see me, now you don't. The arena was in total mayhem, the Taiwanese people witnessed the hit and run, but the referees didn't see anything. Every game we played after that the Taiwanese people booed us vociferously.

After the loss to SMU, we went on a tear, winning seven games in a row before losing to a conference opponent, Alabama. We finished the regular season going 16–12. We marched into the SEC Tournament with a limp. We were heavily reliant on Kenny "Sky" Walker, and everyone knew it. Because Kenny had done all the heavy lifting for us through the season, it was doubtful that he could continue his heroic effort. When every team has you on their board as the man to stop, the pounding eventually takes its toll. We ended up losing the first game of the SEC tournament to Andrew Moten and the Florida gators 55–58. Even though the regular season had been dismal for us as a team, one that none of us expected, we did have to realize we were coming off a Final Four season the year before. That team was dominated by seniors, with two of them going on to the NBA.

Although our regular season was nothing to write home about, we were not giving up yet, as we were to receive a number twelve seed in the West Region of the NCAA Tournament. It seemed that our hope had been revived. We would live to see another day, so to speak. This gave us the drive and determination to keep on fighting.

Our first opponent in the West Region was the Washington Huskies. We felt pretty confident that our tough SEC and non-conference schedule had prepared us for the NCAA Tourney.

Our regional game was played out in Salt Lake City Utah; when you play in Utah, one of the things you have to contend with is the altitude. You get tired quicker because you are thousands of feet above sea level. Our coaches always told us it was a mind thing; it's all in your mind. Well it wasn't all in our mind, it was in our lungs; you would think that your lungs were burning it felt so bad. Nevertheless, we went into our first game on a mission. We ran the Huskies right back to Washington State, beating them 66–58

The next opponent we faced was used to running; they were called the running rebels of UNLV. Jerry Tarkanian, called "Tark the Shark," was their infamous coach. His signature was usually chewing his towel and letting his players run. Coach Tark was an institution; he had been around for a long time and had great success, winning over 80 percent of his games 990–228. Again, we were equal to the challenge. We did not mind running; as a matter of fact, we welcomed the opportunity. At the time, UNLV was rated number nine in the nation. We beat them 64–61 in a barn burner.

In the NCAA West Regional Semifinals, we were matched against the Redmen of St. Johns, and there famous coach, Lou Carnesecca. Coach Carnesecca coached the Redmen's basketball program to 526 wins and 200 losses over twenty-four seasons. He was National Coach of the Year in 1983 and 1985.

The Redmen had Mark Jackson (who played in the NBA and won rookie of the year honors, currently NBA basketball analyst for ESPN and ABC), Chris Mullins (who played in the NBA with the Golden State Warriors and now is the General Manager), and Willie Glass. They were a very talented team. Chris Mullins was their star. Like Kenny, he had not been stopped all year long.

The first half, we did a pretty good job of containing Mullins, and Kenny was doing his usual "Workman"-like job...until he was poked in the eye by one of the Redmen and had to leave the game with a badly bruised cornea. He never returned. We tried to rally the team, but the mountain was too high to climb without our leader, so we lost the game 70–86. Again, I was to face some thrill of victory in the tournament, but ultimately the agony of defeat always loomed nearby, we went a dismal 18–13 for the season. Life for me seemed to be one continuous rollercoaster ride, sometimes up and sometimes down, and sometimes level to the ground.

After the game, we received the stunningly shocking news that Coach Joe B. Hall had coached his last game and would be retiring. It was a move that none of us had seen coming. This was the man that had brought me to Kentucky; I was breathless, and I didn't know quite what to do. Should I leave too or should I stay? After days of contemplating the matter, I thought to myself that the Kentucky program is greater than any one man, although I knew Coach Hall had been an outstanding statesman for the program. I also knew the program would do their best to bring in the best man for the job. So I decided to stay the course.

Coach Hall had been a great coach for Kentucky, winning a number of SEC Championships and the NCAA Championship in 1978. He had done the impossible for the team, replacing a legend and making his own mark on the program. He never really got the credit he deserved for keeping the Cats on top.

Now, a new era was about to dawn in Kentucky basketball.

THE BEGINNING OF
THE SUTTON ERA

In short order, University of Kentucky Athletic Director Cliff Hagan hired former Arkansas Razorback coach Eddie Sutton to be the new head coach at UK. There definitely were mixed emotions about Coach Sutton's hiring. Some people didn't like him because of his Afro. Others thought he might not be able to handle the pressure cooker of Kentucky basketball. Others thought he was too much of a defensive coach and not enough offense. Whatever the case, Eddie Sutton was an excellent coach, having taken his lessons from the legendary coach Henry Iba. (For the layman, Hank Iba is a member of the Basketball Hall of Fame, he was a successful basketball player, and then went on to coach in high school and college. He was the only coach in history to win two Olympic gold medals and also to coach three U.S. Olympic teams.)

Coach Sutton was so effective as a coach that by the time his coaching career had ended he did coaching stints at Creighton, Arkansas, Kentucky, Oklahoma State and the University of San Francisco. Coach Sutton became the first coach to take four different schools to the NCAA tournament, and he reached the Final Four with Arkansas in 1978 and Oklahoma State in 1995 and 2004. He was one of only seven major college men's basketball coaches to have over 800 career victories. Of course at the time, none of us knew he would go on to be such a legendary coach.

Coach Sutton believed wholeheartedly that defense wins championships, taken from his mentor Coach Henry Iba. He felt that we should take it personally if someone scored against us, and upon that principle he was to build a great team.

My junior year at Kentucky proved to be a great one under Coach Sutton.

Again we were led by Kenny "Sky" Walker. We went into our season blazing; we were annihilating every opponent that was placed before us. Our first game was an exhibition against Czechoslovakia. The Czechs were big and very skilled, but weren't very fast, so we ran them into oblivion 98–52. After beating the Czechs, we went on to beat Northwestern State before taking a trip to Hawaii.

Wow, Hawaii was heavenly. It was something that only appeared in my dreams. Seeing the picturesque ocean, the hills, and valleys made you feel thankful for eyesight, this was certainly worlds away from where I grew up in Louisville's west end. The scene was mesmerizing. But again while we were there to take in the sites, the big reason for our trip was to get better and to come together as a cohesive unit.

Our first opponent in Hawaii was a giant killer, called Chaminade University. Chaminade had been known to beat some of the top teams who came to Hawaii, like Virginia when they had 7'3" Ralph Sampson. We were careful not to let the giant killer, kill us. At the time we were rated number ten in the nation. While the scenery was great, we couldn't enjoy it until after our dismantling of Chaminade, which we did in short order 89–57.

The University of Hawaii was our next victim, we never gave Hawaii a chance to think that they could play with us; we beat them 98–65. Our trip to Hawaii ended purposefully. We came with a goal in mind to get better. We achieved our goal and enjoyed the rest of our time in tropical paradise.

We marched through our nonconference schedule that year, taking no prisoners with our only loss coming from number seven-ranked Kansas Jayhawks 66–83. Kansas was always a tough place to play, they seemed to have the loudest fans in the nation, and they had the history of Dr. James Naismith, the inventor of the game of basketball. They were Cameron crazies before there was Duke and the crazies. The sound in Lawrence was deafening. Add to the fact they had one of the best young players in college basketball, Danny Manning (former NBA player who is currently an assistant coach at the University of Kansas). Danny was like a child protégé, like Rex Chapman and Kenny Walker. Those types of players who can take a game over by themselves don't come along very often. The great thing about Danny was he could do it all. He could shoot, but would rather make a great pass instead. He could post up and score, and for 6'11" he could handle the ball like a point guard. He could find open people with pinpoint precision, he was big smooth. Kansas also had big Greg Dreiling. Greg was huge 7'0" tall and just as wide as he was big. There was no getting around him in the post. If he sealed you on the block, forget it, he was laying it in. He wasn't the best of athletes, but he made up for his lack of athletic ability with his hard nose play. It wasn't much of a game; Kansas blew us out of the gym.

After the Kansas massacre, I remember us having a team meeting and Coach Sutton sitting us in the office and giving us each a piece of paper and a pencil. He was still upset over how we lost the game with Kansas. It wasn't the loss that hurt so much; it was the way we lost.

He said, "You guys played like a bunch of pansies."

So he said, "I want you to write down if you were at war and down in a foxhole, who would you want to be in that fox hole with you? Who would you trust to fight for you and with you?"

As we all began to sneak looks around the room, each one with his poker face on, we could see his point. Most of the guys in the room were not fighters; they were finesse players but not fighters. Since I could not pick myself, the only other proven fighter in the room was Kenny "Sky" Walker, so I chose him. I found out later that if it came down to a fight, most of the guys in the room wanted me to fight with them. I was honored.

The team meeting must have left a strong impression, because we came out fighting and won the next three games before playing at home against the number fifteen-ranked Louisville Cardinals. The Cardinals was a game that I always highlight at the beginning of the season, it's the one game we must win. The players who are from out of state don't quite get the pageantry and drama surrounding this game. Some fans have an extreme hatred for one another, for the players its extreme hatred during the game after the game we can be friends. Kentucky is such a marked program for it's over 100 years of excellence. We probably have a little bit of a swagger that make teams like Louisville want to knock us off our high horse, but oh well. Is it really bragging if you can back it up? Another great Louisvillian, Muhammad Ali, use to brag all the time, he would say, "I am the greatest; no one will ever beat me because I am the greatest." But he would also go out and back it up.

The big game was magical for me personally. The Cardinals with their talented big man "Never Nervous Pervis" was the name given to Pervis Ellison the 6'9" super talented freshman who could change the complexion of a game with his ability to block shots and score on the inside. "Superb Herb" was the name given to Herbert Crook, the 6'7 inch forward who had a deadly median-range jumper and could offensive rebound with the best of them. They also had their very talented forward Billy Thompson a part of the Camden, New Jersey, connection that Coach Denny Crum had. Billy usually provided the offensive spark for the Cardinals; it would be my task to guard him during the game. I was always proud to guard the other team's best player; defense and rebounding were the two things that I took great pride in. Jeff Hall was the smart point guard from Ashland, Kentucky, who ran the show for the Cardinals.

The game was classic, the fans were ballistic, and CBS was getting its money's worth as the game went down to the wire. I was able to have my best game as a wildcat by scoring twenty-three points and snatching down seven rebounds, all coming on the offensive end. I also put the shackles on Louisville's best offensive player, Billy Thompson, and held him to eight points. Our usual leaders, Ed Davender and Kenny Walker, struggled this game, so it was good that I was able to step up and provide some scoring punch. But I was not the only one who had a great game, Roger Harden our point guard, and Richard the "Master Blaster" Madison were also major contributors as we defeated the Louisville Cardinals 69–64. The victory gave me bragging rights for the summer when I would go back to the "Ville."

Still riding on an emotional high, we went in and spanked Virginia Military Institute and then went on to Vanderbilt and gave them a good whooping. Vandy was always a tough place to play. They have one of the few old-time arenas where the court sits above the crowd and the teams sit at the end of the court versus on the side like most arenas today. This gives the Vandy faithful a supreme advantage. The coaches can't holler at their players if they are going to the opposite end of the court. Also, the Vandy crowd is probably the loudest in the SEC.

After beating Vandy on the road, we traveled to Auburn. Auburn was always a very scary opponent. They usually always had great talent but never seemed to do anything extraordinary with it. This was the year that Chris Morris, the athletic small forward, took control; he and the "rifleman" Chuck Person the 6'7 inch gunslinger. Chuck could shoot the ball from another area code and make it. He was an extraordinary shooter, and was strong as an ox. We had great success at Auburn in the past, but to our dismay, the Auburn Tigers jumped on us and didn't look back, they beat us 56–60.

After the loss at Auburn, we decided it was time to revisit our goals and objectives. Every year at Kentucky, we set a goal of winning the SEC regular season championship. After winning the regular season, we set a goal of also winning the SEC championship. After winning the SEC conference championship, we sat a goal of winning the NCAA Championship. We were not like other schools that hoped and dreamed of someday obtaining these lofty goals; we expected to achieve all of them. That's why we were the most winning program in history. We expected to win, and prepared to win, while others hoped to win.

When we decided to refocus on our goals and objectives, we went on an eight-game tear, beating every conference opponent in sight.

Our next nonconference opponent was ACC team North Carolina State, led by the talented big man Charles Shackleford. North Carolina State was a very talented team; we were ranked number eight in the nation when we got thumped 51–54. After the game, Shackleford made one of the dumbest comments of all time. He told a reporter, "I can shoot with my left hand, I can shoot with my right hand, I'm amphibious." After losing to NC

State, we regrouped and went on another eight-game winning streak, winning the SEC regular season title with a 17–1 record.

We walked into the SEC Tournament confident that we would win, just as we had in the regular season. Our first opponent was Mississippi; we shredded them to pieces 95–69. Next on the list was Louisiana State (LSU) we had played and beaten them twice already during the regular season, it was a tough game but we pulled it out 61–58.

Alabama was next on the list; this was for all the marbles, the SEC Championship. We had made it this far in dominating fashion, so we continued the beat down, beating Terry Connors, Buck Johnson, and Derrick Mckey's 'Bama team 83–72 in a very tough championship game. Boy, it felt great to be king again. There's nothing like winning, and being on top. The gratification you feel for a job well done is intoxicating. It's a feeling that you hope will never end, even though you know at some point, it invariably does.

After winning the regular season in the SEC, and the conference tournament there was only one thing left to do, and that was to go into the NCAA Tournament field and win it all. Of course, this would be a much harder feat, but it was possible if we took things one game at a time.

As we boarded the plane for Charlotte, North Carolina, for the first round of the Southeast regional, my mind reflected back to our trip to Seattle back in 1984, and how we had a chance to win the big one and didn't. I did not want another episode like that one. This time had to be different. Back then, I thought this opportunity would come again; I thought I might have a chance to make it back to the Final Four. While we were not back at the Final Four yet, this was the first step.

Our first opponent was Davidson University, a quick, crafty team. We went into the game planning to dominate by throwing the ball inside to Kenny, the plan worked to perfection. "Sky walker" dominated the game and we beat Davidson by twenty points, 75–55.

Our next opponent was the cross-town rival, Western Kentucky University. Western at that time had Tellis Frank, a big, versatile big man; and Kinnard Johnson, a workhorse. Of course, the stakes were high in this matchup. Kentucky is always thought of as the big brother to all the other schools in Kentucky. Louisville hates us and so do Eastern, Western, Morehead, and Murray. Why because we have been dominate for a hundred years. We continued our superiority as we began to man handle Western.

One of the plays I remember vividly during the game was when one of my teammates hit me with an outlet pass on the fast break. I caught the ball and dribbled down court as if I had just been shot out of a canon, when I got to the free throw line or there about, I took flight and dunked it over one of the Western players, it was thunderous. It was like I was the human highlight, Dominique Wilkins (the former great NBA player who was known to dunk on opponents). The fans went bananas they couldn't believe what they had just witnessed; the referees couldn't believe it either so he called me for charging. That referee should have been fired on the spot. You don't take away a once in a lifetime dunk on someone and call it a charge; the Western player had just been posturized. Despite the charge call, we beat the Hill toppers 71–64.

Our next game in the Regional Semifinals was against a familiar foe, the Alabama Crimson Tide. We had seen enough of these guys during the SEC conference season. 'Bama had a plethora of talent with Buck Johnson, Derrick Mckey, and Terry Connors. While both teams knew each other extremely well, we outlasted the Tide and went on to a 68–63 victory.

Our next opponent was also a very familiar foe, the LSU Tigers. LSU was a team that was deep and very talented, they had big John Williams, the versatile big man that could handle the ball out on the perimeter and could also post up in the lane. They also had workman Ricky Blanton, and Jose Vargas. We had already played LSU three times during the season and knew we had their number. I can't tell you how difficult it is to beat a team three times in a row, we did that to LSU. The fourth meeting was the most important. It seemed as though Jose, Rick, and John had a different agenda than the first three meetings; they were playing with a renewed sense of confidence.

The game seemed to be back and forth the whole way; Ricky Blanton really gave us fits this particular game. He became the difference maker that won the game and gave LSU a berth to the Final Four 57–59. The blow was crushing, gut wrenching; I had felt this pain before in 1984 with a loss in the Final Four. I didn't deal well with it then and didn't show any signs of dealing with it in a mature way now. Losses are always debilitating, they exasperate you and they cripple your psyche. We finished the season with a 32–4 record, but no NCAA Championship. Was the total season a waste just because we didn't win the big one? I would have the whole summer to think about the tragedy of having lost the big one.

Our lives are not based on the championships we win or lose. I would have loved to have won a NCAA Championship as a player, but for some reason the gold trophy never materialized. That didn't stop me from shooting for it. Don't let your losses prevent you from going for the championship. A lot of us cancel our own victory when we decide in our mind that we can never win the game. You must prepare to win, and then go out and play the game. Victory only comes after many failed attempts. Your failures will lead you to victory if you don't give up. Keep fighting, improve your failure rate, what would happen if you would keep going after you fail, what would happen, if failure didn't matter, how good could you be, what business could you start, what degree could you obtain, what relationship could you have if failure were not an option.

DOOM AND GLOOM

In what was to be my senior year, the 1986–87 seasons, I suffered a tragic and potentially career-ending knee injury in practice. We were in preseason practice when Ed Davender came down court on the fast break with one of his shake-and-bake moves. He took a shot and collided with Irving Thomas in the process. Irving saw Ed's out-of-control nature and took the charge, and Irving came crashing into my knee just as I had landed for the rebound; it was like a malicious hit-at-the-knees clipping play you see in football, Irving hit me as if he were a runaway freight train. The collision proved to be career altering, as Coach Sutton rushed to the court, as if he had just witnessed a hit-and-run accident. I could tell something wasn't quite right with my knee, but I was willing to continue practicing. But Coach Sutton said, "No! We will get you to a doctor, and make sure everything's all right."

I was taken to Central Baptist Hospital in Lexington for an x-ray. Dr. Ray, our team doctor at the time, looked at the x-ray and quickly told me that the prognosis was not good. It seemed that I had a torn ACL, or anterior cruciate ligament. At the time, few players came back from that particular injury, so this news was devastating to me. It surely meant shattered dreams, and the end of my basketball career.

I had worked very hard to get to this point in my life, but now that I could be "the man," this had happened. For three

long years, I had played in the shadows of great men like Sam
Bowie, Melvin Turpin, and Kenny "Sky" Walker, and now that it
was time for my one shining moment, I had suffered as serious
an injury as any player could. It felt like someone had suddenly
snatched the rug out from under me, like I'd had an opportunity
to win the big game, but the coach had taken me out. Was God
trying to tell me something?

As always, when something went wrong in my life, I turned
to God. Was He punishing me? Was this the long-dreaded curse
that would come upon me for my sin? Was I finally paying the
price? If so, I had no one but myself to blame. Everyone had
warned me, and I had chosen not to heed the warnings.

As doctors did more tests, they began to tell me that there
was a slim possibility that I could recover from this injury. It
would not be easy, they said. The surgery would be very painful,
and the rehabilitation would be equally painful. But if I was willing to put forth a lot of effort, I could come back.

For sure, I would miss the entire 1986–87 season, but if I did
eight or nine months of serious rehabilitation work, I just might
be able to play the following year. I was certainly willing to try,
but I would be lying if I said I thought I would come out of this
and be the player that I was before the injury. I knew once an
athlete had suffered a major injury if he did make a comeback,
he was usually a shadow of the athlete he use to be. The odds
were against me coming back like the bull in the china shop I use
to be. Even so, I was not going to give up that easy; the road had
been too long, too many dreams, and too many goals to obtain
to just throw in the towel. I wasn't about to wave the white flag
of surrender.

I received many cards and letters from Kentucky fans as I
was preparing to go under the knife to have the knee repaired.
Then the day came, and I was wheeled into the operating room,

panic-stricken. My parents were there, and prayers were offered up that God would guide the surgeon's hands. I didn't deserve a miracle, I knew, but I was hoping for one anyway.

Dr. Ray began to explain the details of the operation to me and my family before actually carrying out the procedure. I had remembered getting my left knee scoped after my freshman year, and that was tremendously painful (a knee cartilage repair two seasons earlier). This would be a lot more intensive. First, there was the repair of the cartilage tear that required a rather painless arthroscopic procedure. Then the ligament replacement required an eight-member medical staff, two hours of arthroscopic surgery, and a whole chest full of tools. A knife was used to slice away the middle third of the ligament connecting the kneecap to the calf bone. A saw cut off small sections of the calf bone and kneecap that were attached to the dissected ligament. A drill by Black & Decker bored the holes in the thigh bone and calf bone. Through the tunnels, the doctors slipped into place a bone-tendon-bone graft. Finally, a screwdriver tightened the graft into place.

Later that same day it seemed, Dr. Ray and his staff started the excruciating rehabilitation process. I thought to myself, *this must be a bad dream; these people have got to be crazy. You don't saw on a person's knee, put screws and staples in it, and then get them up trying to walk around on it like everything was okay.*

The pain was excruciating. As the rehabilitation progressed, they forced me to do what I thought I couldn't do. It was much more difficult than I could have imagined, and if I could have thrown in the towel, I would have. But something in me just kept telling me to *Fight; fight Winston, if you are going to come back from this one you will have to fight for your life.*

I had to go through, there was no other choice, there was no retreating; there were too many people pulling for me—and, yes, praying for me.

It's amazing what we can do when we have someone in our corner telling us, "You can do it." When our own thought process is saying, "No," that's when we need good, strong, "You can" people around us. As usual, one of the people cheering me on and telling me I could do it was Mom. If she was not able to be with me physically, she was somewhere praying for me. In the darkest moments of my rehabilitation, she stayed right in the hospital with me and never allowed me to give up. She would quote scriptures to me and remind me of God's goodness. Everything was all right as long as she was at the hospital with me, but as soon as she left, things changed dramatically.

As I had done many other times, I took the opportunity of this tragedy in my life to make things right with God. I repented for my many failings and asked Him to help me live a clean and wholesome life in the future, and I meant it.

Then, no sooner had Mom left the hospital, the temptation returned, unrelenting and insistent. At first, I resisted it. How could I sin against God again when He had brought me through this surgery and it looked like I had a fighting chance to make a comeback? That would be lunacy.

And if this injury had been punishment for my sins, what might happen to me if I started sinning again? No, I just couldn't do it again, not the same mistake over and over and over again.

God had been very merciful to me, and I felt at the moment that I could claim heaven as my home, but if I returned to sexual pleasure, I had no such guarantee. And if I stood before God, I knew that I could not blame someone else. There would be no excuses. I would be found guilty as charged. "First-degree sinner, depart from me. I never knew you," I could image Him saying.

I resisted as long as I felt I could, and then I felt compelled to call one of my girlfriends and ask if she could come and show me some affection. We had sex right there in the hospital room. In this way, all of my well-meaning commitments went right out the window. And I was right back where I had started.

Obviously I had not conquered my sexual urges; they had conquered me. Why had I let something that was supposed to be a gift from God become such a shackle around my neck? Instead of me controlling it, it controlled me. I used sex to medicate my pain, to relieve my anxiety, and to calm my fears. It had become my security blanket. Instead of trusting in God to supply all my needs according to His riches in glory, I was trusting in sex. My obsession with sex had gotten so bad that at times, both before and after the surgery, I was having sex with as many as three different women in a single day. I really cared very little about myself at the time. I just wanted to escape reality. Sex was the way I escaped, if just for a moment. Sex had become my god. I had started to believe there was no real reason to live, except to have sex. Everything other than that dealt with pain, unfulfilled hopes and dreams, and major disappointment. It was a wonder that I was able to practice, play, or do anything else, for that matter. Now, more than ever, it seemed, I could not do without some female attention while I was recovering from surgery. What would become of me?

REDSHIRT YEAR

What was supposed to be my senior year became a year of heartache and disappointment. Rehabbing my knee seemed to be an endless process full of pain and agony. Three times a day, I would work with the medical staff and trainers to rehab my fully repaired right knee. The doctors estimated my return date to the court to be nine to twelve months. I can remember one day being in the training room and rehabbing when the old Rod Stewart song came on, "Some guys have all the luck, some guys have all the pain, some guys get all the breaks, some guys do nothing but complain ..." Well, that's about all I can remember. At that point, I wanted to destroy the radio because the song seemed to describe my life to a tee. But it seemed that I was getting all the pain rather than all the luck.

The 1986–87 seasons was to be my time of leadership, stepping out of the shadows of Sam Bowie, Melvin Turpin, and Kenny "Sky" Walker, but it wasn't to be. The injury would cause me to forfeit my date with destiny that year. My return would have to wait. I would use this season as a stepping stone. I would join the staff on the bench and be an unwilling assistant coach.

This season was actually the dawning of King Rex, Rex Chapman, the super guard from Owensboro, Kentucky, who attended Apollo High School. I remember meeting Rex when I was in high school at Male. We were playing at a camp at Kentucky Wesleyan; after seeing me play, Rex wanted my jersey kind of like the old Mean Joe Green Coke commercial back in 1979 (Mean Joe Green played football for the Pittsburgh Steelers; he was a part of the Iron Curtain defense). As the commercial goes, Mean Joe is limping back to the locker room when a kid comes out of the stands and stops Mean Joe and tells him he is the best ever. Mean Joe says, "Yeah sure." The kid says, "Really you are the best ever," so as Mean Joe is limping along, the kid says, "Do you need any help?" and Mean Joe says, "No I don't need any help," and finally the kid offers Mean Joe his Coke. After some convincing Mean Joe finally takes the Coke, and shortly after throws the kid his jersey. The kid goes, "Wow, thanks Mean Joe." My meeting with Rex was similar except he didn't offer me a Coke after I gave him my practice jersey. If I had known then that Rex was going to be as great as he was, I would have given him the Coke and asked for his jersey.

Rex reminded me a lot of Kenny "Sky" Walker in the sense that they both had the uncanny ability of putting a team on their back and willing them to victory. While Kenny played mostly inside and jumped over people, Rex was a 6'5" point guard and shooting guard. The kid could shoot the ball from across the street and make it. He also had springs in his legs; they say white men can't jump, Rex proved that notion totally wrong. Rex would rather dunk on you than stare at you; the boy was nasty. He was the Great White Hope.

While Rex and the team only went 18–11 over the course of the season there were a couple of huge wins. One of those wins was in Freedom Hall against the Louisville Cardinals. Rex almost single handedly beat the Cardinals by himself; the score was 85–51. I really enjoyed that one. It was nothing like beating my hometown Louisville Cardinals.

The other huge win came against Navy. This was the time that "the Admiral" David Robinson was playing. Rex and the Cats totally took the Admiral right out of the game. Actually much like Rex, the Admiral was a one-man show; he didn't have much help, so the Cats won 80–69.

There were no SEC Conference titles this season. We got beat in the first round of the SEC Tournament by Auburn 72–79; we also lost in the first round of the NCAA Southeast Regional to Ohio State 77–91. It was a very trying season for Rex and the rest of the guys; I don't know which was worse, the pain of the knee injury I suffered or watching my teammates struggle without helping them.

While the losses were many during my redshirt season, there were some wins for me personally, as I had plenty of opportunity to sit back and evaluate our team and myself. One of the things my injury taught me was to enjoy the moments, don't take your life and your health for granted. Enjoy every moment. Live each moment as if it were your last. The injury also taught me the meaning of patience. You don't come back from a major injury of this sort overnight; it takes time to heal the brokenness.

The time on the sideline also taught me to take time for introspection, evaluate what's working and what is not. Cling to that which works and make it better.

MY SENIOR YEAR
AT KENTUCKY

Through what came to be described by many as "extreme dedication and hard work," I was able to recover from the ACL knee surgery and was back on the court after nine months. I underwent rehabilitation three times a day and simply refused to give up. Like Jim Valvano, the former North Carolina State basketball coach, said when he was fighting cancer, "Never give up, never ever give up." I figured if a man like Jim Valvano could be so wildly courageous facing one of the most dreaded killers on this earth, I could fight for my right to get back on the court and do what I love to do.

After I had passed my "redshirt" year (a year in which a college athlete is permitted to sit out of competition to rehabilitate an injury without losing eligibility), my fifth and senior year kicked in during the 1987–88 Season. I was back playing Kentucky basketball again.

We had a pretty good year with Rex Chapman leading us with twenty points a game. Rex was one of those all-star players who come along once in a lifetime. He could do anything with a basketball. He was our version of "Pistol Pete" Maravich. Rex, like Kenny Walker before him, was simply unstoppable.

Rex and I were roommates, and the thing I remember most about him was that he was a very congenial and friendly person. He would take me to his grandmother's house in Lexington periodically so that we could wash our clothes.

Rex could have done anything he wanted to do in life, but he was passionate about playing the game of basketball. He chose the NBA and left UK after his sophomore season (Rex played twelve seasons in the NBA, and is currently vice-president of personnel for the Denver Nuggets).

In addition to Rex at the guard spot, we also had Ed Davender, who added 15.7 points a game. Ed was one of those New York City point guards that knew how to get to the rim, but could also step up and take the big shot when we needed it. Ed was also a lockdown defender. He was a defensive specialist.

Also on the team was Sean Sutton. Sean was the son of Coach Eddie Sutton. Sean took a lot of flack from fans playing for his father, but he was very courageous and just went out and did his job (he went on to coach at Oklahoma State after Coach Sutton retired).

Derrick Miller, the sharp shooting 6'6" guard, could flat out shoot with the best of them. He was a pure shooter. He was long and lanky.

Eric Manual was the versatile small forward from Macon, Georgia, who could do it all.

Richard "the Master Blaster" Madison was another very talented forward who could handle the ball as well as shoot.

Reggie Hanson was the 6'7" do-it -all forward from Somerset, Kentucky. Reggie was a great player, but the thing most people talk about when they remember Reggie is his glowing personality and smile.

Robert Lock was our big man in middle from Reedley, California. Rob played hard and gave us much needed help inside. He averaged about eleven points a game.

Cedric Jenkins was the long slender forward, a post player that was hard to get a shot over. We often called him "Big Smooth" for his smooth jump shot. Cedric was also a very intelligent person often making over a 3.0 academically.

LeRon Ellis was also a big man that played center for us. LeRon was tremendously talented. He could do it all even as a freshman.

We called Mike Scott the snowman because he was so big, standing at 6'11," but he was just a tad bit slow, for Coach Sutton's running pressing style. Mike was a great guy, probably a little too nice. Mike was from Green up County Kentucky. Jonathon Davis, Deron Feldhaus, Richie Farmer (currently agriculture commissioner of Kentucky) and John Pelphrey (currently the head coach for the Arkansas Razorbacks) was all redshirt freshman.

This was it, my return to the Wildcat uniform after sitting out a whole year. I was like a caged tiger, or shall I say a caged Wildcat. I was ready; I was not worried about my fully repaired right knee. I felt like Lee Majors, who played the character Steve Austin, in the television series "The Six Million Dollar Man." I was rebuilt stronger. I could run faster, and jump higher. It was my time. I had waited for at least four years for this one shining moment.

Our first game in my inaugural season back in uniform came in the form of a very skilled Soviet Union team. The Soviets are legendary for giving American teams all they want and then some; they have had great success against the USA in the Olympics. They are big, strong, and very intelligent players. They took us right down to the wire, hitting three pointers, after three pointers. We could not stop them from the three-point line. It was a nail biter, not the way I wanted my first game back to start. I did get some glory in that I stepped to the free-throw line late in the game and sank two free throws to give us a two-point lead with seventeen seconds to go. We ended up hanging on to win 75–72. It felt great to get the first game under my belt.

Our next game against Hawaii was a good ole fashion blow-out. We beat Hawaii 86–59. The Bearcats of Cincinnati were our next opponent, it didn't take us long to run them out of the gym 101–77.

Number five-ranked Indiana Hoosiers was our next opponent; we were ranked number two in the nation at the time. Indiana had big man Dean Garrett, and athletic guard Keith Smart (currently the head coach for the Golden State Warriors in the NBA). More importantly they had their Hall of Fame Coach Bob Knight leading the charge. We were fired up for the challenge, playing Indiana is like playing Louisville in my book, and it's a must-win game. Well every game on the schedule is a must-win when you play at Kentucky but when you play against the Indiana's, the Dukes, and the North Carolinas, they are really must wins. So we came in that game with fire in our eyes, it was the Big Four Classic played in Indianapolis. The game was made for television as every point scored was a war, you could see and feel the enthusiasm of the crowd in the stands. The crowd was split half and half, blue for the nation and red for the Hoosiers. One thing you knew about a Bob Knight-coached team, they were going to be tough as nails, and they were going to pick you to death. I never saw a team run the motion offense as effective as the Hoosiers. If you weren't careful and talking on defense at all times, you could quite possibly walk out of the game with a concussion. The Hoosiers was the hardest hitting team in basketball, which I liked; they gave me a legitimate reason to hit somebody. Even though they were tough, we were tougher winning the game in overtime 82–76.

We were so fired up about the season that we won our first eleven games before losing to the Auburn Tigers at home 52–53 on a three-point shot by John Caylor. As time was winding down, everyone in the building knew the Auburn star Chris Morris would take the last shot. Thinking that Auburn designed a play to draw our defense to Morris, Morris got the ball penetrated and kicked the ball to the open man Caylor for the wide-open three-point shot, which he knocked down for the game. We were the number one-ranked team in the country at the time. What a huge letdown; our bubble had been burst. We were deflated. It's not every day you get to be number one in the nation. We were not there for long.

After the Auburn loss, in preparation for our next two games, Coach Sutton made us watch three hours of film. He wanted us to understand how poorly we played against Auburn. He told us there are nights where you will have bad shooting nights, but you should never have a bad night on defense. We shot just thirty-four percent against Auburns slow-down game.

After the strong emphasis on defense and playing hard, we went on a little run to beat Alabama 63–55. Alabama had another dangerous team with Michael Ansley, the 6'7" muscle man, Keith Askins, the 6'6" work horse on defense (Keith went on to have a long career in the NBA with the Miami Heat and is currently an assistant coach for the Miami Heat where former Kentucky great Pat Riley is the president), and Alvin Lee, the talented guard who averaged over fifteen points a game.

We also continued our winning ways by beating Tennessee in Rupp arena 83–65.

Our next game was against the Florida Gators; a win against the Gators could catapult us into first place in the conference.

Florida had a talented team led by DeWayne Schintzius, their 7'0" center, they also had a very talented guard we called "mad max," Vernon Maxwell (Mad Max went on to have a great NBA career). The game was one of those games were nothing seemed to go in for us; we shot 28.1 percent for the game. The Gators capitalized on our inability to put the ball in the hole; they beat us in Rupp 56–58.

Attempting to rebound from the loss to Florida in Rupp, we came back and had a tough game against Jose Vargas and the LSU Tigers. I had a great game this game scoring eighteen points and pulling down ten rebounds; we beat the LSU Tigers 76–61. We were very lucky in this one, in that LSU couldn't hit a three-point shot. After the game, their infamous Coach Dale Brown said, "If we can't shoot the ball better from the three-point line, I will institute a Thou-Shalt-not-shoot-the three-point-shot rule."

Our next opponent was the Vanderbilt Commodores at Vandy. Again, this is probably the toughest place to play in the SEC. The game started out hotly contested with Vandy knocking down three-point shots all over the place. Scott Draud, the little guard from Fort Highlands High School in Kentucky, obviously had something to prove as he hit six three point-shots scoring twenty-two points. Barry Booker (commentator for the SEC game of week) very athletic guard who liked to slash to the basket, shredded us for fourteen points, Big Will Perdue (had a long career with the Chicago Bulls in the NBA) dismantled us inside and had seventeen points, and Barry Goheen had his usual workman-like game with seventeen points. Vandy gave us a woodshed moment, beating us 83–66.

After the Vandy loss, we rallied the troops and went on a five-game winning streak, beating Notre Dame, Mississippi, Mississippi State, Auburn, and Alabama.

After the five-game winning streak, we got a little cocky and ran into a very tough Tennessee squad and lost a close one on the road, 72–70. We also went down to Gainesville, Florida, and got our lunch handed to us by the Gators 76–83.

Again, we managed to reinvigorate ourselves after a couple of humiliating losses. We regrouped and came back with a little fire in our belly and got on a four game-winning streak beating LSU 95–69 at Rupp arena.

Our next opponent was against the highly talented Syracuse Orangemen of the Big East conference. The Orangemen was ranked number ten in the country while we were ranked number twelve. The game was played at Rupp Arena, and the fans were hyped. It was another classic that was close all the way. Syracuse was kept close with their big man Rony Seikaly, and their All-Star power forward Derrick Coleman, and their All-World guard DeWayne "the Pearl" Washington. Of course, Chapman and Davender had their usual workman-like effort, but I was able to circle the wagons and lead the team in scoring in this one with fifteen points and a bushel of rebounds, we marched to victory 62–58.

Our last home game was against Hugh Durham's Georgia Bulldogs. It was the most emotional night of the year, senior night. There is nothing like senior night at Kentucky. It's the night were your name is called, and you walk out to center court with your parents, signifying the end of one journey, and the beginning of a new one. At Kentucky, over 23,000 fans give you a standing ovation that you only see at concerts after you have dazzled the crowd with a virtuoso performance. They stand for what seems like an eternity clapping and applauding as if you are the renowned Pulitzer Prize winner who had just discovered the cure for cancer.

All the adoration and applause soon give way to silent reflection of how far we have come as a team and as a people, as the singing of My Old Kentucky Home by Happy Chandler is sung. Each of my previous four years, I had heard the song sung by Happy Chandler but really did not know the words or the meaning behind the song. Being the slow learner I am, I guess it took me five years to decipher the origin and background of the song. Stephen Foster originally wrote and published the song in 1853 supposedly traveling from Pittsburgh, Pennsylvania, to New Orleans, Louisiana; he stopped in Bardstown, Kentucky, to visit his cousins. The song supposedly describes a scene on a slave plantation. The abolitionist Frederick Douglass believed the song was sympathetic to the slaves. The original version was:

The sun shines bright in the old Kentucky home,
Tis summer, the darkies are gay;
The corn-top's rip and the meadow's in the bloom,
While the birds make music all the day.
The young folks roll on the little cabin floor,
All merry, all happy and bright;
By'n' by Hard Times comes a-knocking at the door,
Then my old Kentucky home, goodnight.
Chorus:
Weep no more my lady
Oh! Weep no more today!
We will sing one song for the old Kentucky home,
For the Old Kentucky Home far away.

In 1986, they say the only black member of the Kentucky General Assembly heard a version of the song performed by a Japanese group of visitors in which they sang the word "darkies." He said the lyrics "conveyed racial discrimination;" soon after, the Assembly made some changes to the original version and replaced the word "darkies" with the word "people." I like this version a lot better:

The sun shines bright in My Old Kentucky home,
'Tis summer and people are gay;
The corn-top's ripe and the meadow's in the bloom
While the birds make music all the day.
The young folks roll on the little cabin floor
All merry, all happy and bright;
By 'n' by hard times comes a knocking at the door
Then My Old Kentucky Home, good night!
Weep no more my lady
Oh! Weep no more today!
We will sing one song
For My Old Kentucky Home
For My Old Kentucky Home, far away.

Time and time again, I swore to myself I would not break down and cry when I saw the likes of Sam Bowie, Melvin Turpin and Kenny "Sky" Walker go through this before me. I guess promises are made to be broken because I had cried every time, this time was no different. Kentucky had come a long way since the days of segregation; now the program was fully integrated, and I was enjoying the fruits of all the players who came before me, both black and white.

The moment marked a time of somberness and yet hope for me personally, being the first African American from Louisville to come to Kentucky as a basketball player since Tom Payne, this must have been what Dr. Martin Luther King dreamed about when he gave his life for racial equality. Maybe my coming would open the floodgates for more Louisville African American basketball players to come to Kentucky.

I also thought about the knee injury the year before that had delayed this moment; I thought about the Final Four appearance in 1984, I thought about all the wonderful relationships I had formed since being at Kentucky. It was a nostalgic moment. Most importantly, I had the two people with me that night who had given me this opportunity, my parents Winston and Shirley Bennett Jr. Where would I have been without them? They were the ones who told me to pursue my dreams, forget about what others say; trail blaze your own path. There were times I wanted to quit, but they kept encouraging me to stay the course. Nothing happens without a fight they would constantly tell me. My mother would always say, "You can do all things through Christ who strengthens you."

The most difficult thing about senior night is trying to play the game. After the singing of "My Old Kentucky Home," you soon discover there is still a game to be played. So you have to dry your four years, or in my case five years, worth of tears and come out and play the game. What a disgrace it would be to lose on senior night. Senior night has to be a must win situation. True enough, after we dried our eyes we came out with the eye of the tiger and beat a very tough Georgia Bulldog team 80–72. The Bulldogs were no pushover, Willie Anderson the exciting guard who went on to play in the NBA, Alec Kessler the mobile post player, and Toney Mack, made the game close the whole night. We were very fortunate to win that night.

After the senior night game, we went on to beat Ole Miss in Starkville, Mississippi 82–64 before moving on to the SEC Tournament.

Our confidence remained at a fever pitch as we went into the SEC Tournament that was to be played in Baton Rouge, Louisiana, the home of the LSU Tigers. We were determined to win, even though LSU would greet us with a real live Bengal Tiger in its cage as we pulled up to the arena. Their fans were there early, always greeting you with true Louisiana obscenities.

LSU fans would have to wait as our first game was against Ole Miss, we had just played them a few days before, we took it right to them, never thinking they could play with us, we beat them 82–64.

Our next opponent was the LSU Tigers; the Tigers were essentially playing at home, and they let us know it was there house. They would turn out the lights and have a stuntman parachute from the ceiling to get the festivities started. We didn't care what they did, they could have played with the Bengal Tiger, we were not going to be beat, and we outlasted LSU 86–80.

We marched into the championship game to play Willie Anderson and the Georgia Bulldogs. The Bulldogs were famous for marching out there real live bulldog on the court to start the game. The bulldog who was gallivanting on the court had a way of leaving slobber on the hard wood, I wondered if he sensed he had some kibbles and bits coming to him. We knew this would be a war, and it was. We managed to squeak out a victory, 62–57, for the SEC Championship. It felt so good to be champs once again. There's nothing like that feeling of winning it all. You work so hard all season long, lifting weights and practicing with no guarantee that you will win. It is an extreme act of faith to see all that dedication, hard work, and discipline come together to win it all. For me, it was even more gratifying after sitting out and seeing the team struggle the year before. This was sweet vindication.

While it was great being champions in the SEC, we wanted to be champions of the NCAA. So there was little time to celebrate as we started to set our sights on winning the NCAA Tournament. We received a favorable draw as we moved to Cincinnati, Ohio, to play in the first round of the Southeast Regional. This was perfect for us; this would be close enough for our fans to travel in droves. We always pack the house no matter where we play, but now it would be for all the marbles, and just an hour and half drive from Lexington. Kentucky has a very strong supporting cast in Northern Kentucky and Cincinnati. Our first victims would be the University of Southern; Southern was small and quick, so our formula for success would be to get the ball inside to Rob Locke, which we did. We went on to beat Southern 99–84.

Our second-round opponent was the University of Maryland and their renowned coach, Bob Wade. Maryland was a very talented team that could be very dangerous. They had a tremendous freshman center in Brian Williams he scorched us for twenty points; they also had Derrick Lewis who was a gifted power forward. It didn't matter; we were firing on all cylinders; we beat Maryland 90–84 to advance to the regional semifinals.

The Southeast Regional Semifinals were played in Birmingham, Alabama. We still had our usual dedicated following of the Big Blue Nation. As a team, we were excited about an opportunity to beat Villanova and go on to the Final Four. The game was frantic, both teams wanted to advance. We did all we could but nothing was working in our favor. We had come so far, but lost to Villanova 74–80. I remember after the game, realizing this was it; my college career was now over. Most of us sat, mesmerized by the fact that we lost another opportunity to advance to the Final Four. Tears began to flow as I began to replay my five-year college career over in my mind. There were moments of extreme adulation, and then there were moments of pain and anguish. I had seen it all in my five years with the big blue. The time had passed as a vapor. When you are on the journey, it seems endless, when you reach your destination it seems that the journey never took place.

WHAT NOW?

As I said before, Dad had asked me when I was still small, if I could see myself playing in the NBA, and all during my teenage years, I had tried to see myself doing just that. Sometimes the dream seemed much too hard to imagine, but I continued to keep it alive in my heart.

In the meantime, I had slowly but surely accomplished some of my other goals in life. Now I had to concentrate on a new one—getting to the NBA.

One of the goals I had already accomplished was to get a college education. I not only played basketball at the University of Kentucky; I graduated from the University with a degree in Business Administration. That meant that I was the first on either side of our family to get a college degree. Wow, what an accomplishment for someone who did not like to read when he was little. Obviously, my affection for reading and academics grew tremendously over time. A word to young people who are reading this book education is your first key to success. It's hard enough to make it in life as it is, without your education you limit your opportunities for success. Treat your education better than you treat your love of the game. Love your education more;

your education will be the foundation that you build your success on.

In June of that same year, another of my dreams seemed imminent. It was time for the NBA Draft, and rumor had it that I would be a late first-round pick. Logic should have told me NBA teams do not draft wounded soldiers first, if at all. Damaged goods are not the preferred order of any professional team.

Expectations were high in my apartment in Lexington, where our entire family had gathered to witness the draft on television. Our excitement had been spurred by the rumors published in the local newspapers that I probably would be picked early. We waited on pins and needles expecting one of the NBA teams to call at any time. We waited, and waited, and waited, but the call never came.

As the draft picks were read one by one, I was not among the first rounders. I suppose I should not have been surprised. I had two strikes against me. (1) I was coming back from a serious knee injury (and I now know that team management never looks kindly on "damaged goods"), and (2) I was a 6'7" inside player, a small forward with no jump shot. There were other more rounded players available.

As the second-round picks were read, surprisingly I wasn't among them either. As I begin to ponder the fate of my career, I began to believe the lie that always haunts me, that I am just not good enough. Had all my dreams been in vain? Had all the pain, the sacrifice, and the commitment been for naught. Was I always going to be a day late and a dollar short? Would anything ever work out like I planned?

After the second round was announced, the later rounds were just scrolled across the television screen. I got up, left the apartment, and took a walk.

Confused and disappointed, I didn't know what attitude to take at the moment. I wanted to be angry with God, yet I knew that He wasn't to blame. I wanted to feel that I had been true to Him, since I continued to go to church, read my Bible, and fasted and prayed. But I knew that I hadn't really been faithful to my convictions in many other ways. I wanted to believe that aside from listening to music other than Gospel and having sex, I was a pretty good Christian, but I knew that wasn't true either. Was God punishing me?

In that moment, I felt like the worst failure the world had ever seen. I just knew that I had blown my chances for greatness by my inability, or unwillingness, to obey God and His Word.

Eventually I *was* drafted into the NBA—by the Cleveland Cavaliers in the third round, the sixty-fourth pick overall. It could have been much worse. God had been merciful to me.

Not long afterward, I left Lexington for the Cavs summer training camp in Richfield, Ohio. I was hoping that this move would represent, for me, more than just a change of scenery. I needed a whole new style of living, a complete change of life.

Being with the Cavaliers was very exciting. Lenny Wilkens, who had been a legend as a player, was the coach during this period. When Coach Wilkens played, it was said that he loved to make his offensive moves dribbling right, and all his opponents knew it, but they still couldn't stop him. Coach Wilkens was one of three elite coaches who was inducted into the Hall of Fame as a player and as a coach (the other two were John Wooden and Bill Sharman). He also coached the Seattle Supersonics to a NBA Championship in 1979, when they had Dennis Johnson, Gus Williams, Downtown Freddie Brown, Jack Sikma, and Lonnie Shelton. Coach Wilkens was the most winning coach in NBA history with 1,332 wins over a 35 year history of coaching in the NBA, until the 2010 season when Coach Don Nelson of the

Golden State Warriors surpassed him (as of this writing Coach
Nelson has 1,333 victories, making him the most winning all time
coach in the NBA). His coaching record speaks volumes about
him as a coach, but the thing that stood head and shoulders
above his coaching record, was his character.

Coach Wilkens reminded me of Tony Dungy, the soft-
spoken former Super Bowl winning coach of the Indianapolis
Colts (Coach Dungy became the first African- American head
coach to win the Super Bowl, when the Colts defeated the Chicago Bears on February 4, 2007). They both were soft-spoken
coaches who knew how to get their point across without getting in your face and screaming and yelling. They both live their
lives with tremendous character and love for people. They both
loved to win, and they both achieved their goal of winning with
a tremendous love of the game, a tremendous love of family, and
a tremendous love of the players they coached. What an awesome inspiration they have both been to me. Sometimes mentors
come not only through our personal contact but sometimes just
hearing a person's story is enough to inspire you to do better.

I loved coach Dungy's book *Quiet Strength,* which spoke
loudly about the importance of not only winning but how you
win. Coach Dungy's success formula of winning with a *Quiet
Strength* that only Jesus Christ can give is the ultimate key to
our success in every area of life. These are two super successful
people who sat the bar extremely high for being great on and off
their perspective courts.

Brian Winters was also a man of great character, who had
been a great guard with the Milwaukee Bucks, was one of Coach
Wilken's assistants. The other assistant was Dick Helm, one of
the nicest coaches I ever met.

Wayne Embry was the general manager of the Cavs. He was an imposing figure, at 6'8" inches and well over three hundred and fifty pounds. He had also been a great NBA player.

In that very first summer with the Cavs, I was injured. I severely twisted my ankle and, because of it, I was not able to prove that I belonged on the team. The team had twelve men under contract, so there was no room for a "blue-collar" player like myself. So I was released from the team.

Again, I was devastated. Did this mean the end of my career?

After many nights of living on the phone and speaking to overseas teams, my agent was able to find me a position with a team called Teorema in Italy.

Remember no matter how many defeats you suffer, remind yourself of the old Destinys Child song, called "Survivor."

(Verse 1)
Now that you are out of my life,
I'm so much better,
You thought that I'd be weak without ya,
But I'm stronger,
You thought that I'd be broke without ya,
But I'm richer,
You thought that I'd be sad without ya,
I laugh harder,
You thought I wouldn't grow without ya,
Now I'm wiser,
You thought that I'd be helpless without ya,
But I'm smarter,
You thought that I'd be stressed without ya,
But I'm chillin'
You thought I wouldn't sell without ya,
Sold nine million.

[Chorus]
I'm a survivor (what),
I'm not gonna give up (what),
I'm not gon' stop (what),
I'm gonna work harder (what),
I'm a survivor (what),
I'm gonna make it (what),
I will survive (what),
Keep on survivin' (what),
I'm a survivor (what),
I'm not gonna give up (what),
I'm not gon' stop (what),
I'm gonna work harder (what),
I'm a survivor (what),
I'm gonna make it (what),
I will survive (what),
Keep on survivin' (what).
(Verse 2)
Thought I couldn't breathe without you,
I'm inhalin'
You thought I couldn't see without you,
Perfect vision,
You thought I couldn't last without ya,
But I'm lastin'
You thought that I would die without ya,
But I'm livin'
Thought that I would fail without ya,
But I'm on top,
Though it would be over by now,
But it won't stop,
You thought that I would self-destruct,
But I'm still here,

Even in my years to come,
I'm still gon' be here.
[Chorus]
I'm a survivor (what),
I'm not gonna give up (what),
I'm not gon' stop (what),
I'm gonna work harder (what),
I'm a survivor (what),
I'm gonna make it (what),
I will survive (what),
Keep on survivin' (what),
I'm a survivor (what),
I'm not gonna give up (what),
I'm not gon' stop (what),
I'm gonna work harder (what),
I'm a survivor (what),
I'm gonna make it (what),
I will survive (what),
Keep on survivin' (what).
(Bridge)
I'm wishin' you the best,
Pray that you are blessed,
Much success, no stress, and lots of happiness,
(I'm better than that)
I'm not gonna blast you on the radio,
(I'm better than that)
I'm not gonna lie on you or your family, yo,
(I'm better than that)
I'm not gonna hate you in the magazine,
(I'm better than that)
I'm not gonna compromise my Christianity,
(I'm better than that)

You know I'm not gonna diss you on the Internet
Cause my momma told me better than that.
[Chorus]
I'm a survivor (what),
I'm not gonna give up (what),
I'm not gon' stop (what),
I'm gonna work harder (what),
I'm a survivor (what),
I'm gonna make it (what),
I will survive (what),
Keep on survivin' (what),
I'm a survivor (what),
I'm not gonna give up (what),
I'm not gon' stop (what),
I'm gonna work harder (what),
I'm a survivor (what),
I'm gonna make it (what),
I will survive (what),
Keep on survivin' (what).

This song has been the testament of my life and I am sure of your life, too. If you are reading this book you are, as Destiny's Child sings, a survivor. You have been through countless catastrophes and you are still here, you have your health, your strength, you are in your right mind, hey baby keep on surviving. And hopefully by now you realize the reason we are survivors is because we have one who is fighting for us who has survived all that life can throw at you, his name is Jesus Christ. He not only survived but mastered all that life could throw at Him. And He said the same power that dwells in Him dwells in us.

PLAYING IN ITALY

Playing in Italy had its definite pros and cons. The pros were that the pay was excellent, I had my own flat or apartment, and I was given a car to drive. Our games were played on Sunday nights, so I had a lot of time for other things. The cons were that I didn't speak a word of Italian, didn't understand the money system, and couldn't drive the five-speed, stick-shift Saab the team gave me to use. I really had nowhere to go and was afraid to get lost if I tried. I didn't have a church to attend, and wasn't playing at home in the NBA before family and friends. All of these thoughts weighed heavy upon my mind during the next few months.

When pretending as a child to block socks, and shoot baskets in a garbage can, I did not see Italy in the picture. All I could see was capacity filled NBA arenas, I could smell the freshly popped popcorn, and I could hear the man say, hot dogs for sell, get your hot dogs and coke. The words being verbalized in Italy, I couldn't even pronounce nor understand. I was in a foreign land with no exit. I am sure you too may seem like at times in your life you are in a foreign land, you are in a place that you didn't dream about. No matter where you find yourself take heart, things do change. Nothing stays the same. Your dreams and aspirations will take shape, but you have to get in the game and stay in the game. Win or lose stay in the game. Great things happen to people who stay in the game. Your only true losses are the ones that you refuse to play. Play the game and the game will give you the wins you deserve.

Coach Tubby Smith (former Kentucky basketball coach, currently the head coach with the Minnesota Golden Gophers) gave me some great advice once when I asked him how to be successful as a head coach; Coach Smith's reply was, "Work hard and stay in the game. You can't be successful at coaching or anything else if you don't stay in the game." So I pass the same advice on to you: first discover which game to get in, in other words do your research; once you have done the research, get in the game, and compete. Play to win, and then stay in the game. You will lose some games, but keep playing. If you continue to practice and watch the film of your games (take inventory of what's working and of what's not working), you will find a way to win.

Because I was paid so well by Teorema (and it was all tax-free money), I was able to do something I had dreamed of doing for a very long time. I made a down payment on a small house for my parents. And, like "Griff" before me, I bought them a new Cadillac. Doing this gave me a lot of satisfaction. My parents had always taught me it was better to give than to receive. I felt a sense of responsibility to do more since at that time I had more to give.

The flat (or apartment) I stayed in was immaculate; it was two bedrooms, one bath, kitchen, and a great room. But I was lonely being away from home, and I made a lot of expensive long-distance phone calls.

Italian was not my favorite language, but not being able to speak it made life very difficult for me. How I wished I had taken Italian in high school. Instead I took French as a foreign language, I thought a little *parlez-vous francais* would give me a leg up on the honeys. I always wondered why teachers taught a foreign language anyway. I wasn't planning on going to any foreign country, after all America was the land of opportunity; it was the place that flowed with milk and honey. Boy life is full of surprises. When I wanted to eat at a local restaurant, for example, all I could do was point to someone's food, like a little child. While I thought, I was perfectly clear as to what I wanted, I pronounced every syllable, I made every word come out loud and clear, but the matradee didn't understand a word I was saying.

Italian food was delicious, I loved it, but I missed my American food. When I went to the grocery store, it was hard for me to find sliced bread and the ingredients to make the peanut butter and jelly sandwiches I loved so much. I had taken for granted the convenience of McDonalds, Burger King, and Wendy's just a few miles away from our house in the states. I was really craving some White Castles (commonly known as sliders for the after effect it has on the digestive system), where I would usually order about five double cheeseburgers, fries, and a Big Red soda.

Also the money in Italy did not have the pictures of Benjamin Franklin or Andrew Jackson on the front. I couldn't even describe the images on the Italian currency, all I know was their money was not dollars and cents, but lira (since 2002 the Italian money supply is been changed to the euro)—whatever that was. Neither could I turn on my favorite investor shows, like CNBC or "Mad Money" with Jim Cramer. I didn't even care who they had as their investment guru, I knew in the states we had the wizard of Omaha, Warren Buffett (Warren Buffett took a $105,000 investment and turned into a $40 billion fortune, which makes him the second richest man in the United States).

Because I didn't understand the language, it was very difficult to meet people, and this included pastors and other church people. And since local services were in Italian, I didn't attend church while I was there.

But the worst thing about playing in Italy was that I was not playing in America, and I was not playing in the NBA. For a young player who still had great aspirations, being in a foreign country was devastating. But I decided that I would have to make the best of my time in Europe, honing my skills and keeping my game sharp, and hoping for an NBA invitation the following season. In retrospect, I wish I had ventured out more. Italy was so beautiful and so full of history; I was also not very far from Milan, the fashion capital of the world.

(As a note on the underlying theme of this book, I was able to meet and romance a local Italian girl under these difficult circumstances. I always found a way to do that.)

Each of the Italian teams were allowed to have two American players, and since the Americans earned much more than their European counter-parts, we were expected to be the best. With every win, the American players received the credit, and with every loss, we received the blame.

My American teammate on Teorema was an older player named Floyd Allen. Floyd had his whole family with him in Italy. They had been there for a number of years and spoke fluent Italian. I will always be indebted to them for their hospitality. In my loneliness and isolation, they made me feel welcome in that foreign country.

Floyd played the center position for the team. He was about 6'8" and had very long arms, and he had a nice medium-range jumper. I will never forget seeing Floyd doing his one hundred crunches every day after practice. As a result, he had great abs.

For an older player, in his mid- to late-thirties, he was in great shape.

Another of the highlights of my time in Italy was having a chance to hook up with Michael Ray Richardson. Michael Ray was a NBA legend who had been banned from the league because of a drug problem. He was a superb player and played for the best team in Italy. Because he could put on a show with a basketball, people from all over the country would come to see him play, and they would chant his nickname, "Sugar ray;" the people would just call him "Sugar."

PHOTO GALLERY

WINSTON BENNETT JR. (MY DAD), ME ENJOYING MY
PARENTS, SHIRLEY ANN BENNETT (MOMMY DEAREST)

ME ENJOYING MY POPS

ME AND MY IDOL MY MOTHER

ME AND MY FRIENDS AT MY 5 YEAR BIRTHDAY PARTY

ME AT 6 ALREADY THINKING ABOUT
THE THEORY OF RELATIVITY

ME, MOM AND DAD, AT A WEDDING

My FIRST Doss Optimist Basketball League

My High School Male Bulldog Teammates 1983

My Male High School Graduation May 1983

Me with fellow Male High classmates

MOM AND ME AFTER ONE OF
MY GAMES AT THE
UNIVERSITY OF KENTUCKY

COACH JOE B. HALL SIGNING ME TO A LETTER OF INTENT
TO ATTEND THE UNIVERSITY OF KENTUCKY,
MY PARENTS LOOK ON IN AMAZEMENT

My Golden Goose, Peggy Denise Bennett on
our wedding day December 23, 1989

Senior night when Happy Chandler sings my
Old Kentucky Home, me with my parents.

ROGER HARDEN HITTING ME WITH A PASS IN THE POST AGAINST
INDIANA AND THERE ALL WORLD POINT GUARD STEVE ALFORD

ME TRYING TO GET A SHOT OVER HAKEEM
OLAJUWON AND THE HOUSTON COUGARS IN 1984

ME WITH THE BEST COACH WHOEVER COACHED THE GAME OF
BASKETBALL, COACH JOHN WOODEN ("THE WIZARD OF WESTWOOD")

MY 2001-2002 KENTUCKY STATE THOROBRED TEAM

1995-96 KENTUCKY WILDCATS
NCAA NATIONAL BASKETBALL CHAMPIONS

Front Row (L-R): Assistant Coach Delray Brooks, Head Coach Rick Pitino, Allen Edwards, Derek Anderson, Jeff Sheppard, Tony Delk, Anthony Epps, Cameron Mills, Wayne Turner, Associate Coach Jim O'Brien, Assistant Coach Winston Bennett.
Standing (L-R): Equipment Manager Bill Keightley, Administrative Assistant George Barber, Jason Lathrem, Oliver Simmons, Nazr Mohammed, Mark Pope, Walter McCarty, Antoine Walker, Jared Prickett, Ron Mercer, Trainer Eddie Jamiel, Assistant Strength Coach Layne Kaufman.

ME AS AN ASSISTANT WITH THE NCAA
CHAMPIONS KENTUCKY WILDCATS

ME CLOWNING AROUND WITH FORMER
KENTUCKY GOVERNOR PAUL PATTON

ME AS AN ASSISTANT COACH TO RICK PITINO
AND THE 1998 BOSTON CELTICS

ME AS AN ASSISTANT TO RICK PITINO ALONG WITH
DELRAY BROOKS ON THE KENTUCKY STAFF 1996

Me meeting former President Bill Clinton in 1996

Our 1996 Kentucky Wildcat Team visits the White
House after winning the NCAA Championship

My family: my wife Peggy, my daughter Princess
and her daughter Kassidy, my daughters Jasmine
and Stephanie, and my son Leontay.

Me and my girls in Florida

My late grandmother Josephine Lawless ("MoMo")

Pops, Peggy, Me and my daughters at my
mothers funeral, May 12, 2008

ME AND THE GOLDEN GOOSE

GETTING CLOSER TO PEGGY JONES

One result of my time in Italy was that I became much closer with a lovely lady friend back home. Her name was Peggy Jones, and she was a member of our church in Louisville. Peggy and I had started seeing each other every once in a while before I left for Italy. She was a very attractive young lady who captivated me with her attention to detail. She was always one of the best-dressed women in the church.

Peggy was thin and walked like a model—so thin that she reminded me of Olive Oil in the Popeye cartoon. Her hair was usually worn straight on the sides in the Cleopatra look.

Peggy and I had been on a few dates, but it was nothing very serious yet. But before I left for Italy, she threw a going-away party for me. It was the first party any girl had ever given me, and I was very impressed—especially since it had come so unexpectedly. Peggy Jones had swept me off my feet. As a result, while I was in Italy, the two of us began to write each other. Each week, I would write her a love letter. My only connection to the love of the states was through Peggy and my parents. I would often have Peggy describe a day in the states, was the weather cold or hot, were the leaves green or were they beginning to change. I declared in my mind if I ever touched back on American soil I would be sure to kiss the ground that gave me this dream that I can be and do whatever I put my mind to.

My time in Italy was to be much shorter than I had imagined. I had been in the country only three or four months when suddenly the team stopped paying me. This is a common practice in some over seas countries, I'm told. If the team starts losing, the owners stop paying the players. These foreign teams expected every American player to be Magic Johnson, Michael Jordan, and Larry Bird all rolled into one, and if a player could not deliver, he soon stopped receiving checks.

When my checks stopped coming, I panicked and began making urgent phone calls back home to my business manager, Billy Wilcoxsen. He told me to stay put and he would work it out.

Then things got worse. One day when I arrived at practice, I noticed a new American player on our team. He shocked me when he said that he had been brought in to replace me. It was a traumatic experience. I had been doing all I knew to do to help my team win, and yet they were firing me—and announcing it in this very curious way. I was flabbergasted, I was disturbed, and I felt defeated. I was thousands of miles away from home, with no help in site. I wanted to be back in the states. Italy was a great country, but for me it was the one thing standing in my way of getting back home. I felt like E.T. the Extra-Terrestrial, but I not only wanted to phone home, I wanted to go home.

But I had to stay in Italy a couple more months (without pay) while the whole matter could be worked out in court. Eventually I was paid, although not what I had been promised; but in the meantime, it was a terrible time in my career as a professional athlete. I didn't belong anywhere at the moment, and I didn't know what my future might be. There I was, stuck thousands of miles from home and unable to move. This seemed like a no-win situation.

Eventually the matter was resolved, and after spending some six months in all in Italy, I flew back home. I left Italy with mixed feelings. It had been an interesting experience to play there, but I was certainly happy to be back in the land of opportunity.

Now what? It seemed that nothing came without a fight.

I had been back in the States only a short time when I was able to team up with the Pensacola Tornadoes of the Continental Basketball Association (CBA). The late Joe Mullaney was their coach. Joe had been the coach of the Los Angeles Lakers at one point in his career.

"Big Bob" McCann's was the star of the Pensacola Tornadoes. At 6'7" and two hundred and fifty pounds, he was a dynamite inside player who played his college ball at Morehead State University in Morehead, Kentucky. Bob went on to play five seasons in the NBA.

We also had a nifty little guard named Mark Wade (who played for the University of Nevada-Las Vegas). Mark wasn't the quickest guy in the world, but he knew how to get to where he needed to be on the court. It was amazing being back in the states, and playing basketball on American soil. It was also great to be able to attend church.

I found a fiery little church to attend in Pensacola and was happy to be visiting the House of God once again. I would keep the faith that another opportunity would open for me to play in the NBA. At the same time, as was my habit, I developed a couple of female companions.

In general, playing in the CBA was no picnic, but it was known as a league in which you could hone your skills. And if you were lucky, the NBA scouts would see you and call you up to the big leagues. I played with the Tornadoes for about three months before being invited to again attend the Cleveland Cavaliers' summer training camp.

CONSIDERING MARRIAGE
AS A WAY OUT

This was my big opportunity, and I was elated by it. Now I must not allow anything to destroy it. As I made the move to Cleveland, I renewed my commitment to God. Somehow I would live for Him. Somehow I would resist temptation. Somehow I would lead a better life. Somehow I would be an overcomer.

And what was that "somehow" that had eluded me until now? I wasn't sure, but I had to find it. I prayed and studied the Word of God searching for an answer.

I'm not sure that I totally understood at this point the temptations I was about to face in the NBA. I had completed the previous camp and must have had a glimpse into it, but soon the groupie aspect of NBA life or of stardom in general would become a reality for me.

In short, NBA players had hoards of eager women waiting for them everywhere they went, and many of the players developed a reputation for wild sex. In later years, it would become public knowledge Magic Johnson, the former leader of the Showtime Los Angeles Lakers, had contracted AIDS. Another star, Wilt Chamberlain, wrote a book in which he claimed to have slept with over twenty thousand women during his career. Later on, it was published that Kobe Bryant had been accused of having an in appropriate relationship with a woman in Denver, Colorado. Steve McNair, the long time NFL quarterback for the Tennessee Titans and then with the Baltimore Ravens, was gunned down by his alleged mistress on July 4, 2009. The stories are rampant of extra-martial affairs from former presidents like Bill Clinton and JFK, to politicians and preachers. Sex has been one of most pervasive demons since the days of King Solomon, who had over 700 wives and 300 concubines. Since I did not want to go to Hell for having sex before marriage, I began to think about marriage. Little did I know that marriage would do nothing to curb my appetite for women.

Slowly I came to the conclusion that I needed to get married, and when I did, one name stood out above all others—Peggy Jones. Despite having other female companions in Florida, Peggy and I had still been communicating by phone, and I was growing closer and closer to her. I liked her as a prospect for marriage for several reasons.

One of the big pluses on Peggy's score sheet was her strong relationship with my parents. My mother absolutely adored her. But the most important plus was her love for the Lord. This was the most important credential to me. We had always been taught, to marry in the faith. Finally, I wasn't sure how much I knew about love, but I felt that I could learn to love Peggy over time. My thought of marriage at this time wasn't about love, it was about lust. If I got married, I could have sex without feeling condemned because this was my wife. She could help me get my life together.

A word of caution here: never get married to cure your weaknesses or shortcomings; the only reason to get married is because you love your mate dearly and deeply. I was one of the lucky ones, even though my motives weren't ideal for marrying the

Lord did bless me with what I needed in a mate. Through the test and trials of life, I have grown to love and respect my wife unconditionally.

Somehow, some way I had to overcome this larger-than-life monster called sex. It was continually sabotaging my spiritual relationship with God. It seemed that no matter how hard I prayed and vowed never to have sex outside of marriage again, I would always go right back to it. I was living in a continuous cycle of up today and down tomorrow. I was trying to beat this thing on the outside while the real work that needed to be done was on the inside. I had to make a radical change in my mind about the situation. I couldn't go on thinking that the way to beat this sex hungry demon was on the outside. I needed a spiritual change. Trying harder and doing better would never last it was not the formula for this problem. I knew I couldn't continue in fornication and expect to get to Heaven. It's just like that old saying: you can't keep doing the same thing expecting different results; that's insanity.

The only way our circumstances change is if we change. Don't expect to make millions of dollars if you don't change your mind set about spending, don't expect millions if you know nothing about how to invest and compound money. Even if you won the lottery, which is a one in a million chance, the odds are great that you would be right back where you started if you have not changed your mind about how you do things. Our mind is the starting point of change. Whether your change is a change of environment or a change of attitude, you will find the desired outcome begins in your mind.

I love to win, but my problems with sex made me a constant loser. It kept me down and defeated personally. I had to overcome that somehow—and now I thought I had found the way to do it.

My obsession had grown so intense that sometimes, even when I was down lying prostrate before God in prayer, the thought of a young lady would flash through my mind like a news bulletin. Instead of being able to resist such a crazy impulse, I would give in to the compulsive inclination, and act out the thought I had in my mind. I felt like I was in between the proverbial rock and a hard place because I felt doomed if I had sex, and I felt doomed if I didn't. The Bible was very strict on this point. It said:

> But I tell you that anyone who looks at a woman lustfully has already committed adultery with her in his heart.
>
> Matthew 5:28 (NIV)

That was tough! Even if I hadn't yet slept with a girl, the very thought of doing it meant to God that I'd already performed the act. Wow!

Whenever I had sexual relations with a woman, I always felt very depressed afterwards. It was common for me to make an appointment to go and see a pastor to confess my sins and seek forgiveness, but somehow I felt like it was all for nothing. The next time temptation came, I was again unable to withstand the stranglehold sex had on me. I had to do something radical; I couldn't continue to travel the road I was on. I knew it could only lead to destruction.

I have learned through my constant battles in attempting to overcome weaknesses that if we don't resist our weakness they will persist. It has taken me years and years to learn that I have to resist, in other words I have to fight. Nothing is easy in this life except quitting. It doesn't take too much effort to quit, all you have to do is just give up and give in. I have had many days of giving up and giving in. It was only after I decided to resist and defend that I started to win some victories.

AT LAST, MY NBA DREAM
IS FULFILLED

During that summer of 1989, I had a great camp with the Cleveland Cavaliers and was later signed to a one-year contract with the team. I felt greatly relieved to have finally made it into the NBA. This represented another of my major long-term goals accomplished.

Of course, it wasn't enough for me just to make it into the NBA; I wanted to enjoy a long career in the league. While with the Cleveland Cavaliers, I would be playing with such greats as Brad Daughtery, from North Carolina; Craig Ehlo, from Lubbock, Texas; Larry Nance, from Clemson; Mark Price, from Georgia Tech; "Hot Rod" Williams from Tulane; Ron Harper, from Miami of Ohio; Terrell Brandon, of Oregon; Chuckie Brown, from North Carolina State; John Morton, from Seton Hall; and John Battle, who had previously played with the Atlanta Hawks, was also a big part of the success of the franchise. It felt great to be among these great men. I was very blessed to be a part of this group. We did not have the problems that some teams have with drug and alcohol use. I cannot recall any of these players being involved in any excessive behaviors.

Now, I simply had to get serious. I couldn't allow anything to damage my future with the Cavaliers. And I had to show appreciation to God for having gotten me this far. I had to do something to change my way of life. Shortly after making the team, I came to the conclusion that my only hope was to take the leap into matrimony.

In some ways, I could hardly imagine myself as a married man, and, with my reputation, I certainly wasn't a good catch. But I wanted to live right and not be a fornicator any longer. With all my heart, I wanted to please God. If I could get married, I could make love to my wife and cut off all the other relationships with old girlfriends. The Bible had said:

> Marriage should be honored by all, and the marriage bed kept pure, for God will judge the adulterer and all the sexually immoral.
>
> Hebrews 13:4 (NIV)

My intentions were honorable, but, of course, what I was about to ask of Peggy was totally unfair. Before I went forward, my mind began to play tricks on me, as I thought about the sexual healing that Peggy and I had before popping the question. Even though we both knew the way of truth, the sex had still caused us to fall a time or two together. What was the difference between Peggy and the other women I had slept with? Was there a difference? We made the same mistakes. I rationalized the difference being when Peggy and I had sex in one of those moments were we couldn't keep our hands to ourselves, the next day she would feel convicted and go tell our pastor about it. It was like a setup, one of those kiss-and-tell moments. Just like the enemy does to us with all the lies about sex and how it will soothe the pain; it will make all your fantasies come to reality; it will make you feel

FIGHT FOR YOUR LIFE

like a real man to have sex with as many women as possible. It's all a big lie.

I hated when Peggy would report me to the pastor; I vowed to never make the same mistake with Peggy again. Bishop Little was very intimidating; I never wanted to end up in his office, but that is just were Peggy had me, as she sobbed uncontrollably because she had fallen again to her sexual urges. What she didn't understand was I was a master at pleasing women. I knew the right words to say and I knew when to say them. Was this the woman I wanted to marry and save me from sexual sin? We were doing the same thing, having sex before marriage, so what was the difference, was there any difference between Peggy and the rest? The difference was Peggy cared greatly that she was disappointing God; the other women either did not know any better or did not care that what we were doing was wrong. Maybe to them it wasn't wrong; maybe they did not have the spiritual foundation that I had.

I thought enough about her passion for doing right that I decided to propose to her on the phone from my room at the Holiday Inn in Richfield, Ohio. But first I asked her a litany of questions: How many children did she want? What type of lifestyle did she want to live? Since she already had a son (Leontay, who was eight years old at the time), how would she feel about another man other than the boy's natural father raising him? How did she feel about working outside the home? She must have thought I was Central Intelligence (CIA) with all of the detailed questions about her finances and everything else.

Nothing Peggy said that day in answer to my many questions changed my mind about her, and after getting her answers to this laundry list of queries, I went on to ask her if she would marry me. Thankfully, she consented. Her mother, Doris Roberts, and her son, Leontay, were both excited about the proposal.

Only a few days after that telephone call, I flew back to Louisville, where Peggy and I had a small wedding at my parents' home. I had always been very impulsive and spontaneous, and this wedding was no exception. We were married on December 23, 1989, we had a one-night honeymoon at the Executive West Hotel in Louisville, and the next day I flew back to Cleveland (because we had a nationally televised game coming up with the Atlanta Hawks on Christmas Day).

I was very happy. My long nightmare was finally over.

Or was it? The next night, I made the serious mistake of going into a club at the Holiday Inn where I was staying. A live band was playing at the hotel, and I wanted to hear them.

The manager of the band turned out to be a very beautiful woman. She was tall and brown-skinned and reminded me of Vivica A. Fox (actress and television producer best known for her role in the movie Independence Day), with her long hair and her beautiful shape. I could hear my mind as if it was the robot in the science fiction television series Lost in Space (the television series ran from 1965–1968). There was a robot that whenever Will Robinson, the little kid who starred in the movie, would get in trouble or would face impeding danger the robot would say, "Run, Will Robinson, run." Just like the robot my mind was telling me to run, but my body was telling me to stay, there would be no running out of my robe like Joseph running from Potiphar's wife, no sir I was in it to win it. We hit it off right away and ended the evening back in her room having sex.

When it was over, I couldn't believe what I had just done. It had been both a wonderful and a terrible experience for me—wonderful, because, as usual, I enjoyed the sex, and terrible, because it represented for me a colossal failure. I had just married precisely to avoid this type of behavior, and now here I was doing it all over again. Nothing had changed. I thought marriage was supposed to change everything. I thought it was the final frontier, the fortress, that hedge of protection I needed. What happened? Absolutely nothing. I thought marriage would change my life from a life of lies, sex, and video tape, to a life of wholeness, purity, and love. But instead the bricks, the fortress, the foundation, all came tumbling down at the sign of sex. There was no barrier between me and sex; it was all a façade.

This incident also raised anew my fears of not being ready for marriage. In this area of life, I seemed to be totally ill equipped. Although I hadn't been sure of how anyone could feel totally prepared to face the challenges of marriage life, I had held out hope that it would cure my sexual appetites. Obviously it wasn't working. I had been hoodwinked, bamboozled into thinking all my problems would be solved by marriage. As I look back, I realize that there is only one problem solver, His name is Jesus Christ. No matter what the problem, He can solve it.

I knew that Peggy cared very deeply for me, and I was not concerned that she had married me just because I was an NBA basketball player. She had the same spiritual desire to please God as I did. We were equally yoked, so I thought everything would be all right. What had happened? Usually, most of us grow up with a dream of one day marrying the person of our dreams. We dream of having a wife who wakes up with no scarf on her head, no warm-up suit, but instead adorned in a sensual and provocative Victoria Secrets negligee. We dream of having someone with the perfect hair, the perfect body, and baby smooth skin. Guess what? It doesn't happen. There is no one who has everything. We have to make the best of what we have. We all go into marriage with these false assumptions of what we think marriage should be like, of what we think our spouses should be like. We sat ourselves up for failure when we have these grandiose assumptions. No one can live up to a picture of Julia Roberts or Halle Berry in their mind: the perfect body, the perfect smile, and fresh breath when you wake up. You would think that Halle Berry would be every man's dream, but for Eric Benet the popular R&B singer song writer, Halle was not enough as it had been reported that Eric himself had been treated for a sex addiction just before their break up. It's all a big lie. The first thing you should do when you wake up in the mornings is run for the Scope and the Right Guard, no matter how beautiful you are. Beauty is in the eye of the beholder. Besides beauty doesn't hold up over time, we all age and begin to sag, and bulge in places that we were once proud of. Father time gets us all at some point. Godliness with contentment hath great gain. That's the tough part is being content with what you have. We are always looking for better, sweeter, more attractive. The eyes of man are never satisfied.

OUR FIRST YEAR
OF MARRIAGE

Our first year of marriage was turbulent—to say the least. Peggy and I were reunited sometime in late January, having spent a month apart. This was not good for our marriage—especially when my sex drive was at its peak, and I was so out of control.

With Peggy now with me in Ohio, my lifestyle did improve somewhat at home, but when I was on the road, it was a very different story.

With every road game, I developed the goal of meeting and grooming new women. If I didn't have sex with them on the first meeting, I knew I would in future meetings. I always traveled alone; I thought this improved my changes of meeting a nice young lady. The group always travels in packs; I never wanted to be a part of the group when it came to meeting women. I thought that would mess up my opportunity to score.

If there was a favorite place in the NBA to travel and meet exotic women, it was Los Angeles, California. Tony! Toni! Tone!, the rhythm and blues group, used to sing, "It never rains in Southern California." The sun was always shining and the stars were always out. Everybody in the league loved L.A.; the potential to meet a star was endless. Of course, there was no telling who you might meet at the games; Janet Jackson, Donna Summers, Diana Ross, the list was endless. The lifestyle in L.A. was totally different than anywhere else in the league with the exception of maybe Miami, and New York City. People there seemed to be more liberal and open.

My favorite spots in L.A. were Venice Beach and Aunt Kizzy's, the Soul Food Restaurant. And of course, Friday's Restaurant in Marina Del Ray was *the* meeting place, it was like Don Cornelius and Soul Train in that place; the music was hip-hop and rhythm and blues, and the clientele loved it. It didn't matter what night you went to Friday's, you were assured to meet a beauty. And when the team went to L.A., we always stayed at the Marriott, just a stone's throw away from Friday's.

We loved being in L.A. so much that we never wanted to leave. It was definitely not the place for a married man to be without his wife. I witnessed the fact that many married men forgot their vows once they arrived in the City of Angels. In reality it was anything but a City of Angels. It was more like sin city.

Now that I was married, my status sometimes complicated my ability to groom (to meet new women and prepare their minds for sex). Some women I met resented the fact that I was married, and others even wanted to cause me harm because of it, then there were others who didn't care. For instance, I was having sex with a lady in Milwaukee, and everything was going great...until she learned that I was married. Then, she became bound and determined to find my wife and make sure she knew that I'd had an illicit affair with her. Needless to say, I was terrified. Even though I wasn't sure about being married, I did know that I didn't want to lose my new family so soon. In the end, I told Peggy about the relationship myself, and asked her to forgive me. Of course, forgiveness is never immediate, if it happens at all. Peggy had been so patient with me in dealing with this life-altering problem. It had to be God and godly people to help influence her not to give up on someone that should have been thrown away a long time ago.

Peggy eventually forgave me, but the thought or the memory of past moments of infidelity always had its way of creeping back into our relationship. I was like a city with no walls. I couldn't say no. Or maybe I didn't really want to say no. It's hard to give up something that you love and enjoy. Sex became my hobby. It was my play time, if nothing else was working the way I wanted, I could always turn to sex for fulfillment, excitement, and pleasure.

There were times when Peggy was finding girls' phone numbers and she was tracking my phone; since she paid all the bills, she had access to everyone who called me and who I called, there was no need for a private investigator, she had that role down to a tee. I wasn't really doing a great job of hiding my infidelity; one might say I wanted to be caught I wasn't thinking of the consequences of my actions, I was just satisfying the craving; once I had my fix, I would settle down and become a very sedate person. I was selfish beyond belief; it was all about satisfying my craving at all costs.

It was a terrible cycle, and I couldn't understand it. I was constantly embarrassed and demoralized, wondering what would happen next.

There were days when I did overcome, and it felt great. If I could be faithful to Peggy for an entire day and go home from a day's practice and not hunt a woman that day, I thought I had accomplished something great. But, inevitably, the very next day or the next week, I would wake up thinking about how I could satisfy my sexual urges.

Usually after I'd had sex, then I was a different person, calm and collected; but beforehand, my stomach would be in knots, and I was very spontaneous, very impulsive, could not be still, but fidgety. This was a sure sign that I was headed in the wrong direction, and if I could only have heeded those early warning signs, the outcome might have been very different. But I couldn't seem to do it. Instead of fighting the feeling I would just give in to them.

There were always certain numbers I could call; when the girl knew it was a passionate plea for sex. Most of the women seem to want the affection as much or more than I did. There were so many times that I felt so convicted and tired of tripping over the same problem, that I would actually throw my little black book in the garbage can. Days later I would be frantically rummaging through the garbage like a hobo looking for food trying to retrieve my little black book. In the black book were my fix, my fantasies, and my escape from reality. While I tried to rid myself of the promiscuous activity, something inside of me just would not let it go. It's difficult to give up someone or something that you know will satisfy your every desire. Of course in today's society little black books are a thing of the past; now the mode of communication is texting, Facebook, and MySpace. The advances in technology have made it increasingly easier to socialize and meet new people, or to reacquaint yourself with people of your past. Danger Will Robinson. Run.

Once I got home from one of these encounters, I usually didn't want to be bothered, and I often fell into a deep depression. It deeply troubled me that my life was such a contradiction. Why couldn't I overcome?

I knew what the Bible promised:

No temptation has seized you except what is common to man. And God is faithful; he will not let you be tempted beyond

what you can bear. But when you are tempted, he will also
provide a way out so that you can stand up under it.

1 Corinthians 10:13 (NIV)

Why wasn't I able to take advantage of that promise? Often,
I had felt that God was trying to warn me and to provide an
opportunity for my escape. Just before I was about to consummate the act of sin; for instance, my cell phone would ring, and
I knew that this could be my opening to escape the pleasures of
sin for a season.

But if the truth be told I didn't really want to escape. Yes I
wanted to do right and yes I wanted to be dedicated to my wife
and family, but I wanted it to be easy. I wanted someone to pray
for me and make it go away. I did not want to have to work on
me, particularly the inside stuff. The NBA use to have a program
called the Inside Stuff, where they would take you behind the
scenes of a NBA player's life. When you want to get to the root
of the problem, you have to go behind the scenes. I was firmly
in the clutches of sin and had come to the point of no return.
Where would it all lead?

THE POINT OF
NO RETURN?

It seems totally absurd now, but many times, after my sexual encounters with females, I would then try to witness to them about God. How absurd must that have seemed to them? Here I was just finishing sex with them, and suddenly I was telling them that they shouldn't do this anymore because God didn't like it? I would often confess to the young lady, "I can't do this anymore; it's causing a curse to be on my life. I am displeasing God every time I have sex with you." The young lady would look at me as if I was some crazed lunatic and say, "Okay I will see you next week." The cycle had been so pervasive that they knew the routine better than I. She knew I could not withstand her sexual healing.

Because of my constant unfaithfulness, I also developed a serious spirit of jealousy about Peggy. On several occasions, I left her and Leontay at the church we attended in Cleveland because I thought she was making eyes at some other man in the congregation—just to get back at me. I couldn't help myself. A furious jealous rage came over me every time I thought she was looking elsewhere. The problem on these occasions at the church was that we lived forty minutes away, and Peggy had to ask the pastor to give her and Leontay a ride home when this happened.

On another occasion, a friend and his wife came to visit us. We were all sitting in the great room—my friend and his wife on one side of the sofa, and Peggy and I on the other. Peggy was lying in my lap, lying still as if she was sleep. But I could see that she wasn't sleep; she was looking at my friend. When I would look at her, she would close her eyes quickly. After carefully watching this for a few minutes, I broke into a rage, pushing Peggy off of my lap. Everyone was startled by this and asked me what was wrong. Finally, after I'd cooled off a little, I told my friend that I thought my wife "had a thing" for him. When I confronted Peggy on the matter, she said she was just admiring the relationship that my friend and his wife had together. A few years later, the two would divorce. What looks good on the outside may not be so good on the inside. It's that old saying: the grass always looks greener on the other side. But the converse is also true; it still has to be cut.

The truth is when things got this bad, I sometimes lost all thought of God and how important He was in my life. This was a sad commentary. I later realized when we are at our lowest point, that's when God seems to show Himself mighty, if we will let Him. I noticed that even though God has the power to do anything, He will not superimpose His will on us. He has given us the awesome and sometimes self-destructing power of choice. He says, "You chose life or death, blessings or cursing, but the choice is yours." He said the power of life and death is in the tongue.

What a powerful statement. The words we speak can either make a life or destroy a life. We have to be so careful with the words we speak. Let's determine that we will speak life and not death, let's speak victory and not defeat. Whatever you send out will come back, whatever you plant will grow.

GUARDING
MICHAEL JORDAN

My other love in life, basketball, was proving to be memorable. My most treasured moments would be those spent playing against the other teams' best player at the three, or small forward, position in the NBA. I had to guard the likes of Dominque Wilkens of the Atlanta Hawks, Larry Bird of the Boston Celtics, "Magic" Johnson and James Worthy of the Los Angeles Lakers, Charles Barkley of the Philadelphia Seventy-Sixers, and, of course, the infamous Michael Jordan of the Chicago Bulls.

My first opportunity to play was one of the most memorable. Coach Wilkens came to me that day and said, "Hey, Winston, I've been noticing how hard you work. You show up for practice an hour early, and you stay a couple of hours after the others. That's the type of attitude we want the rest of our players to have. So I'm going to reward you for all your diligence and hard work."

Immediately dollar signs began to pop up before my eyes. "Rewards" meant big bucks in the NBA, but Coach Wilkens had something very different in mind. "I'm going to start you in your first NBA game today," he said. I was overwhelmed with excitement. This was better than receiving a million dollars.

I ran from the meeting to the nearest pay phone and called my parents to tell them the good news. "Hey, Mom and Dad," I said excitedly. "I've got some great news. Coach Wilkens says I'm going to start in my first NBA game today."

They, too, were overjoyed. Dad said, "See, I told you when you were just eight years old. Remember? I asked you the question, "Can you see it?" How well I remembered that statement, as dad would pose it over and over again, "Can You See It?" and now I was about to see it. My parents said they would call all the other members of our family and have them all gathered at their house to watch the game.

I had been so excited about the idea of playing that day that I neglected to ask who exactly we were playing. Now I ran back to the locker room and searched frantically for a schedule. After looking the schedule over, I decided that what I saw printed there must be a mistake. It indicated that we would be playing the World Champion Chicago Bulls that day. The team was at its height, and no one else could compare to them at the moment. Surely Coach would not be putting me into my first NBA game against such a difficult team!

This cannot be happening to me! I thought. *Why couldn't we play the lowly L.A. Clippers or the Minnesota Timberwolves? Was the timing of Coach's "reward" right?* After the initial shock, I settled down and began to think more calmly about facing this formidable opponent.

Soon, the whole team had gathered in the locker room, and Coach Wilkens began putting assignments on the board for the game. He said, "Brad Daughtery, you guard Bill Cartwright. Larry Nance, you guard Horace Grant. Craig Ehlo, you guard Scottie Pippen."

In my mind, my hand went up instantly into the air, and I said, "Hey Coach, aren't I the small forward for the Cleveland

Cavaliers today? And isn't Scottie Pippen the small forward for the Bulls? So shouldn't I be guarding Pippen instead of Craig?" I only internalized all of this, because I didn't want to do anything to blow my big opportunity.

He continued: "Mark Price, you guard B.J. Armstrong."

In my mind, my hand went up instantly again, and I said, "Hey Coach, you promised me you were gonna start me today. Did you change your mind? There's only one guy left to guard and I know you're not putting me on him."

Then he said it: "Winston Bennett, you guard Michael Jordan."

With that, I nearly went into cardiac arrest. I lost all the functions of my body, and my blood seemed to have stopped flowing. When I revived, I asked (again in my mind), "Do you mean the guy who appears on the Wheaties Box? Is it the same guy who walks around in Hanes underwear? Yes? The Great Michael Jordan, God in Basketball Shoes?" I couldn't believe it. I was assigned to guard Michael Jordan in my first ever NBA game.

As we headed out through the corridor for the court, I could see the members of the Bulls team heading the same way. I was very interested in what Michael Jordan was doing—since I'd been given the unenviable assignment of guarding him. Mom had always told me to pray to God when I got into trouble, but she hadn't warned me that I might meet Him face to face on the basketball court. Michael seemed to be very focused, as he and the rest of the Bulls proceeded to the court.

As the Bulls warmed up at the other end of the court, I continued my fascination with Michael's routine. I couldn't help but notice that he was hitting everything he threw up. As we say in basketball, it was "nothing but net." Everything he touched seemed to be going in. He was, as we say, "in a zone." And me? I was shooting air balls, thinking about how I was going to guard God on the court. Not only that, I had been so nervous about guarding Mike that I had come down with diarrhea. So the trainer was rushing back and forth to the locker room for the Pepto-Bismol to calm my stomach. Finally, after a few healthy spoonfuls, my stomach was feeling better.

After what seemed like a lifetime of warm-ups, the introductions were called. When the announcer called out "Michael Jordan," it seemed as though the Heavens had opened and God was saying, "This is my beloved Son in whom I am well pleased." At that point, I knew that I was in over my head.

Finally all the preliminaries were over, and the referee tossed the first jump ball to start the game. The Bulls got the tip, and the first play of the game went to Jordan. Out came that famous tongue and saliva dripped off of it, as if he had just seen a big porterhouse steak with a baked potato in front of him. He looked as though he was going to carve me up and eat me for dinner.

I could tell he was thinking, "This is gonna be a hundred-point night, Wilt Chamberlain's record will be a thing of the past after tonight. I'll break every record that has ever been set. This first-year rookie shouldn't even be on the same court with me."

I felt totally helpless, and all I could think of was to stay down in my stance—like Joe B. Hall and Eddie Sutton had taught me at the University of Kentucky.

The ball went to Pippen, then to B.J. Armstrong, and finally back to Jordan. Jordan gave me a little shake-and-bake move and pulled up from fifteen feet for a jump shot. But I was all over him, and he missed the shot.

"Thank you, Lord!" I had stopped Michael Jordan on his first possession. This gave me a little confidence.

Next, Mark Price hit me with a pass for an assist as I was streaking down the right lane for a bank shot. I had just scored on the Almighty, and my confidence soared. For a moment, I didn't know whether I was in the body or out of the body. It felt as though I had been caught up to the third Heaven.

Back in reality, the Bulls had the ball again and were running a play for Michael. He pulled up to shoot from three-point range, but I was all over him again, and he missed.

All sorts of things were running through my mind by this time. Among them was the thought of a big score when my contract came up for renewal the next time, and that I just might be the next guy on the Wheaties box, I started thinking of Jerry Maguire when he said, "Show me the money." "The Man Who Stopped the World-Famous Michael Jordan" might be a proper caption. I even pictured myself posing in my Hanes underwear commercial.

The magic of that first quarter continued, and Michael was able to score only two points. In the second quarter, he again only scored two points, four points for the half...not bad defense from the little kid from Kentucky who use to play basketball in a garbage can.

In the locker room at halftime, we were celebrating like we had just won the World Championship. Our guys where high-fiving one another, and Coach Lenny Wilkens, who was usually quite reserved, was bouncing off the walls; he was so excited.

But there was a slight problem we had not given thought to. There was still another half of basketball left to play.

Just as with the first half, as both teams walked through the corridor to reach the court, I checked to see how Michael was doing. This time he had a different look in his eyes. They sparkled. I couldn't imagine what that might mean—but I was about to find out.

As play began for the third quarter, we got the ball first. We ran a play for Brad Daughtery in the post. I threw the ball into Brad, and he turned for his little skyhook. But somehow Michael had left me and now grabbed Brad's shot out of the air; he didn't block it out of bounds like you see most guys do, he grabbed it right out of mid-air. Then it was a foot race, as Michael controlled the ball and headed for the other end of the court like a man possessed. He cleared for takeoff from the free-throw line, as Brad Daughtery, Larry Nance, and I pursued. But it was too late. He had performed one of his Space Jam renditions, and there was nothing we could do to stop it.

I wasn't much worried. Michael still only had six points. I was still pretty confident...until we ran another play for Brad, and Jordan left me again and was able to block Brad's shot from behind. As he raced for the other end, Brad, Larry, and I again pursued him feverishly...only to suffer the same disappointing result—a thunder dunk in our faces.

Now my confidence was nonexistent. Maybe I had hoped too high. Maybe I wasn't going to be the next guy on the Wheaties box after all. Maybe my Hanes underwear commercial wasn't as imminent as I had imagined. We had been beating the Bulls by ten points at the half, but Michael went on a rampage over the next two quarters to score sixty-five points in the second half (for a total of sixty-nine points for the game). We lost by twenty points.

We were disappointed, but what could we expect when playing against the legendary Michael Jordan? We would just have to keep fighting for our lives, and hopefully we would win another day.

But wait just one minute. Yes we lost the game, but when I think about the picture in its totality, I had just played against the world's greatest basketball player. Here is a man that made

$300,000 a game and played in over a 100 games a year. Michael Jordan made $10,000 dollars a minute. I was in the same game as the world's greatest player. Compare this to the fact that 60 percent of NBA players go broke within five years of retirement. Professional basketball players are the highest paid players in the world with an average salary of over $5 million a year. Compare this figure with the $770,000 average pay of a NFL football player. The average NBA basketball player makes almost $4 million more than the average football player. When you compare the NBA figures to the figures for the NBA development league the disparity is even more glaring. The average minor league basketball players make between $12,000-$24,000. Wow!!! By being in the NBA, I was in the right game, with a chance to make all my dreams come true. So what, I failed against the great Michael Jordan, just my competing against him was proof I was in the right game.

Are you in the right game? Are you in a game that you just can't seem to win, are you failing, are you struggling to win, usually this means you are in the right game. If you don't have any challenges you can't be the leader you were destiny to be. Great leadership is built through adversity, through failure. Jack Welch (former leader at GE) became the great leader at GE (General Electric) through great trials and adversity. Steven Jobs became the iconic leader at Apple through tremendous conflict and adversity. Bill Gates the visionary leader at Microsoft has experienced greatness only through extraordinary problems. It's playing against the Michael Jordan's of the world that stretches us and forges our philosophy of leadership. Games you win by 40 points do nothing to build a winners mentality. But when you have to fight against an opponent who is more skilled and better prepared then you, this will stretch you to do better. We become great when we are face to face with our greatest competition, our greatest obstacle.

Do you have days, where you feel like you are playing against Michael Jordan? You know those days where you know at the outset that nothing will go right, everything goes wrong. What do you do when you are matched up against your most feared opposition and competition? Well the first thing I do is pray that the Lord will lead and guide me throughout the day, help me, as I can't defeat the Michael Jordan's of the world on my own. With Christ in my life I have a chance, it does not mean that I will always win in my eyes; the most important thing is that I win in His eyes. The other thing I do is take on the challenge, I have to get in the game, I know in the end I will win if I get in the game. I know you are saying but hey you can't beat Michael Jordan so how do you think you will win. I will win because the score board is not the real score; the real score is how God sees the game. Do I believe that I can win, am I trusting in Him, and am I Fighting? If I keep fighting there is no way I can't win. If I trust in Him the game is already fixed. I can only lose if I stop fighting.

LIFE IN TRANSITION

I played with the Cavs for three seasons, and during that time, I suffered another traumatic knee injury. This time, I tore my medial and lateral ligaments. I underwent surgery immediately at the Cleveland Clinic, and then I worked hard, rehabilitating the knee over the next six months. Only then was I able to reevaluate my dream of having a long career in the NBA. I went on to play some more, but toward the end of my third year, I sprained my ankle rather seriously, and the Cavs, wanting to avoid renewing my contract (and paying me more), decided to release me.

What a horrible day that was! I went through all of the usual guilt and self-loathing, repenting and renewal of commitments. Was my career over?

It was so difficult for me to give Peggy the news that I had been let go. Would she blame me? What did the future hold for us? I earnestly prayed and begged my agent to somehow find a place for me with some other team.

I was able to play several games at the end of that season for the Miami Heat (yes that's the same Miami Heat that LeBron James, DeWayne Wade, and Chris Bosh now play for. I guess you could say I paved the way for those young guys. Just kidding), and I worked out that summer, expecting to be invited to their tryout camp the next season. God had been merciful to me. My repayment to Him was to take up with some other women while living alone in Miami. When you think of Miami, you think of the television show "Miami Vice," with Crockett and Tubbs the flashy undercover police agents, South Beach, and the beautiful women that reside there. That summer I worked out, preparing myself for the Heats' camp, and one day I heard a popping sound in my knee. I iced it, and it seemed to be okay.

During the one-week camp, my knee suddenly ballooned up on me and became very painful, although I iced it and did everything else I could to get it to work properly, I was unable to finish the camp. I had to return home in defeat.

The doctors who examined the knee had some very bad news for me. It was all over. I would never play again, and I would be forced to take an early retirement. I cannot describe what a devastating blow that was. I had fought my way to the top, and now I was out in the cold. Three years of play had not been enough to really get my career going and to establish myself in the league. I would never reach the level of play I had envisioned for myself. It was just not to be. That fact left me in a deep depression, blaming myself for everything and wondering just what I would do with myself in the future, and how I would support my family.

Have you ever lost something that was near and dear to your heart, maybe it was a love one, a job, or a business. Life is constantly changing, we have love ones and possessions that come into our life, and then for whatever reason they disappear. This is a fact of life; this is why we are not to trust in our jobs, or our possessions. Our trust should remain in the Lord. He is the only one that will be by our side in our ups and downs of life. He is always there. As a matter fact every good and every perfect gift comes from God. He knows the outcome of every person and possession. After all He made them both so no matter where you find yourself, trust in the Lord. If I have a job I will trust in the Lord, if I don't have a job I will trust in the Lord. If I have a wife I will trust in the Lord, if my wife leaves me I will trust in the Lord. No matter what I face today I will trust in the Lord, because He is the giver of Life. He is my sustainer, without Him I can do nothing; with Him I can do all things.

MAJOR ADJUSTMENTS

Basketball had been a major part of my life for more than twenty years, and suddenly it was taken from me. What do you do when the fans stop shouting and the ball loses its air? Many athletes in my position had experienced difficulty in transitioning to the next phase of life, and I was no different. Even though I had my degree in business, life without basketball seemed bleak. What would I do, my whole life had been immersed with playing the game of basketball since I was six years old.

You often see prize fighters stay in the game too long and end up getting severely hurt or even brain damaged. Why do they go beyond their set time? One of the reasons is the game is all they know. They have given their life to a sport, and once you have given your life to anything it becomes all encompassing. My pastor Anthony Walton would say, "once you grab something, that something grabs you back making it almost impossible to unleash its grip on you."

Peggy and I decided to move back to Louisville, and there we found a nice ranch-style house in the Copperfield Subdivision in eastern Jefferson County. It was located near the lakes I had frequented as a boy. This was interesting because when I had fished there, I had always noticed the fine homes in the area and could only look and admire then. Now, I owned one of them. How would I pay for it?

After a long search into what exactly I wanted to pursue as my next career, I eventually decided to try my hand at banking. PNC Bank was the most aggressive in their offer for my services as a novice banker, and I accepted their offer. The offer would include six months of intensive training in Pittsburgh, Pennsylvania, where the bank had its corporate headquarters. During that time, I lived in a local hotel, and that was just what I didn't need. Far from home and away from my wife, I fell back into the same old habits.

I had already met quite a number of young ladies in the city and was romancing them when Peggy decided to come for a visit. From the first day we had married, her visits had always been a tense time for me, because I always seemed to have someone else on the side, and I never wanted her to discover them. I also didn't want to arouse suspicion among my lady friends. How could I call them and tell them not to call me for the next few days? It was a tense time all around.

Everything went smoothly with Peggy's visit...until she prepared to return to Louisville. As she was checking out of the hotel, the clerk handed her a list of calls she had made since being in town. The only problem was the list also contained many of my calls as well. The little "come to Jesus" meeting we had on that day was heated to say the least, and I was unable to deny that I had been seeing other women. This dealt our marriage relationship another dramatic blow.

There is something irrevocable about losing trust in another person, especially the person you love; it is almost impossible to retrieve. The effort and work involved in building the bridge of trust is an endless construction job, and that's only if you don't further damage the bridge. I had destroyed the bridge of trust over and over and over again. My building project will forever be under construction.

After my training period, I went back to Kentucky. Somehow or other, Peggy and I managed to stay together—despite my infidelities. It had to be God working on us both, not allowing us to give up on a marriage that was doomed to fail. Why else would she put up with me?

I worked for about a year for PNC Bank in Louisville. At the same time, I traveled back and forth to Lexington doing pre-game and post-game radio shows called "Cat Calls" for the University of Kentucky basketball program. I was working with Tom Leach of WVLK. It was a wonderful experience and a way for me to stay close to the game.

This work became more important to me than my real job. I had never been a numbers person, and my job at the bank was to evaluate financial statements. Years before, I had become a big fan of Warren Buffett, the world's most successful investor, but I could never get excited about the numbers on a balance sheet the way he did. My love continued to be for the game of basketball. That was the blue chip stock I loved. Soon an opportunity would open for me to return to basketball on a higher level.

If you are not doing what you are passionate about, quit. Yes, you heard me. Grab your stuff and run. You will only be astronomically successful working in your passion. My job at the bank was pure drudgery; it was like watching paint dry. I was stuck in a situation that I found no enjoyment, no stimulation, and no passion. Your passion is the gateway to your success. I love coaching, I love the game of basketball; it's my passion. No matter how many hours I put in recruiting, or practicing my players, it doesn't matter it's a labor of love. Find your labor of love. I am not saying you may not have to do something you don't like for a while; I did that in banking until I found my true passion still was the game of basketball.

RICK PITINO CALLS

About this time, I heard that two positions had come open at the coaching level on Rick Pitino's staff at the University of Kentucky, my *alma mater*. Billy Donavon (currently the head coach at the University of Florida, and has one two NCAA Championships), an assistant coach, had just left for Marshall University, and Bernadette-Locke Maddox, the head assistant, had gotten the Kentucky women's head coaching job.

The head assistant's position was quickly filled by Jim O'Brien (currently the head coach for the Indiana Pacers in the NBA), the former Dayton Flyers head coach. Coach O'Brien had also worked with Rick Pitino when he was coaching the New York Knicks.

I made it a point to show up whenever I heard that Coach Pitino would be in the area. I wanted him to know how serious I was about working with him as his assistant coach. As Les Brown (the great motivational speaker and author of *Live Your Dreams*) would say, "I was hungry;" I was willing to do whatever it took to get back into the game of basketball. I would have slept on Coach Pitino's doorstep. I was like a crazed Doberman. I was ready to sink my teeth into something I was deeply passionate about—basketball.

Coach Pitino was a very loyal person and would not just hire anyone. For example, he didn't like hiring ex-NBA players because he felt that they didn't have the work ethic required to be a successful coach, he thought all professional players were spoiled by the glamour, the money, and prestige that comes from being a top notch athlete. He believed that success was in outworking everyone else. I didn't let that bother me, because I wasn't worried about having to work hard. Hard work was all I'd ever known. It was the way I made it to the NBA. I didn't have any extraordinary talent to run, jump, or even shoot the ball. I just tried to outwork everyone that came across my path.

One day, Coach Pitino called me at the bank and asked if I would come to Lexington to meet with him. I was so shocked that I couldn't reply for a few seconds. This was serious business; he wanted me to bring Peggy with me.

After a moment of hesitation, my lips began to move, and my tongue uttered the words, "Okay, we'll be there."

Our meeting was a short one. Coach Pitino outlined what my responsibilities would be if I accepted the job and asked Peggy if she could handle me putting in long hours at the office. She said she could, and I indicated that I was delighted and was ready to get started. My persistence and determination paid off. I was ready to go back and help my alma mater win a championship, not as a player but now as a coach.

There was one serious drawback to the offer. The university could only pay me $12,000 a year, I would be the restrictive earnings coach; in other words, I was the last man on the totem pole. This represented a monumental step backward financially, since I had been making thirty-five thousand at the bank. But in spite of the fact that it would require this substantial financial sacrifice, I still decided to accept the position. I was sure that the long-term benefits would outweigh any short-term sacrifices we would have to make.

My decision to accept the lower salary was not a frivolous one. Coach Pitino had a wonderful track record of putting his assistants in head coaching positions. Ralph Willard (who is now the first assistant at the University of Louisville) was previously at Holy Cross and Western Kentucky University. Herb Sendeck was the former North Carolina State head coach (now at Arizona State). Tubby Smith was the former coach at Georgia and at Kentucky (and now at Minnesota). Billy Donavon was at Marshall (and now at the University of Florida). And, of course, there was Jim O'Brien (former Celtics head coach, now with the Indiana Pacers).

It was a wonderful blessing from God to have been given such an opportunity. I thanked Him. The money, I was sure, would take care of itself. In fact, I was able to get speaking engagements at schools and basketball camps to help supplement my salary. I was always taught that if you love what you do, and you do it with passion, the money will eventually follow. Don't be fooled into thinking money will make life pain-free. Money is good to have, but it is not the cure all. Jesus Christ is the only answer to all of our wants and needs. Often, money is used to pacify our wants, our needs, and our desires. If a desire is good, then God gave it and it will take God to fill it, not money. I had to learn this lesson the hard way. I had chosen at an early age to fill any pain, rejection, or disappointment with sex. Instead of believing that God is the one to fill any void in our lives I believed the lie that my void could be filled with sex.

After so much heartache, I now had a chance to start life all over again—and, hopefully, to do better this time around.

When you are trying to do what you love, most times it will take extreme sacrifice. You will have to be willing to do what most people won't. Most people will not take a drastic cut in pay to do what they really love, most people will not work endless hours at what they really love for less pay. In order to get what you really want sometimes you have to do what you really don't want to do. But do it anyway.

MY FIRST ASSIGNMENT

I accepted my first coaching position at the University of Kentucky in 1994, with the official title of Restrictive Earnings Coach. My assignment was to work with the big men during individual instruction period. It's a great feeling to know that you've had a hand in developing great players like Mark Pope (currently an assistant coach at Wake Forest University), Nazr Mohammed (currently playing with the Charlotte Bobcats in the NBA), Jamal Magloire (currently playing for the Miami Heat in the NBA), Antoine Walker (currently working to make a comeback to the NBA as a player), Scott Padgett (currently assistant coach at the University of Manhattan), Tony Delk (currently an assistant for the Kentucky Wildcats), Derek Anderson, and Ron Mercer.

Usually three times a week, Coach O'Brien, Delray Brooks, and I would put the players through individual instruction. This was not some go-through-the-motions session. This was all-out war for forty-five minutes between the players' classes. The players would put up hundreds of shots during these session. The hardest workers among them were usually Tony Delk, Derek Anderson, and Ron Mercer (in the guard group), and (among the big men) Mark Pope, Jamal Magloire, Scott Padgett, and

Nazr Mohammed. While Antoine Walker was the most noted, he was lazy and didn't like to work hard. Although in time, he would understand to play for Coach Pitino, it was all or nothing. Somehow or other, Coach Pitino would convince Antoine to work like no one else would now, so he could live like no one else could later.

Antoine did live like no one else as he was projected to have grossed more than $100 million dollars over his twelve year NBA career. It was said that during Antoine's heyday as an NBA player he was taking care of more than 70 relatives and friends. Antoine built his mother a mansion in the suburbs of Chicago with ten bathrooms, indoor swimming pool, full court basketball court, etc. Antoine had a show room of automobiles with Bentley's, Hummers, and Mercedes, you name it, he had it. In October of 2009 an article appeared detailing Antoine's bankruptcy troubles and debts. Presently Antoine is fighting for his life to make a comeback in the NBA.

The story of Antoine Walker is not only his story but my story as well. No, I didn't make hundreds of millions of dollars, but I have hit rock bottom just like Antoine. We all hit rock bottom. When we realize that we cannot control our unmanageable situations, it's during those times of discontentment that we need the Master the most. The part I like most about Antoine's story is his humility, Antoine has always been very cocky and precocious, but problems have a way of humbling us all and making us understand, that life is really about doing the right things, treating people the right way, and living for the Master.

These guys all knew that in order for us to win, they had to improve. In reality, they had no choice. Coach Pitino would not let them settle for mediocrity. And to be fair to the players, they were there because they had a vision for greatness. They knew that if they fought for their lives, Coach Pitino would make a

FIGHT FOR YOUR LIFE

way for them to get to the next level, whether that next level was the NBA, or an MBA.

Coach Pitino was the fire that lit the torch that made everything go. He was one of the most intense coaches with whom I have ever been associated. On several occasions, when Delray Brooks and I would come in a few minutes past our normal 6 a.m. starting time, we incurred Coach Pitino's wrath. He told us in no uncertain terms that arriving late, even a little late, was unacceptable and threatened to fire us if we did it again. It seemed like I was fired daily for as little as coming in one minute late. The guy was from another planet; his intensity, and his passion for the game was off the charts.

Coach O'Brien, whom Coach Pitino called "OB," would usually get the brunt of Coach Pitino's wrath. I suppose Coach Pitino knew that Coach O'Brien could take it. "OB," Coach Pitino would shout. "What are you doing? Why didn't we defend that last play? You're not a coach; you're an imposter."

Coach O'Brien took these tongue-lashings in stride, knowing how fortunate he was to be working for such a great man.

THE PRE-GAME PREPARATIONS

Pregame, for those who are not familiar with game preparation, is an important process that takes place the day of the game. We usually had brisk walkthrough sessions on those days. These walkthroughs were worse than most coaches' regular practice. They usually lasted a full hour, and the intensity of them was simply breathtaking. We would go through all of our own plays full speed, just as if we were playing the game.

Then we would go through all our planned defenses against the opposition's plays. Coach Pitino's philosophy was: How can we defeat an enemy if we don't know that enemy's proclivities? Our team had to know the opposition as if they themselves were the opposition, and he was not satisfied until they did. This intense preparation gave our team a tremendous leg up on the competition.

As in life, most players and coaches were not willing to put forth this type of effort just to win a ball game. Some might do it for a game or two, but if they lost, they quickly abandoned it as "too much work for too little results." Coach Pitino would not allow his players to abandon it. They measured up...or else.

Next, we turned to the blackboard. Delray was in charge of the first section. Each coach put his assignment on the board. The board was broken down into four sections. Delray's section listed the opposition's best three-point shooters and their shooting percentages, underneath that came the best field-goal percentage shooters, then came the best free-throw shooters (and the worst, just in case we needed to foul someone at the end of the game). Lastly, we would put on the board a list of the opponents' steals leader, and best offensive and defensive rebounders. The reason for the unparalleled precision was we wanted to be ready for anything. We wanted nothing to surprise us during the course of the game. Now it's virtually impossible not to run into some new play a coach could have put in or some new wrinkle, but we tried to control the things we could control with meticulous detail. We knew that people are creatures of habit, a coach would stick to things he was use to, even if it meant running it over and over.

In the next section, Coach Pitino would concentrate on offense, putting up on the board the bread-and-butter plays we would be using for that particular game. The third section was also his, and he would use it for the planned defensive strategies. He made notes about trapping in the post and trapping baseline.

The fourth section was Coach O'Brien's. He would write down the three or four main plays the opponent liked to run and how we were going to defend against them. He would also list three or four keys to winning the game.

Before taking the court, we would show the players a two-to-five-minute videotape of something positive they had done in their previous game. This got them thinking in terms of success. For them, there was nothing like going out onto the court on a positive note. If they were positive, and their self-esteem was high, they could do supernatural things. We wanted them to visualize victory before they ever stepped on the court. We wanted them to take ownership of their vision. You can do whatever you think you can.

When our team had a roaring crowd behind them and not against them, they felt like nothing was impossible; and, of course, they were right.

Think about that for a moment, are you adding this type of precision to your business, your company or your life. Are you watching the game film of what has worked or what has not worked for you in the past? Have you charted the competition, do you know your competitor as well as you know yourself, if you can't answer yes to this question then you are cheating yourself and your business. What plays have worked for you continuously, what plays need to be changed. As a coach I am constantly changing my play book. You will have to constantly stay on the cutting edge of change if you are to meet with success in uncommon hours.

GAME TIME

During the game, each coach had his individual area of concentration. Coach O'Brien was to look at every play the opponent ran against us and to devise a strategic plan to stop it. He also kept track of timeouts—how many we had and how many the opposing team had.

Delray kept every offensive play we ran on a chart and had to document the success or failure of each one. He also kept track of the fouls each player on our team had, as well as those of our opponents.

I was to chart the success or failure of every defensive play we had. We had our black/white press, our man defense, our zone defense, our five defense, and others.

I also kept all the stats on the players' hustle. Who deflected the ball or tipped it away from the opposition? Who drew a charge from an opposing team member? Who dived after a loose ball? Coach expected us to have at least thirty-five deflections per game, and if we got them, he told the players in advance, we would win.

Making these charts was serious business, and if a chart was later found to be inaccurate, Coach would call us on it immediately. He was uncanny in this regard. If he discovered an error, he would give us a tongue-lashing we could never forget. When it happened to me, I felt like crawling under a rock and never coming out again.

Many times, Coach tested our will to survive as one of his assistants. He told us, "When I was with Hubie Brown (former NBA coach and analyst), I had to keep the offensive *and* the defensive charts—all at the same time—and you can't even keep the defensive chart? What good are you? I'll send you back out on the streets. I don't care about you or your family. You'd better get the chart right." Well I knew he didn't mean everything he said, but he sure made you think he did.

During each game, Coach was meticulously dressed like a model out of GQ fashion magazine. He always wore dark-colored business suits. These were actually two-thousand-dollar designer suits. Coach Pitino was a businessman at heart, no different than Warren Buffett or Bill Gates. He dressed for success, he was always prepared, and he was meticulous about everything he did.

Coach was so intense that before every game, he could be found sitting on the toilet, suffering from diarrhea. I never understood why he got so nervous before a game...that is until I became a head coach myself. Then I quickly understood, and I experienced the exact same thing. His will to be the best drives him relentlessly.

After he ascended from that toilet, Coach was a madman, and everyone knew not to bother him before the game. He was like a caged tiger ready to pounce on his prey, and anyone could fall victim to his wrath. If any of us showed the least sign of weakness, he would eat us for lunch. If someone were easily shaken, he would chew them up and spit them out. This was a man consumed with one thought—winning.

Perception is a big part of winning. People often make perceptions based on what they see. If you are not dressing for success how do you expect to be successful? You can't leave the house unshaven, or with your pants hanging off your butt and expect to be perceived in a positive manner. Perceptions are always being formed; there is the old saying that you only get one time to make a good impression. In order to be successful in your life or your business, dress for success. There's something about putting on a suit that makes me feel more successful. There is something about getting a fresh haircut that makes me feel really good about myself. I feel like I can make the billion dollar deal if I am already dressed for it. Ladies, go to your favorite beauty salon and get your hair done, go to your favorite nail salon and get those fingers and toes manicured. Your performance will follow your dress. Dress for success.

CHAMPIONS

In 1996, Kentucky was rated number one in the nation for most of the year, and we were expected to win the national championship. We had the confident sophomore, Antoine Walker, who was 6'8" and could handle the ball like a guard. His only negative was that he wanted to shoot three-point shots rather than be unstoppable in the post.

We also had Derek Anderson, who had transferred from Ohio State, and Ron Mercer, the high-flying freshmen, who had a wonderful mid-range game. (For the layman, the mid-range game is the ability to hit the in-between jumpers, from fifteen to seventeen feet away from the basket).

Tony Delk was a shooting machine. He could get thirty points on an opposing team from anywhere and on any given night.

Anthony Epps was the smart point guard who kept everyone happy. He wasn't the most athletic guy in the world, but he was a winner and a true leader. Although Anthony was rather moody, Coach knew the right buttons to push to get him motivated to be the best he could be.

Wayne Turner was the back-up point guard. He was the exact opposite of Anthony. Wayne was fast and strong and could push the basketball up the court. His only problem was his unorthodox jump shot. He was a right-handed shooter, but he brought the ball to the left side of his head to fire off his jumpers. Bad habits are often hard to correct, and we were never able to correct this one.

Big Nazr Mohammed was our man in the middle. He had come to Kentucky at over three hundred pounds, but Coach put him on a diet with vigorous exercise—and I do mean vigorous. Nazr lost the weight, but it cost him to do it. I would arrive at the office at six in the morning, and Nazr would already be on the Stairmaster, hitting it hard, trying to change his body. Eventually he succeeded.

Mark Pope was a versatile big man, 6'9," who could step out and hit the three-point shot. He was one of the nicest guys you ever wanted to meet. Always upbeat and positive, he was one of those players whom every coach needs. Mark was also one of the top students on the team.

Jared Prickett was our blue-collar worker, and Walter McCarty was our Mr. Energizer Bunny.

We won the national championship in the Meadowlands that year, and it was no surprise to anyone; we were loaded with talent. Talent promises you nothing, but without it, you don't have much of a chance. Talented young men who are willing to push themselves to get to the next level provide the key to winning the big one.

In the Meadowlands, we beat a hard-nosed Jim Boeheim's Syracuse Orangemen. It was one of the most gratifying moments in my young coaching career. I had never been part of a NCAA Championship team until that moment. I was amazed. God had fulfilled my dreams, although in a very different way than I had imagined. We all rejoiced and celebrated.

Later, I was often asked what I did with the suit I wore during the championship game. It was a bold black and white pinstripe suit, and with it I wore black and white wingtip shoes. I must have looked like a character out of the movie *Scarface*. I thought the look was really sharp at the time, but I later came to the conclusion that it wasn't, and I learned the wisdom of dressing in conservative business suits. Coach Pitino made sure of that. He said later that he couldn't figure out if I had been part of his staff or one of the referees. I got the message.

With the victory in the Meadowlands, Coach Pitino finally had the monkey off of his back. The talk had been that he could never win the big game. It had taken him seven years to move a program that was in shambles and bring it back to respectability by winning the national championship. We were all very happy for him.

I was also very happy for him for another reason. The summer of 1995, Coach Pitino had taken all of us on a trip to Italy; it would be a trip to develop team chemistry before the 1995–1996 season began in earnest. A lot was expected of the team that year, nothing less than a championship would due. So our trip to Italy was an opportunity for us all to get on the same page of winning a championship. The highlight of the trip was going to Rome and seeing the Vatican and meeting Pope John Paul. I remember Coach Pitino going up and kissing the Pope's ring, it was a humbling site to see coach Pitino kneeling down to anyone. As Coach knelt down to kiss the Pope's ring, the Pope took Coach's hand; it looked as though he was going to kiss his finger but found he had no ring, so the Pope said, "I would kiss your ring but you don't have one." So winning the 1996 Championship gave Coach Pitino the opportunity to go back to Italy and have the Pope kiss his ring. Whether he ever did, I don't know.

The other highlight of winning the national championship was arriving back home at the Lexington airport. Thousands of raving fans were waiting for us there, as if Santa Claus was coming to town. They had come to congratulate the team, but they were also very appreciative of the job Coach Pitino had done. It felt like we were the Beatles coming home from our farewell tour.

The Kentucky fans and students were fanatical. We went from the airport to a bus that took us to a giant pep rally in Rupp Arena. I remember the bus cruising through the streets of Lexington with a legion of police cars. The police cars had their sirens blasting and their horns on high pitch. Pulling into the arena and seeing the fans going "ballistic" in their jubilation, palm palms were waving, fans were cheering, and we were just blessed to be a part of it all.

The highlight of the rally was pulling down the banner and hearing the song "We are the champions. There's no time for losers, for we are the champions of the world." Tears flowed as we realized that this accomplishment was an once-in-a-lifetime dream come true. My mind began to reflect on all my failed attempts as a player to win a championship: there was the 1984 loss to Georgetown; there was the loss to St. Johns in 1985; there was the loss to LSU in 1986; and of course there was the loss to Villanova my senior year in 1988. All that paled in comparison to this one shining moment in 1996.

Do you know when your one shining moment will appear? Let me answer that for you: no you don't. That's why you must stay in the game, that's why you must continue to evaluate what's working and what's not working by watching the game film of your life. I never won a NCAA Championship as a player, but I was blessed to be a part of a championship team as a coach. That's why you never stop improving, that's why you must work in your passion, passion breeds success. Dress for success, dream of success, get in the game and be a success.

MASTER OF THE GAME

Working with Coach Pitino and Coach O'Brien was such a rewarding experience; I have many memories of them during this time. Coach Rick Pitino was (and still is) a master of the game of basketball. He was flawless on strategy and execution, and he was also a genius at motivation. This was shown very clearly one year when we encountered a problem keeping Roderick Rhodes focused on the present.

Rod's whole aim of playing college basketball had been to go to the NBA and become a star. He was a great post-up player and a great slasher, but the people he had surrounding him kept telling him that he had to prove to the NBA scouts who attended the games that he could shoot three-point shots. Rod would go out onto the court and try to prove to everyone that he was a good three-point shooter, and it made him and the whole team look bad. It wasn't that he couldn't hit them occasionally, but it wasn't his mastery. He had a mastery at driving the ball to the hoop and posting up. It was hard for anyone to stop Rod when he put the ball on the floor because he had great court awareness. He was either going to score, get fouled, or dish to an open teammate.

After we had failed to bring this conduct under control, Coach Pitino, in an attempt at reverse psychology, decided to read the team a story called *The Precious Present,* by Spencer Johnson. The story was about a young man who was never satisfied with life. He was always concerned about tomorrow and about what the future held for him.

An old man who lived next door noticed the young man's preoccupation with the future and kept telling him that he had a present for him—if he could only find it. The young man looked everywhere for the promised present, but he was never able to find it. As much as he searched, it remained elusive.

After a year of searching, the old man died. When the younger man went to the funeral, he found a note attached to the old man's body. It said, "You have found the precious present. By this, the old man meant that we must all live in the present; tomorrow will take care of itself. We should live today with such zest and vigor that tomorrow will not be a concern. Yesterday is gone, and tomorrow never gets here, for when it does, it's already today. So we must live in the present."

This story seemed to have the desired effect...for a time at least. Eventually, Rod reverted to his former behavior.

Coach Pitino is the standard by which all other coaches should be judged. He's not only a great coach, but also a great motivator. I count it a great blessing to have worked with him.

One of his favorite sayings was, "It's important to know what to do, but it's even more important to know what not to do." I was to learn the meaning of this statement in the near future.

Are you always preoccupied with the future? We negate the present by always worrying about the future. Successful people make their future by working their present. All we have is the right now, today. One of my mentors would tell me all I want to do is to make it today if I can overcome today then I have victory today. I can't worry about tomorrow; the successful tomorrow is predicated on a successful today. Work in the moments of today, if we succeed in the moments we will succeed in the future. Moment by moment I will be great. Moment by moment I will do great things.

A GIVING MAN

Surprisingly, Coach Pitino turned out to be a very giving man. Once, when we were in Philadelphia for a game, he asked me to go shopping with him. Coach "OB" always declined these invitations, because he knew that Coach Pitino would still require him to have all of his scouting responsibilities done to perfection even if he went. So he would stay in his hotel room and watch game films.

Coach and I went that evening to a store where all the NBA players shopped. It was my first time there, and I was amazed by what I saw. There were plenty of nice clothes on the rack in larger sizes. When you are 6'7" and above, it's a rarity to find clothes particularly suits that you can buy off the rack. I usually have to get clothes special-made. So I began looking around hungrily.

In the end, I picked out three nice suits with ties to match and laid them on the counter for the sales person to ring up. I had just taken out a credit card to pay for them (I was thinking to myself that I probably couldn't afford them, but that it was so seldom that I could find my size in anything that I probably should go ahead and splurge). Just then, Coach Pitino came over and insisted on paying for everything. I was so shocked by this demonstration of generosity that I cried like a baby. I had never seen this side of the man before, and it was something I hadn't expected from one who was such a perfectionist. In the years to come, I would see this side of Coach more and more.

Once, for example, when my daughter, Princess, was collecting money for a church program, Coach Pitino gave her five thousand dollars. Another time (this one after he had fired me), I was again favored by his generosity. Peggy and I had met with Kathy Debour and C.M. Newton (the former athletic director at Kentucky) and talked about my son, Leontay, possibly going to Kentucky for his college education. We explained to them that I had lost my job and we had no money right then, and asked if there was anything they could do.

C.M. later told me that the matter had been taken care of. The school would give Leontay a scholarship because I had given so much to the school as a student athlete. Needless to say, Peggy and I were very grateful to know that the program thought so well of me as to pay our son's way through college. It was months later before we learned it was actually Coach Pitino who paid Leontay's way through school. Such was the generosity of the man. He expected and demanded the most from you, but he also gave the most of himself. Its one thing when a superior expects the most from his subordinates, and gives little, but it's a whole different thing when that superior expects the best but also gives the best of himself. That was Coach Pitino. He didn't expect any more from you than he expected of himself.

Are you a leader in your organization, your church, or your house? What are you expecting from others that you are not giving yourself? Great leaders do more than what is expected. Great leaders give of themselves to others. We all know it's better to give than to receive, but we live in a society that teaches us to be the receiver and not the giver. The great ones, from Mother Teresa to Mahatma Gandhi, gave their all, and in doing so changed the world. Learn to give and success will overtake you.

COACH JIM O'BRIEN

As they say about a successful marriage, "behind every great man is a great woman," the same can be said for a great coach. Behind every great coach is a great assistant. Jim O'Brien was the great man behind Coach Pitino.

Coach "OB" was a wizard at breaking down the opponents' every move and he was a great model of what every coach should be. He would often ask Delray and me what we would do in certain defensive and offensive situations—even though we were both still young in the coaching game. It's impossible to describe how good that made me feel. That one question, "What would you do?" boosted my self-esteem in coaching in a major way.

Coach "OB" gave us confidence and self-worth. He kidded us by saying that we all had to stick together if we were going to survive Coach Pitino's temper tantrums.

I knew that one day Coach O'Brien's time would come again as a head coach. He was patient, yet he knew how to get the best out of the players. He was more laid back than Coach Pitino, but he was still very demanding.

Jim O'Brien was the most organized coach I've ever known; he approached his passion with a laser beam focus. He had a folder for everything. He had big black binders for each recruiting service that we ordered, and his desk was always meticulous. I still haven't learned his secrets of organization.

I found Coach O'Brien to be a very loyal man. He would often take up for me if he thought Coach Pitino had chewed me out wrongfully. Everyone should have a friend like Jim O'Brien.

In fact, the only bad thing I ever heard said about Jim O'Brien was that he didn't smile enough. But I can't complain. The same observation had often been made about me.

Smiling is an infectious attitude. As a young player, I thought it was cool to be known as an intimidator, so everywhere I went I had a scowl instead of a smile. The scowl was okay for the basketball court but once off the court, a smile would have been more impressive. People who are successful know the power of smiling, and laughter. The good book says a merry heart doeth good like a good medicine. While we are striving for success we must have a balanced attack, which includes enjoying family and friends. What good is it to get to the winners circle and find that there is no one there to share your success? Let's work hard, play hard, and let's smile.

THE 1997–98 SEASON

By the time 1998 came around, we had lost Antoine Walker to the NBA, as well as Mark Pope, Tony Delk, and Walter McCarty. The biggest blow came during a regular season game, where Derek Anderson tore his ACL. With him and Ron Mercer working together, we had thought we might have another shot at winning the championship. Without him, our chances would be slim.

The news was bad. Derek would be out for the rest of the season.

But Ron Mercer surprised us all. Deciding that this was his opportunity to become a real leader, he put the team on his back and carried us back to the Final Four.

Who could have imagined that we would reach the Final Four after having lost five players to the NBA draft and our best player to injury? It was a moment of great victory for the team.

While we were glad to be back at the Final Four, we knew that we had a monumental task ahead of us. Could Derek possibly play to help us? He had been tenacious in his rehab, and it was thought by the team doctors that he could probably play if we needed him. But Coach Pitino wasn't about to take the risk that Derek would be reinjured and miss his opportunity in the upcoming NBA Draft. This had been his second ACL surgery, and team owners would be asking themselves whether he could survive the strain of an eighty-two game NBA season.

We were not to be so lucky this time in the Final Four. Arizona, our opponent, came into the tournament loaded. Coach Lute Olsen could rest easy with Mike Bibby and Miles Simon running and gunning, and the Arizona defense completely shut down the Big Blue Attack. Ron Mercer had done all he could, but he was only one man. His heroic efforts were not enough to defeat the Arizona Wildcats. Our season had come to an abrupt end.

From the start of my time at Kentucky, I had been determined to change, but that hadn't happened. In fact, my lifestyle became so objectionable that one day Coach Pitino called me into his office and warned me about my propensity to pick up women. My activities were embarrassing the coaches and players. If I didn't change my ways, he warned, I could jeopardize my career.

That was about as stern a warning as I could imagine, and I knew that it had not come from Rick Pitino, but from God Himself. I was on the road to disaster, bringing my soul down to Hell. This simply had to stop.

And I wish I could say that it did...but it didn't—again.

THE NBA CALLING

At the end of the 1998 season, several NBA teams came court-
ing Coach Pitino very seriously. This was nothing new. Every
year, there had been rumors of his going back to the NBA. This
time, however, the rumors were to prove true. We were in San
Jose, California, for a NCAA Tournament game, and Coach and
I had gone out for our usual daily run, when he told me that he
was seriously thinking about going back to the NBA. If he did,
he said, he wanted me to go with him.

I was so excited by this news that I didn't know what to do. I
thanked God for being merciful to me and moving on my behalf.
In many ways, I hadn't deserved it.

In other ways, I did. I'd been working hard as a coach, preparing for precisely this day. I had taken careful notes of everything
Coach Pitino did, somehow knowing that if I stayed the course
and did what I was supposed to do, my opportunity would come.
My father would have a favorite saying along those lines, "Son,
if you do what you are supposed to do, God will do what He is
supposed to do."

When I say I took notes, I mean it literally. I took index cards
and a blue felt-tip pen with me wherever I went. Many times,
Coach would ask for one of my index cards and would borrow

my pen. He was always making notes and drawing up plays. I had a lot to learn, so I put it on paper and proceeded to memorize it. Coach Pitino believed very strongly in memorization.

This philosophy of always being prepared has been indelibly stamped on my forehead. I always carry an ink pen in my pocket just in case I am asked for a pen. I always wear a watch; our practices were so early (6 a.m.) that we dreamed about Coach Pitino in our sleep; as a matter of fact I never slept. I wear a watch so much that I forget to take it off when I am sleeping; there is a permanent imprint on my left wrist as if it were a tattoo. I am still haunted by the ghost of Pitino. I was terrified of being late, being late in Pitino's system is the equivalent of murder, you will be placed before the firing squad, and you will be sentenced to the guillotine. I could hear Coach Pitino's voice cussing me out in his most melodious Italian dialect every time I came in just a minute late, "you F.....ing no good son of a b..... You either get here on time or go back to the rock from which you crawled." I was so self-conscience of being late that I would go to sleep in my clothes, fully dressed for the next morning's early bird practice, I would walk into practice looking like Bullwinkle, my socks was missed matched, my clothes were wrinkled, I looked like a street person, unshaven, wrinkled, ashy legs the whole bit. But none of that matter, the only crucial element was to get to practice before time, not on time, before time. Fifteen minutes early was the Wildcat Way, anything less would not be tolerated.

I have never seen an assistant return to work for coach Pitino. Once you leave you never go back. Not because we don't love the guy it's just we know the pressure to be great is so all consuming that we feel the only option is to secum to the pressure of mediocrity. Coach Pitino is a perfectionist of the highest order, anything less than perfection is a loss in his book. And the one thing that Coach Pitino will not tolerate is a loss in any form or fashion. Memorization was a must with Coach Pitino.

When Coach O'Brien would go over the scouting report on the court, he was not permitted to look at a single note. The team might have thirty plays they ran during the course of the game, but Coach O'Brien had better have them all memorized. And he always did.

If a team ran a play during the game that was not covered in the scouting report, we were all given a death sentence. If he asked you who we were recruiting in any of the fifty states—seniors, juniors, underclassmen, and junior college players—you'd better know the names, the addresses, and the contact people at that very second. There was no looking at notes.

One day Coach Pitino came into my office and said, "I want you to do the scouting report for the LSU game."

"Coach, I can't do it," I said.

He said, "Don't tell me you can't! You *will* do it!"

It was about noon, and we had practice scheduled for 2:45 p.m. He said, "Get it done." So I had two hours and forty-five minutes to look at five game films and to memorize everything that LSU did—both offensively and defensively. If it had not been for Coach O'Brien that day, I would've suffered a nervous breakdown. With his help, I got through it.

This was typical of the ways Coach Pitino stretched us. He forced us to do more than we thought we could do and wanted us to see that there was more in us than we thought there was. He expected us to go the extra mile, not just do what we were told to do. "Be a person of initiative," he told us. "Be proactive rather than reactive. Be a self-starter, don't wait to be told, do what you think needs to be done."

He did not demand more of us than he was willing to give himself. He was, in every way, an intense person. In the three and a half years I had worked with him, I had never seen him either eat or sleep. He would always make sure *we* would eat, but he would never eat himself. It was as if he got joy by seeing us gain weight, while he remained in tiptop shape.

Coach Pitino seemed to have a phobia about gaining weight, he was always moving. We would run a few miles, and then he would go back to the gym and run some more on the treadmill. We would play ball at six in the morning, and when he was finished, he would go get on the Stairmaster or the treadmill. The man was so relentless that we would lose weight just watching him.

I never saw him in his office for very long, usually just a little while before practice. He was like a ghost—now you see him, now you don't—always on the move.

Another amazing thing about Coach Pitino was his sense of what was going on. When we were together at Kentucky, he could be in Miami and we would be in Lexington, and he would call us and tell us what was happening with the players there at the university. He would say, "Did you know that Anthony Epps beat up a guy at the nightclub last night? What are you guys doing back there? When I get back to Kentucky, you're fired." The television networks tried to make it seem like this phrase "you're fired" was made famous by billionaire real estate mogul Donald Trump, but I was being fired daily by Coach Pitino way before "the Donald" made it famous.

This was Coach Pitino, a man of excellence who demanded excellence of us all, and the thought of working with him now at the Boston Celtics was thrilling.

Are you waiting to be told what to do next? The great ones figure out what needs to be done and do it. Great companies evaluate themselves and take action. If you are to rise through the ranks of the company you have to evaluate your strengths and weaknesses. In business they call this SWOT analysis. This is the evaluation of strengths, weaknesses, opportunities and threats. If you are to be the greatness you are designed to be you will have to evaluate every area of your life and take progressive action to correct unwanted activity. Evaluate your strengths and make them stronger, evaluate your weaknesses and see if you can make them strengths, evaluate the opportunities presented to you, don't run from opportunities that are masked as problems, run to them. Figure out what the threats are, those things that are stopping you from being the great "you" you are supposed to be.

CELTIC PRIDE

Coach Pitino thus took the head coaching job at the most storied franchise in NBA history—the Boston Celtics. And true to his word, he invited me to join him. What a major task that was to be—attempting to redirect the greatest team in sports history! Coach had done a masterful job in all the other rebuilding programs he had undertaken—Boston College, Providence, the New York Knicks, and Kentucky—and now he would work on repositioning the Celtics back to glory.

I remember the day I met all the greats who worked in the front office for the Celtics: Red Auerbach, the former coach and club president; Bill Russell, the best block-shot artist the game has ever known; John Havlicek; "the magician," Bob Cousy; and Tommy Heinsohn. It was going to be a wonderful experience to work with such legends of the game.

For the first month or two of my stay in Boston, I was in a downtown apartment paid for by the club (at $2,000 a month) until we could find a suitable house and bring our family East. This arrangement couldn't have been better for a womanizer like me. I was like a pig reveling in the slop again and finding it impossible to disassociate myself with all the females in Boston. I was dating chicks like crazy, until I began to kill myself physically. Still, the obsession grew. It's amazing how blind we get when sin dominates our lives. I had not given any thought to the fact that God had been merciful to me. It was only a few years ago that I had just had a career-ending knee injury and had to give up my dream of having a long and productive career in the NBA. Now God had given me another opportunity by repositioning me as an assistant coach, but I was acting as if I had amnesia, not remembering any of the horrors of defeat that I had faced in my past. The skeletons were still a live and walking out of the closet. Instead of being thankful, I ran back to being the womanizer I had been for most of my life.

Every morning, I would walk to work at Merrimac Street, about a ten-minute walk, and before I had arrived, I was already focusing on a couple of girls at work I wanted to date. I was like a shark that smelled blood, I was in a feeding frenzy.

I wasn't on the new job long before Coach Pitino called me into his office one day and warned me about my behavior. "I've been hearing rumors that you're trying to pick up some of the girls here in town," he said. "If you don't cut it out, I'm gonna have to fire you. And if you keep going outside of your marriage, I'm warning you that something embarrassing is going to happen."

Needless to say, his words frightened me. I had been in his office at UK for this exact same thing, but this time his warnings seemed ominous and somehow prophetic. Oh, how I would later wish that I had heeded them. I knew I should, but I seemed incapable of doing so.

Are you doing things that could destroy your prospects for a bright future? Are there things in your life that are controlling you, drinking, smoking, sex, etc? It does you no good to dress for success, or to evaluate and watch the film of your life if you don't take notes on what the film is trying to tell you. If you have life controlling issues that are making you feel out of control, get help. Don't wait, do it now. Don't be prideful; beg if you have to, but get the help.

THE BOSTON MASSACRE

Eight months after I started working for the Celtics, I was approaching the Brandeis campus one day, where, for some reason, the Celtics practiced. Peggy had come to town, and I no longer had the apartment. But I was in a sexual mood that morning and decided that I would like to meet some college girls. I wasn't aware the team had an agreement with the university that the players and coaches would never be seen on campus other than to use the gym for practice. I should have been aware of the rule. I was the one, who passed out the rulebook to the players, but I never read it; it was for the players.

No sooner had I gotten onto campus, the students learned that I was one of the Celtics coaches, and treated me like a king. Oh what a feeling to be king.

Before long, I spotted a group of girls off to one side openly smoking marijuana, as if they were a part of the hippie generation of the sixties. This surprised me, that a student would be smoking pot openly on a college campus. When one of the girls waved me over, I gladly complied. I was like a dog going back to his vomit. Again, I had no walls, no fortress, my house was made of straw and not bricks.

This girl seemed to be the ringleader of the group. We talked for a while, and then I asked if she would mind giving me a private tour of the campus. My look told her that I was seeking more than a history lesson, and her look told me that she was open to more. She said she would love to show me around, and we set off together.

The "tour" was short and sweet, and all paths led back to her dorm room. There I had the first of many sexual encounters with her that would take place over the next four months. This was madness, of course, and I suppose I knew it, but I felt I needed it so much that I couldn't care at the moment.

Of course, I cared when that fateful phone call came from Coach Pitino one day in early January that I had been fired for sexual misconduct. Just like that, it was all over; everything I had worked for had been lost. The house and cars would be the smallest loss. My reputation would surely be irreparably damaged, and my profession set back many years, if not forever. But more so, would my marriage survive this? Would my relationship with my parents survive it? And would my relationship with God survive it? Was my soul lost forever because of what I had done?

All of these thoughts ran through my mind on the forty-five minute drive home. Over and over, I struggled to find the words to explain to Peggy what had happened, but there didn't seem to be many innovative ways of telling my wife that I had just been fired for sexual misconduct. I was an emotional wreck when I finally pulled into the driveway.

Peggy was in the kitchen holding our daughter, Jasmine, in her arms. She smiled when she saw me, thinking that Coach Pitino had, for some reason, given us the day off—a rare occurrence. She stopped smiling when she saw the look on my face.

"Peggy, you'd better sit down," I told her when I could speak.

She sat, suddenly apprehensive, and waited for me to continue.

It took me a moment. I still didn't know where to begin, what to say, or how to say it. Finally, I just had to plunge in. "Peggy, I've just been fired from my job."

"What?" she asked incredulously. "What do you mean you've just been fired?"

"Peggy, I've been unfaithful to you again. I've been sleeping with a young lady on campus. She's gone to officials at the school, and they've gone to the Boston Celtics organization. Coach Pitino says that he has no other recourse but to fire me."

There was so much more I wanted to say, but I didn't know how. I tried to say how sorry I was, but Peggy seemed near to fainting with despair at what I had said, and then her mask dissolved into sobs and screams. It looked like a scene in Amityville Horror.

"Why?" she demanded. "Why did you have to do this?"

"I hate you! I hate you!" were among the many other things she proceeded to shout at me in her hurt and utter despair.

In that moment, I felt as if the very fiber of my being was ripped to shreds. I hurt so much for her, but I didn't know what to do about it.

I was sure that Peggy must feel like killing me, and I didn't blame her one bit. She was a wonderful lady, and I had put her through this same torture time and time again. This was just the latest in a whole string of shocking revelations. I had known all along that I was doing wrong, but somehow I had never foreseen it ending like this. Why hadn't I been more concerned about her feelings?

Aside from her screaming and lamenting this great tragedy, I could somehow hear my mother's voice, as she had warned me a number of times through the years, "Son, if you don't stop this sexual acting out, it's going to destroy everything you've worked for."

I could also hear coach Pitino's voice, "I told you that if you didn't stop having sex outside of marriage something would happen to embarrass you and your whole family."

When they had spoken these words, I heeded their advice—for a little while, that is—until the I-have-to-have-its would set in. Then the cycle started all over again. What would it take for me to change?

Mrs. Pitino was devastated by the news, and she was worried about Peggy...and rightfully so. Peggy fell into a deep depression and took to her bed, not wanting to be disturbed by anyone for any reason—especially by me. Mrs. Pitino came over to the house to console her, and when she saw Peggy's state, she actually climbed into the bed with her, held her like a child, and assured her that she would get through this ordeal. The two of us had to stick together, she wisely counseled.

It was hard for Peggy to see any future ahead for either of us at the moment—let alone any future for us together. I felt exactly the same way. And yet what would I be without Peggy and my children? I couldn't imagine life without them, but surely I would lose them now. I was firmly in the clutches of what Tyler Perry, the great writer and movie producer, called *The Diary of a Mad Black Women.*

Peggy had been scheduled to pick my parents up that day at the airport. Surely she wouldn't feel like it now, I imagined. I would have to do it, and I would have to explain to them what was wrong with her and why I wasn't at work. How ironic it seemed that all of this should happen just as they were arriving for a visit.

When the time came, my parents took the news very hard. They had made great sacrifices to help me be successful, and now this. Mom called Bishop Ford (our pastor from Louisville) to let him know what had happened, and he flew to Boston on the first flight he could catch to be by our side.

Over the next few days, I had a couple of meetings with Coach Pitino at his house, mostly to discuss the details of my firing. He was sorry he had to do this, he told me, but it was settled. All that remained was for me to sign some legal papers required by the lawyers for the team.

I signed, and then suddenly it was all over. My career had vanished into thin air, and like a flower that fades my dream of eventually being a coach in the NBA also faded. Would I ever be able to get back on my feet—morally, personally, and professionally? If I did, I would have to fight as never before. I had created a mountain of problems that would not be easy to overcome.

Have you ever lost a job that you thought was everything that you dreamed of? Sometimes we cause gigantic waves with one mistake. Our character is the one thing that can make us or break us. Character takes a lifetime to build and a moment to destroy. Someone said our talent will take us where only good character can keep us. When you detect character flaws, seek accountability right away. One of the down falls of my life has been isolation. I would always rather travel and be alone rather than be accountable to someone. This has been a grave mistake. Accountability helps us to get in line and stay in line. Like it or not it could be the very thing that saves your life.

PART 2

STRUGGLING TO GET UP

MOVING BACK HOME

After a week or two of confused activity in Boston, I decided to accept the advice of Coach Pitino and move back to Louisville. Although things were shaky with Peggy, it seemed that we just might be able to stick together. I would go ahead of her and stay with my parents, while she stayed behind in Boston and tried to sell the house and get Leontay through this period of his studies.

At first, Mom was adamantly against my moving back to Louisville because there were already a lot of hideous rumors circulating there about my dismissal. One of the most vicious of these rumors was that I had been let go because I was gay. What, me gay? What a preposterous statement. The thought that anyone could think such a thing was baffling to me. This foolish thought gave me a relentless resolve to chase skirts even more. I had one goal and that was to sleep with as many women as I possibly could stand.

This rumor got started when a Celtics player, who was well known around Louisville, was also released. But his release had nothing to do with my firing. He had suffered a whole series of injuries, and he was also thought to be a drain on the salary cap instituted by the league. But soon afterward, someone started the rumor that this player and I had been caught in bed together and this had led to the downfall of both of us. It was a ridiculous rumor, but many chose to believe it. I am always amazed how people make up their own story when they don't have a story to go on.

When I arrived back home, these rumors had preceded me, and I was treated as an outcast. When people would see me on the street, they would point and whisper to one another. The common refrain seemed to be, "He used to be a coach in the NBA, but now he's a "fag." I wanted to bash heads every time this lie was repeated, and eventually I did go to the *Courier Journal* newspaper and have them print a story that should have silenced the rumors. But people continued to believe what they wanted to believe.

In more than one way, my world had been destroyed. When I tried to find some type of meaningful job, I found instead that no one wanted to hire me. In time, I decided to go into real estate, but I also decided to get some serious help for my problem.

On several occasions, Bishop Ford had told Peggy that he thought my problem was a "sexual addiction." She had been very skeptical of such a thing, and I was even more skeptical. What I was doing was what most men did. Of that I was sure. The only difference was that, as a Christian, I felt condemned. I don't know of a man who when he was a teenager didn't try to collect as many phone numbers as possible. It was the manly thing to do. I liked it so well that once I grabbed on to the habit, the habit grabbed me back and wouldn't let go. I felt like Michael Douglas, who played Nick Curran in the 1992 thriller *Basic Instinct*, when the sensual and sexy Sharon Stone got involved with Nick. Once Nick had one fling with Catherine it was over; he was caught in a web of sexual healing. One scene was captivating when Nick was interviewing Catherine in a room, Catherine had on a white mini dress and as she was talking she opened her legs so that Nick could see she had on no panties. I too was in a web of deceit, captivated and mesmerized by chicks all with miniskirts and no panties. I could not leave the web. I was stuck and couldn't get out.

If I had not known the ways of God, having sex with the Sharon Stones of the world would have been perfectly legitimate. Most men with my pedigree would have crowned me king, for having slept with numerous women. But my knowledge of God says I am a wretched sinner who needs grace and mercy. Even with a major weakness I still desired to please God. I didn't want to constantly give in to my every whim for sexual pleasure.

Now, Bishop Ford asked me to participate in a program he had located in New Orleans, Louisiana, that dealt with this issue. It was hard to say no to him. After all, I did have *some* kind of problem. That was for sure. Was it a sex addiction? I couldn't imagine that such a thing existed, but, for the time being, I decided to swallow my pride and agree to attend the sessions he had arranged.

What else did I have to do at the moment? I was unemployed, and my future was looking very bleak.

Also, the idea of getting out of town, going somewhere where I could lay low for a while, appealed to me. My story would surely be hitting the newspapers any day now.

When you are faced with any type of major decision with your life, seek Godly counsel. Bishop Ford was a spiritual advocate for helping Peggy and I in the time of our most urgent need. I don't know what we would have done without his divine counsel. If you don't have Godly people in your life, seek help from wise people who you admire and respect. None of us have all the answers and none of us are as powerful as all of us.

SEEKING HELP

The program in New Orleans was conducted under the auspices of the famed sex researchers Drs. Masters and Johnson. It was a six-week program designed to help those suffering any type of compulsive disorder. At the time, these two doctors were considered to be the foremost authorities on the subject. I sincerely hoped that the people at this clinic could help me understand why I felt that I had to have sex so frequently and with so many women in order to be happy.

It proved to be a very intense program in which I was shut in with other people who had the same problem. I first sat down with a doctor, who tried to assess the seriousness of my case. Then I and the other patients attended classes that taught us tools to use whenever we began to fantasize about sex. We were taught, for instance, to wear a rubber band on one wrist and to pop that rubber band when we needed to. That, we were told, would give us an unexpected jolt and bring us back to reality, when we would fantasize about sex.

We were also given ammonia capsules and told that we could break them and smell the ammonia if we needed a jolt of reality. I immediately thought, okay, I guess the worldly population of men is all walking around with ammonia capsules in their pocket, and rubber bands on their wrist.

We were encouraged to remember the specific incident that had brought us to the point of seeking help. For me, it was not hard to remember. I had been fired as an assistant coach with the Boston Celtics because of sexual impropriety. How could I ever forget? I had not only lost my job, but I was about to lose my house, my cars, and my most prized blessing, my family.

I could adamantly relate to Tiger Woods, the most celebrated golfer of my generation, when the story broke that he had over one hundred and twenty affairs. On December 11, 2009, Tiger announced that he would take an indefinite leave from the game of golf after two dozen women had come forward to say that they had affairs with the world's greatest golfer. Tiger was listed by Forbes as the richest sportsman in the world in 2010, making an estimated ninety million dollars. Addictions have no prejudice. You can be the neighborhood mailman or you could be one of the richest men in the world. Our only hope in overcoming any life controlling issue is to first believe that we can overcome our issue. Shortly after Tigers admission, my wife and I were approached by ESPN to do an interview discussing Tiger's dilemma. Because Peggy and I have experienced similar circumstance, ESPN felt the interview could be helpful to Tiger and his former wife, Elin. One of the main questions ESPN wanted to know was did I consider Tiger to be a sex addict. Because I am not a registered clinician I didn't feel comfortable placing the tag of sex addict on Tiger; however, it doesn't take much to see that he has a problem. I am sure he feels like I have felt for a long time about myself. I was just a guy that had an insatiable appetite for women. I can't image what it must be like to be Tiger Woods, the greatest golfer to ever play the game. A young superstar thrust onto the world stage at such a young age.

He is a man with everything, money, power, and prestige. There is nothing he can't have; it's all at his fingertips at his beck in call. The first stage in overcoming weaknesses whether you call the problem a sexual addiction, or sexual compulsiveness, you first have to admit there is a problem. Tiger never admitted that he was a sex addict, although he did admit to the affairs. And he did have the wherewithal to get help. I wondered if the facility in Mississippi taught Tiger some of the same things that I had been taught. I wondered if Tiger wore a rubber band on his wrist during the Masters or if he took a break at the 9th hole to break an ammonia capsule because of the beauty he saw in the gallery.

Now I understood what the Bible meant when it said:

A good name is more desirable than great riches; to be esteemed is better than silver or gold.

Proverbs 22:1 (NIV)

Reputation and character take a lifetime to build and only a moment to destroy. Oh, if I had only realized and appreciated this earlier. Character never crossed my mind when I was in the web of supreme sexual thought, at least not until after the act had been consummated. I was immersed in the deception of this grandiose feeling of pleasure, Janet Jackson made a song about this feeling of extreme satisfaction and called it *The Pleasure Principle.*

During the time I was in the Masters and Johnson Clinic, I remained skeptical about the idea that I had a sexual addiction, but I did accept the term because everyone there agreed that this is what I was—a sex addict.

Whatever was wrong with me, it was serious, and after the six-week program, it was obvious to me that I needed more help. Peggy and I together attended another program located by Bishop Ford, this one in Colorado. The program was taught by Harry Shaumberg, author of the book *False Intimacy*. Dr. Shaumberg approached the subject of sexual addiction from a Christian perspective and posed the question: "Where is God in all of this?" Later, I couldn't remember much of what had been said in the program, except that we needed to trust God.

Again, I objected to the term sex addict, but I went along with it because everyone was using it. I wasn't a sex addict; I was sure, just a Christian who had a weakness that was sex. I had plenty of friends who chased women for the express purpose of having sex.

The clinic in New Orleans had set out for me a course of therapy that would last for the next two years, and, as part of that required therapy, I now had to locate some local counselors who could help both Peggy and me. One who was recommended to us was Jerry Leach in Lexington, and I began seeing him once a week. I also was able to contact Dr. Schmidt in Louisville, and he accepted me for a weekly session as well.

I also got involved in a local SAA (Sex Addict Anonymous) group. Attending all of these meetings was a big step, because (1) It let me see that I was not the only person around with this problem, and (2) Because everyone involved in these sessions used the term "sex addict," I slowly began to accept the idea.

I'm not sure just when I accepted the fact that I was a sex addict, and when I did, some thought that I had done so just to have a convenient excuse for what I was doing. What the truth is I cannot say. What I can say is that my problem was not getting better, only worse.

GETTING WORSE BEFORE
GETTING BETTER

I'm not sure what I expected to happen with the counseling sessions, but just because I was getting counseling didn't make the temptations disappear. In some respects, the counseling only seemed to focus me more on the issue. It wasn't long before I began to tell Peggy that I no longer saw the need of attending the SAA meetings. "It's a waste of time," I explained. "Just a bunch of sex addicts talking about their problems. That doesn't help me, and sometimes hearing the lurid stories these people tell can be arousing." There were more opportunities to set up sexual escapades in those sessions than anywhere else. Just by hearing the stories I already knew there were women in the group struggling with the same issues I had. Birds of a feather flock together.

I also decided to stop going to the counseling sessions. For one thing, they were very expensive, and I wasn't sure they were doing me any good. If I just went to church faithfully, surely God would deliver me. Or so I reasoned in my own mind.

I remember reading the book *Straw: Finding My Way*, by Darryl Strawberry (former big league baseball player for the New York Mets and the New York Yankees). He came to some of the same conclusions I did after his long and destructive bout with drug, alcohol, and sex addiction. While he attended meetings with other addicts and thought the meetings were useful, eventually he came to the conclusion that what he needed most was a committed relationship with Jesus Christ.

I hadn't been back in Louisville long before I discovered that my old girlfriends were still around, and I began to visit them again. I was just like an alcoholic; if you go around the bottle you will drink, if you go around women and you know you have a woman problem, guess what? You will fall back into the habit again, which I did. I somehow convinced myself that I could play around with fire and not get burned.

As at other important junctures of my life, this was appalling to me. I had lost everything because of this activity, and didn't that mean something? It did...until the temptation, that I had often heard called the "I've-Got-To Have-Its" kicked in. Then I went running to find sex. As before, I tried many things to control myself, but my flesh wasn't trying to hear any of it and insisted, "Give me what I want."

If this turn of events had not been enough to cure me, would I ever be free? I became convinced, through listening to several of the counselors, that I was in a lifelong battle, and I needed all the help I could get.

One of the things that soured me on individual counseling sessions was when I was told that I simply must tell Peggy about every girl I had ever slept with. A key to being released from "sexual addiction," my counselor insisted, was to end the secrecy, so this was an important step that I simply had to take.

I was very hesitant. These kinds of revelations would surely stir up a lot of vindictive feelings in Peggy. When I was urged to continue, I reluctantly agreed to reveal all during the next session.

Peggy so dreaded this session that she asked our pastor to go with her for support. She had every right to be concerned. These revelations was so crushing to her that the two of us argued vehemently right there in front of the counselor and our pastor, the President could have been in attendance that day, and it would not have mattered. We were engaged in full combat. Words were coming out like AK47's shooting rounds and rounds of ammo. Finally, after a few choice expletives, I got up and walked out and didn't go back. I came to the conclusion that such confessions were not worth the emotional and physical turmoil they caused. But the counselors were right, it did end the secrecy, but I wondered at what cost. We were close to killing each other in that blood and guts session.

Most of the counseling I received during that early period was good, but how to put it into practice I didn't know. After each counseling session, I had to go back to my day-to-day reality and face the demons that constantly haunted me.

The counseling did, at least, serve one purpose. Until then, as I have said, I had continually minimized the problem, saying that it was something most men experienced, and hadn't liked the phrase "sexual addiction" at all, because it sounded like far too serious a term for what I was experiencing. It was only after being forced to take inventory of my life that I could see the difference between what I was experiencing and what most men experienced. Now I was more convinced than ever that I needed help. But what could I do about it?

Perhaps the worst thing that happened to me about this time was that news began circulating around our church about me being a sex addict. Sexual addiction was a problem that most Christians could neither understand nor forgive, and suddenly I found myself very uncomfortable in the church I had attended all of my life.

Do you need help with the struggles you face in everyday life? Is there no one to administer to your call for help? The church should be the answer for a dying world. In many cases our churches have become places for the pure, the clean, and the Holy. Church was made to be the hospital, the place were sick people can go and get help just like the hospital. If there were no sick people why would we need hospitals? If there were no people with problems, why would we need churches? But now we make our churches Heaven, where only the pure, the clean, and the mistake free people can attend. Let's get back to the old time way where people can run to the house of God in their time of need, once we get in the house and get clean, then we can go out and lead others to the house of cleansing.

HOW I OCCUPIED MY TIME AND FED MY FAMILY

As I Struggled to Recover

After many rejections of trying to find work, I became interested in real estate through attending a Paul Semonin open house. There I was presented with the idea of owning my own business, so to speak. Why not? Nothing else seemed to be on the horizon. Not long afterward, I prepared myself and passed the real estate exam.

Howard Stacey was my real estate coach at Paul Semonin Realtors, and he had also been a basketball coach. He was a great leader, continually motivating the troops to be the best sales people they could be.

This was my first introduction to any type of sales. I knew from reading about sales, the number one reason why most people do not like sales was the fear of rejection. In some respects, I had already been acquainted with rejection upon being fired by the Celtics. We were taught that in order to be successful, we would have to be relentless and persistent. We could not accept no for an answer. Every no had to become a doorway to a yes.

One of my many sales tactics was going door to door in various neighborhoods, asking people if they were thinking of selling their home. I walked so much and knocked on so many doors that I actually wore holes in my shoes. This method was very personal, and I liked the idea of meeting my clients face to face, but it took too much time and gave too little results.

I eventually came to the conclusion that the telephone was my road to success, and I began making what were called "cold calls." I spent long days and nights making calls to people's homes trying to befriend them and then trying to convince them to list their home with me, or to let me sell them a new one. This was not easy work by any standard.

It was also a very difficult time for Peggy and me financially. We had lost so much in Boston and had to start over, and now I was spending on several counselors each week. We had a little savings, but it was dwindling quickly. My pay for selling houses was based strictly on commission. I had to sell a house before I could receive a commission check. It was a feast or famine business.

Actually, being in the real estate game gave me ample opportunity to chase women. The sex was my way of medicating the pain I felt, from all the loss, the fears, and the rejection. I felt needed and wanted when I was in the arms of a woman. All my inhibitions and fears seem to dissipate while I was living in the moment.

For the first months after I moved back home to Louisville, Peggy remained in Boston, and I lived with my parents. During this time, I was completely out of control.

Women had become my God. It didn't matter where I went or what woman I saw, it was the same. I got to the place that I could tell just by the way a woman looked at me whether or not she would eventually have sex with me. I had become a master of what sex therapists call "grooming." This involves a process of preparing a woman for sex.

Oftentimes, the ladies I met had heard of my basketball exploits. This posed a special danger. I was treated like a trophy of sorts, and after having sex with me, ladies wanted to tell other people about it. "Guess who I was just with?" It was the old teen theme, kiss and tell.

If they told a close friend, that friend would tell another friend, and that one would tell another, until soon the news would be spread far and wide. This, of course, was devastating, so I was no longer interested in having any kind of relationship with another woman. I just wanted sexual gratification, and then I could move on.

Eventually, I began to do a little better at the real estate business, but it never brought us enough income. When Coach Pitino got word that we were really struggling and having a tough time, he stepped in and helped us. This amazed me because he had shown such confidence in me by taking me to Boston with him, and I had betrayed his trust. I was shocked that he even wanted anything to do with me.

He reminded me that firing me had not been his choice. He hadn't wanted to do it, but was forced to do so by the circumstances. Now he not only gave me some scouting assignments for the team, but he also provided me with a vehicle to use while I was doing the scouting. I would attend all of the Indiana Pacer home games in Indianapolis to gather stats so that the Celtics could better defend against them in the future, and I was sent to scout a few college games as well.

Dad accompanied me to many of the Pacers' games, and we enjoyed ourselves. Indianapolis wasn't too far from home, so we could drive there in two hours and come back home the same night. That was better than having to fly all over the country, staying in hotels, and renting cars to get around.

For the layman, scouting consists of watching an opponent play and then noting down the plays they use. This included defensive, as well as offensive plays. Scouting helps you to know the competition, so you can develop a plan to be victorious. But while I was helping the Boston Celtics learn how to defeat their enemies, I still seemed powerless to defeat my own.

THE ANSWER WAS SO SIMPLE THAT I HAD MISSED IT

In the end, I was amazed at how simple the answer to my dilemma proved to be. As is often the case, it was so simple that I had missed it for years. It was right before my eyes. In fact, it was within me.

I had God's power; I just needed to use it. And no one could do that for me; I had to do it for myself. A story I once heard serves to illustrate the point:

An old Indian who lived in one of the small towns of the Oklahoma oil fields had been very poor all his life...until oil was discovered on his property. A well was drilled, and when it began to produce oil, the man decided to buy some of the things he had always wanted in life. For instance, he had always wanted an Abraham Lincoln stovetop hat and a tuxedo with tails. He had also wanted a box of Cuban cigars and a Cadillac touring car, the kind with the wheels on the back. The largest one he had ever seen had two wheels on the back, but he wanted four wheels on his.

The old Indian was able to buy everything he wanted, and every day he would go through town dressed in his tuxedo and top hat, smoking a Cuban cigar and waving to everyone in sight from the seat of his Cadillac touring car with the four wheels on the back. The only problem was—or so the story goes—that the old Indian never learned how to put the key into the ignition and start the car. His luxury touring car was always pulled by a team of horses on the outside, when on the inside the car had over a hundred horse-powered engine, but he never inserted the key and turned on the engine.

I, like many, was just like that old man. I had everything inside I needed to overcome my weaknesses, but I wasn't using it. The Scriptures had taught:

> You, dear children, are from God and have overcome them, because the one who is in you is greater than the one who is in the world.
>
> 1 John 4:4 (NIV)

He was in me, and through Him I could overcome.

It wouldn't be easy. I would have to face a daily battle with my flesh and my carnal desires, but I must never give up on myself, no matter who else decided to abandon me. I had to decide that I was worth fighting for. If God had allowed me to live to see another day, no matter where my eyes may have opened, then I had an opportunity to do better.

As I thought about it, I realized that most every character in the Bible had wrestled with some kind of *"thorn in the flesh"* (2 Corinthians 12:7). David, for instance, had taken another man's wife, killed the man, and then made the woman his own wife. That was pretty bad, but God still used David—after he repented for his sins.

Moses had apparently been a "hot head." One day he saw an Egyptian mistreating one of the Israelites, and it made him so angry that he killed the Egyptian. Still, Moses had gone on to become Israel's great deliverer.

There were also notable cases in the New Testament. Paul, who became the greatest missionary of the first century, had been on his way to kill more Christians when he had his Damascus Road experience. He later wrote:

> What shall we say, then? Shall we go on sinning so that grace may increase? By no means! We died to sin; how can we live in it any longer?
>
> Romans 6:1–2 (NIV)

It was Paul who experienced the *"thorn in the flesh."*

In all of this, I could see that God's redemptive power was limitless; all I had to do was tap into it. Most Christians wrote me off as impossible to be saved, but I knew that my sin was no greater than another. Christ had died to atone for sin; surely He could handle my sin.

I knew that I could not just live any way I wanted and get away with it. God would repay me for my deeds—good or bad. But if I sincerely, with all my heart, wanted to change, I had the Change Agent at my disposal, the Almighty God. He had taught us the secret:

> I lift up my eyes to the hills—Where does my help come from? My help comes from the Lord, the Maker of heaven and earth.
>
> Psalm 121:1–2 (NIV)

This revelation turned my life around. My help would not come from sex counselors, or recovery programs, or from talking to other troubled individuals about their experiences. I had to live out the Christian life (depending on the One I had within me). No one else could do it for me. That is not to say the recovery programs and the sex counselors are not needful, because they are. I had just gotten to a point were I needed to find God.

It was an earth-shattering and life-changing revelation.

DISCOVERING DIAMONDS

This revelation reminded me of a story I heard by Russell Cromwell, the founder of Temple University. As the story goes there was a poor farmer who settled in southern Africa who was discouraged by how difficult his land was to till. When he heard rumors of the discovery of diamonds, he sold his land cheap and went off in search of the gems. But for many years he searched in vain, until he was so distraught that he took his own life.

What he could not have known was that the man who had bought his farm found a large stone in a stream that crossed the property. That stone turned out to be a very valuable diamond. He had experts look at other parts of his land, and it was discovered that it was covered with similar stones. On that land, he opened what would become one of the largest diamond mines in the world.

The point is that the first man could have been wealthy, but he just didn't know what he had. He sold his property for next to nothing, considering it to be worthless, and went to seek his fortune elsewhere...when all the while, he was sitting on a rich bed of diamonds.

Many of us, I'm afraid, make the same mistake. The answer is within us, and we seek everywhere else but within. We turn to man and to money, when God is our only Source. We turn to drugs, alcohol, and sex, when only Christ can satisfy the longing within.

I came to realize that no matter what our situation in life happens to be at the moment—an addiction, depression, sickness or disease—God is able to deliver us and keep us. We must never give up on Him because He never gives up on us. If we have the faith to believe, He has the power to deliver.

Donnie McClurkin (Gospel music singer who has won 3 Grammy Awards) said it best in his song *We Fall Down, But We Get Up*. A saint is just a sinner who fell down, but got up. Our greatest attribute is having a God who is able to pick us up when we fall.

This also reminds me of the song that Marvin Sapp (Gospel music singer and song writer) sings, *He Saw The Best In Me*, when everyone else around could only see the worse in me. If we have the Lord and Savior on our side which we do, He only sees the best in us, even when we can only see the worse of ourselves; He still sees the best in us. He sees all the potential, all the purpose and destiny on our lives. He can see it because He put it there. So He tells us, "You work it out."

Everything that I had accomplished in life had come only after much prayer, faith, and a mindset to fight for my life. I knew that my fight was not yet over. Now that I knew the answer, I would have to put it into practice. Now that I had taken a stand, I would have to prove to the world, to the devil, and to myself, that I could win this fight.

Nothing was to come without a knockdown, drag-out fight, I was saying, "Okay, Satan, put your dukes up and start swinging, because I'm determined to win this battle."

I would have to be ready to take a punch and then to deliver the knockout blow at just the right time.

It's comforting to know that we have the greatest fighter who ever lived on our side—and I don't mean Muhammad Ali. We have the Great I Am, the Lion of the Tribe of Judah, the Rose of Sharon, and the Lilly of the Valley. His name is Jesus Christ. If I could just put my hand in His and keep it there, I knew that I could survive and win.

PART 3

AT LAST, SUCCESS ON EVERY HAND

REBOUNDING FROM TRAGEDY

After about a year of scouting for Coach Pitino, in March of 2000, I was approached by Derrick Ramsey, the former athletic director at Kentucky State University. He told me that they were looking for someone to fill the head coaching position for men's basketball at the school. He said that Kentucky State had been a powerhouse in basketball in the early 1970s, with Elmore Smith and Travis "Machine Gun" Grant. I wondered if I had possibly been too young to remember those glory days. KSU was a black university with a lot of history and tradition. Would I consider coaching them? He said that he had other candidates to interview, but I was his first choice.

There were many things about this offer that appealed to me. More than anything, I was thrilled with the idea of getting back into coaching, and this, after all, was a head coaching position that I was being offered. There was one major concern. I was doing much better in my personal life, and I didn't want to do anything to hinder or slow down my progress. KSU may have had a lot of history behind it, but it also had a lot of beautiful black women in it. This became a concern for both Peggy and me.

I had no doubt that I could get the job done on the court. After all, I had been groomed for the position by the best—Rick Pitino himself. The question was could I be faithful to God and to my wife and family and not cause them another public, or even private, humiliation? We prayed long and hard about this, because we didn't want to take any unnecessary risks.

After a serious time of prayer, I decided to take the job. I will have to admit Peggy wasn't totally sold on the idea. She had seen me fail too many times and wondered if the temptation might be too great.

Derrick Ramsey himself was one of my counselors in this decision. He had been an All-American at Kentucky, and the first black quarterback the school ever had. He went on to play in the NFL with greats like Art Shell and Ken Stabler. He knew what I was going through, and his advice was invaluable. He, too, was sure that I was making the right decision. So it was settled. I would accept the position of head men's basketball coach at Kentucky State University.

MY FIRST
HEAD-COACHING JOB

I was very anxious about my first head-coaching job, and I needed God to help me. Assisting a head coach and being a head coach were two entirely different jobs, so I knew I had a lot to learn.

I hired Tom Patterson (who now owns a restaurant in Louisville) to be my associate coach. Tom had coached at Shawnee High School in Louisville and also at Spalding College. I had known him for a long time and, in fact, I had told him eight years before that if I ever got a head-coaching job, I would want him on my staff.

Tom is a great person, a man of integrity, and an extremely hard worker. He works from morning until night, trying to be the best he can be at his jobs, and is a great example of what relentless hard work can accomplish. I also retained J.D. Coles, who had been the assistant to the previous coach, Thomas Snowden. J.D. wasn't looked upon very favorably in those days. Whether or not this was his fault, I can't say. What I can say is that J.D. has always done a great job for me.

We did have one little flare-up between us. I got on J.D. one day about something, and he took it personally, and tried to come back at me, as if to say, "I'm doing the best I can, and you're still on my back." But like any other head coach or CEO, I expect excellence from both my players and staff, and when I don't get it, they can expect to be corrected. After that one incident, J.D. and I got along fine. He was responsible for scouting our opponents and for helping to recruit.

In my newness to the job, I made several mistakes. One of the early ones was moving into my office before we had actually finalized my contract. I really didn't think I had done anything wrong at the time, but looking back, I suppose that I was a little overzealous. "If I was already promised the job two months ago," I reasoned. "Why not get a head start?" I didn't realize how much red tape there was with university positions.

When a member of the board learned that I had not only moved into the office, but had already changed the greeting on the office telephone system, he was upset, to say the least. Reportedly, he called one day and was greeted by the message, "Hello, this is Winston Bennett, head men's basketball coach of the Kentucky State Thorobreds." The next thing I knew I was the subject of a newspaper headline.

Mr. Ramsey was understandably angry about this. He had warned me to be patient and let the process run its course. But, as usual, I had a problem with waiting. I've always wanted things to happen *now*. Not waiting on the process proved to be a costly mistake.

Another big mistake I made during this time was to go on the road and recruit—again, before I had a signed contract. Since I had not officially been signed as Kentucky State's coach, the rules said that I could not be out recruiting for that institution. I hadn't been trying to gain an advantage; I was just trying to catch up. I was being hired late in the recruiting period, and no records were left by the previous coach that would help me with the recruiting process. So I had a big job on my hands, because I would be starting from scratch.

Another mistake I made was watching our guys play in an open gym situation. The rule was that I was not to see our men play until October 15, when the season officially began. But again, the previous coach had not left a tape that I could watch to see how my own players performed. This was another innocent mistake of a novice who was trying to learn all he could about how things worked in NCAA Division II basketball. I was quickly learning some of the dos and don'ts of coaching, but I was learning them the hard way. It was very difficult to come in as a first-time head coach and know all the rules.

The flurry of criticism over these incidents made it seem that I was doomed to fail before I ever got started. I was suddenly fighting just to keep my head above water. This made me very uncomfortable. I'd had enough negative publicity in the last few years already, and I didn't need more.

MY FIRST TEAM

Sadly, my new players had heard about me losing my job with the Boston Celtics and the reasons commonly circulated. In my first meeting with the players, I had to let them know that I was not gay. In fact, I told them, my attraction to women had been so powerful that it had become like a drug for me. In this way, from day one, I was very honest and upfront with my players about my fight with sexual promiscuity, and I quickly made them partners in holding me accountable and helping me to walk a straight line.

After such a gut-wrenching summer, we were all determined to have a successful season. Our program was nothing like our players had ever seen before. It was predicated on discipline and an unrelenting work ethic. Our conditioning program was right out of an Army boot camp. We lifted weights three times a week and ran hills and sprints on alternate days.

This was particularly important to our star player, a senior, Jason Lewis, or "Big J," as we called him. Our success or failure lay largely in his hands. That summer, "Big J" had become seriously overweight—more than three hundred pounds. He was down to two hundred and seventy-five pounds as the season began. I wish I could take credit for "Big J's" transformation, but I can't. My assistants proposed a special diet for him, and he was willing to stick with it and to put in the time and energy necessary to condition himself. Fortunately, Jason really wanted to change his life. This was critical because we needed him to play like an all-star. Like the rest of the team, "Big J" had under-achieved in his previous three years at the school. It was my job to light a fire under him (and the others), and fortunately I knew how to do that.

The other important cog in our wheel was Jonathan Johnson. Jonathan was a two and three man from Tennessee. It was our job to make him believe that he was the best scorer in the con-ference—even though he wasn't. This is always a challenge for a coach—to cause his team members to see themselves doing more and being more than they have been in the past.

Jonathan was our "silent assassin." He was very quiet and unas-suming, but he was also very effective.

Steve Reese was our two guard, or shooting guard, from Cin-cinnati, Ohio. He had attended Sinclair Community College before coming to Kentucky State and was vital to our success. I made him think he was Tony Delk, the great shooter we had at the University of Kentucky (former player in the NBA). Steve wasn't as athletic as Tony, but he did have that same type of deadly shoot-ing touch. He became our zone buster.

The only problem we had with Steve was that he shot the ball when he was open, and he also shot it when he wasn't open. He didn't know the difference, but that was okay with me. I preferred having a player who was a great scorer that I could tone down a bit than someone who had to be taught how and when to score.

We also had Carl Hutchinson from Lexington, Kentucky. He had attended Bryan Station High School before coming to Ken-tucky State. Carl's nickname was "Red." "Red" was the coach on the floor. He was our Anthony Epps (the point guard at the University of Kentucky who led us to the NCAA Championship in 1996). "Red" was not quick and he couldn't jump, but he knew his limitations and he would not stray from his circle of competence. He knew how to lead.

One of the hardest things to teach young players was to stick to their area of mastery. "If you're a rebounder," I told them. "Be a Dennis Rodman and major in that area; meaning, if you're a rebounder, be an expert rebounder. If you're a three-point shooter, then that's your gift to the team." This is never an easy lesson for a youngster to learn. Most young players want to flourish in areas of deficiency. You don't go out and shoot a bunch of three-pointers in a game if you are a post player. If you are a great three-point shooter, you are probably not the best post player. It is possible to get better in areas of deficiency, if the person is willing to work on the areas of weakness.

Essien Jackson, from Jessamine County, Kentucky, was another of our sharpshooters. Like Jonathan Johnson, Essien was very quiet, and I wasn't able to get him to talk much during the season. I suppose, though, that he let his game do the talking. He was another of our zone busters.

Chris Duckworth, from Manual High School in Louisville, was our elder statesman. Chris, or "Duck," as we called him, was a warrior. The oldest player on the team (at twenty-six), he could still jump, and he did whatever was necessary to win. If we needed him to score, he could do it. If we needed him to block shots, he could. His specialty was taking charges.

For the layperson, this happens when a man on offense is driving the ball to the other end, and he gets out of control. Then a defensive player stops in front of him, and he can't resist charging into that player and committing the foul. "Duck" was a master at taking charges, and he was also our Mr. Hustle.

All in all, it was a good team.

A BURNING DESIRE BRINGS
A CHAMPIONSHIP

But this group of young men had another quality that all championship teams must have, and that was a will to be great. They had a desire to be champions. They had suffered through losing season after losing season, and they were tired of being labeled as losers, so tired of it that they were ready to find a way to win. They had a hunger, a burning desire, to succeed. That fire would propel them through the rough times to come.

My players reminded me of the story I heard about an Idaho potato farmer. It is said that in Idaho all the farmers were accustomed to bagging their potatoes, loading them onto a truck, and taking them to market to see what price they could get. One farmer bypassed the bagging process, and he always received more for his potatoes. When he was asked the secret of his success, he told a strange tale. "When I put all of the potatoes together in the back of the truck and drive the rough and tumble seven-mile trip into town, the potatoes are shaken around so much that the small potatoes end up on the bottom, the middle-sized potatoes are in the middle, and the big potatoes end on top. People seem to be willing to pay more for them sorted in this way."

When I heard that story, I thought, "That's exactly right. Big potatoes always end up on top, just as cream rises when milk is churned." Most of us try to avoid problems like the plague, but they are the very thing that will make us stronger. In fact, we are all big potatoes; sometimes we just don't realize it. We allow our life circumstances to tell us we are mediocre, we are average; we allow our past to dictate our future. I don't know about you, I am tired of allowing my past mistakes to dictate who I can be in the future. My future is up to me and God alone. I have the choice of making the right decisions; if I am able to do that, I will have a promising future unrelated to my past difficulties. You are not your past. You can be anything you want to be. Just believe that it is possible. I refuse to let my past dictate my future; the future is in the hands of my decisions and choices today.

In my very first season as head coach (2000–01), we won the Southern Intercollegiate Athletic Conference (SIAC) Tournament Championship. This conference is comprised of historically black schools like Tuskegee, Morehouse, Lane, Paine, Clark Atlanta, Miles, Fort Valley, Albany State, and Lemoyne Owen Colleges. It's a very athletic conference, with many young men who can run and jump and knock down three-point shots. I give God the glory for allowing us to win the conference championship that very first year. It was a wonderful sight to see our guys, who had worked so hard during the season, end the year cutting down the nets. It was definitely a surreal moment for me personally. I had been through so much, with the knee injury at Kentucky and in the NBA, the job loss with the Celtics, and now to win a championship was an incredible feeling. I thought I might be getting back in God's good graces.

After winning the conference championship, we received an automatic bid to the NCAA Division II Tournament. Kentucky State had never won the conference on the Division II level, nor had it ever gone to the NCAA Tournament. So we were breaking new ground for the school on both fronts. When the school was in the NAIA division in the 1970s, it was a powerhouse; it had not seen that kind of success since.

All of our regular season and conference travel had been by bus, but now we were flown to St. Petersburg, Florida, for the NCAA Tournament, and our players and coaches were placed in First Class. It reminded me of my days at the University of Kentucky and with the Boston Celtics, where everything was first class.

But this would be the end of our Cinderella season. In the first game of the regionals, we played a Tampa team that had a dominant six-nine center who was blocking everything we brought to the basket. Although we played hard, our opponent was too much for us. They clearly had the better athletes.

But I was thrilled with our championship season. It was an once-in-a-lifetime experience for a first-year head coach to get that far. We considered it to be a banner year.

Besides winning the championship, one of the most gratifying pleasures a coach can have is to see his players graduate and become productive people. Coaching is much more than just the X's and O's we use in charting plays. We're actually parenting these young men, and are, in large part, responsible for the success or failure of their futures.

What's stopping you from winning the championship? Don't let what people say about you make you quit doing what you know you should. If I had quit during the preseason when negative reports were being written about me personally, I would have never experienced the championship run. Stay the course, know what you are playing for and go for it. Know that times will get hard, and you will feel like quitting, but keep striving, keep working. You will have negative quarters, but just realize one quarter doesn't make a season. Companies have down quarters and even down years, but the ones that become household names keep striving to get better even in recessionary periods.

2001–2002 SEASON

Our 2001–02 seasons were one of great expectation. Coming off a banner year, our goal was to duplicate the success of the previous season, and to go even further in the NCAA Division II Tournament.

This time we had a more talented team, but it was made up of a very different cast of characters. The previous year's team had been together for at least three years and had been a senior-dominated team, most of whom started playing together as true freshmen. This team was more talented but less cohesive.

Our 2002 season ended with a loss in the second round of the SIAC Tournament to Paine College. Paine College also went on to win the Tournament Championship. It had been a year of rebuilding and we would do better in the future, I was sure.

2002–2003 SEASON

Before long, I was hit with a flurry of bad news. Campus police called to say that they had found evidence of marijuana in a room shared by two of our players. When the players in question refused to confess, we had no choice but to drug test the entire team. When this happened, my heart was at its lowest point. As I went to God in prayer and asked Him what I should do, I again felt in my heart that somehow I must make a difference in the lives of these young men. I could not abandon them to the streets. It would have been easy for me to just throw these guys off the team, but would that be best for their purpose and their destiny. None of us make it without someone going to bat for us. If I had not had coaches, teachers, and preachers, that were willing to stand in the gap for me, I would have never made it this far. It was my time to stand in the gap for them.

One of the biggest blows of the season came when I felt that I had to throw one of our most tenacious players off of the team. He was talented, but his bad attitude was destroying team chemistry. The thing I knew about negative attitudes was attitudes were contagious; if you have a cancer on your team its best to go in and cut away the cancer before it spreads to the rest of the body. I didn't want one bad apple to spoil the whole barrel.

The worst trial of all came when another player led a sort of attempted mutiny, inviting me to a team meeting (just after we had lost five games in a row) and there calling into question my integrity as a coach. Fortunately after a mild discussion, we were able to squash the discontentment.

With all of these test and trials, we finished the season with thirteen wins and sixteen losses. Still managing to make it into the conference tournament, we won our first-round conference Tournament game against Clark Atlanta, a team that was young and athletic and had beaten us earlier in the year. Our season ended, however, when we lost the second-round game to Lane College, a school that had made a remarkable turnaround from the year before.

The eventual winner of both the regular season and the conference championship was Morehouse College.

One of the crucial lessons you learn as a coach is no matter what your plan is to make your team better, sometimes it only ends up getting worse. We thought we made the right recruiting decisions, we thought we had the right plan in place, but it still didn't work the way we thought it would. Sometimes things just don't work out in your business, in your company and in your family, you count it as a learning experience and you keep moving. You go back to the drawing board and try again, but you don't give up or give in, just keep working.

PRE-SEASON PRACTICE

In October 2003, my world as I knew it was about to change, just as it did in 1998 with the Boston Celtics. Seemly, when everything seems to be going great, beware, the messenger of misery is soon to follow.

In 2003, I was going into my fourth season as the head men's basketball coach for the Kentucky State Thorobreds. We had come off a subpar season the season before and were gearing up for a great year; it had been two years ago that we had won the SIAC Championship. It was preseason practice; the part that everyone dreads. We were accustomed to early morning practices, 4:45 a.m., which meant I had to leave Louisville by 3:45 a.m. to make it to Frankfort on time, not the easiest thing to get motivated for. I could certainly think of better things to do than practice at 4:45 a.m., like sleeping, but as a coach you have to make some tough decisions, and this was one of them. Ever since the first day I started at Kentucky State, we have had 4:45 a.m. practices. The reasoning was very simple. I wanted to get to the players before the girls did.

Our practices were like boot camp, no nonsense. When we practiced, we practiced hard; constant motion, no sitting around doing nothing, and no congregating; just work, pure and unadulterated work. This must have been the picture of perpetual motion James Naismith envisioned when he created this great game called basketball in 1891.

Everything we do in practice helps us to simulate game situations. We are practicing end of game situations, so when we are down by one point with one second to go, we will know what to do. I tell my players there may be a more talented team in the world, but there will not be a more conditioned team, we will be the hardest working team in the world.

But this particular morning was different. We were going hard as usual, but for some reason one of my best offensive players had an attitude, and that not a good one. I have always told my players that your attitude will control your altitude, so always try to be positive and see the bright side of things. This particular player was a great talent; he had transferred to us from a NCAA Division I school. So already there was a feeling of superiority. He felt like he was better than the people he was playing with, and that's okay, as long as you understand these are your teammates and you have to learn to fit in with the team concept. Every great player I know, Magic Johnson, Larry Bird, and Michael Jordan, all made the people around them better. I would always tell them there are no I's in team. We are an army of one. I like what John Maxwell, the great author and speaker says, "Teamwork makes the dream work."

NO FREE LUNCH

In this day of instant gratification, where guys are going one year of college and then straight to the NBA and becoming millionaires, we all want it now. There is no real gratification without perspiration. You don't just wake up one morning and find yourself in the NBA. It only comes after many years of practice, millions of shots, hours and hours of ball handling, and passing until it feels like your arms are about to disengage from your body.

If you are going to be great, there will be a huge sacrifice of your will, your perseverance, and your ability to stay the course. You realize only after you have put money in the bank, can you pull money out. Only after you have done the preparatory work to be great can greatness reward you. There is no such thing of getting anything great without paying a very dear price.

After going hard for about two hours, we had started to scrimmage. This is the part that most players live for. They'd much rather scrimmage than do a lot of drill work. This particular player, who we will call Tony, came down court, made an aggressive move to the rim, and thought he had gotten fouled, but my assistants never called the foul. My assistants will do this at times to get our players accustomed to playing on the road where fouls can be overlooked or not called. Tony immediately went into severe pout mode. Instead of running back and playing defense, he just stood at the other end of the court leaving his teammates to defend by themselves. But as soon as his team got the ball off the rebound, he started playing again. When he got the ball this time, he drove it hard across mid-court; one of his teammates tried to stop him and attempted to take a charge but was called for a block. Both players fell with thuds that seem to rattle the whole gym. Action stopped with complete silence. Just as if the Lord had split the sky the mood changed, Tony got up with fire in his eyes, and you could see his discontentment. He took the ball, reared back and with all his might, threw the ball at the young man who attempted to take a charge on him. At this point, I thought there would be another Thriller in Manila. I thought the young man that was on the ground who had just got blasted with the ball would get up and kill the smaller but more mature Tony. As quick as I could, I moved in between both players feeling a little outraged myself at Tony's actions. Tony was reacting from the previous non-call and thought he would take it out on one of his teammates.

This was not the first rambunctious action from Tony; his attitude and regard for others had been the worse. We thought he could really come in and help our team both offensively and defensively. He was such an explosive talent; on any given night, he could explode for twenty to thirty points if he got hot from the three-point line. But it was really all about Tony; Tony wanted the ball, Tony wanted his play called every time down court, and if he didn't get it, he would go into severe pout mode again.

This morning, he got hot, not because of his shooting, but because of his attitude. After throwing the ball with supreme velocity and accuracy, I stepped in and grabbed Tony, asking him why he did it. While reacting in a rage over the incident, I swung at Tony, landing numerous punches. While this was transpiring, I could hear one of my players saying "No Coach, No!" He could see I was at a point of no return. In a split second, I was engulfed with rage; I had crossed a line that should never be crossed with a player. Every coach knows that at no point, do you ever put your hands on a player; I had crossed the line. The scene reminded me of the famed former football coach Woody Hayes of the Ohio State Buckeyes, who grabbed a player running down the sidelines and started hitting him. The difference was the player had on pads and a helmet. It also reminded me of Coach Bob Knight, former Indiana Hoosiers coach, who had lost control on many occasions, one time throwing a chair across court attempting to hit a referee.

After a couple of quick blows, the moment had faded as if nothing had ever happened, except for the blood that dripped profusely as if a water faucet had been left running from Tony's nose. I immediately asked my assistant to run practice the rest of the way as I went to my office, crushed about what had just transpired. I asked one of my other assistants to check on Tony to make sure he was all right, but he had disappeared in the wind. No one could find him.

Moments later, as if out of an Alfred Hitchcock thriller, standing before me was the campus police with a written statement from Tony, who said I had assaulted him. At that moment my life flashed before my eyes. I didn't know what to expect next. I told the police from my viewpoint what had happened; he then went on to record the statements of the players and coaches. Some of the players vehemently sided with me, but most did not; they said I had attacked Tony.

SELF-DESTRUCTION

Oh how I wish I could go back and change that moment, just as when I lost my job with the Celtics. I wish I could hit rewind and change everything. But in life, there is no rewind button to push; the only constant is forward, sometimes fast, sometimes slow, but always forward. As long as we are alive, life stops for no one, it keeps going. I have always maintained since the sun keeps rising and setting, I should do the same. There have been times in my life when the last thing I wanted to do was rise, but rise I shall.

It would take what seemed to be lifetimes to rise from this colossal mistake. There would be three years of legality to sift through. Tony was asking for astronomical amounts of money to drop the charges that were levied against me. When you have name recognition, you become a target; people have a tendency to think you are made of money. Unfortunately, we were not. We were just rebounding from the Boston Massacre, where I had lost my job for sexual impropriety. Also because the legal battle with Tony lasted three years, there were three years of unaccounted expenses that had to be paid. My penalty for such heinous action was over two hundred hours of community service and over six weeks of anger management.

I took my punishment very seriously; I never wanted to be in a position to lose my temper again. The incident had cost my family and I dearly, it was another public disgrace. There are great and wonderful privileges that accompany being a public figure. You sometimes sign autographs, you sometimes are recognized at events, but then there are times if you have made mistakes honestly or foolishly that the adulation turns from applause to rejection. Your persona has not changed, but the way you have been received has changed. My mother would tell me, "When you are endowed with great gifts and callings, there is more responsibility to do the right thing, to whom much is given, much is required."

I met many wonderful people during this time of turmoil. I thoroughly enjoyed working at the soup kitchen helping to feed people who themselves had been down and in despair and needed help. I told them like Peter said,

> Then Peter said, "Silver or gold I do not have, but what I have
> I give you. In the name of Jesus Christ of Nazareth, walk."
>
> Acts 3:6 (NIV)

Do you ever stop and wonder, "Why me?" I wondered continuously why all this was happening to me. It seemed that in a split second, my life changed from doing the thing I loved, coaching, to worrying about what my future would be without it. Whenever things seem to be heading in the right direction, something would happen to take the entire positive and turn it negative. I was back coaching, something I figured would never happen.

But the Lord gave me another opportunity to do what I love, and what happened, I blew it—again, I hit the self-destruct button.

My former pastor would say, "God continues to do great things in our lives even after we have made mistakes, but when he does we tend to hit the self-destruct button."

Why do I continue to thwart my own success? All I could think about was the sex. It was the thing I held onto. No matter what was going on in my life, sex was the medication. I could depend on it to make me feel better. The relationships continued outside my marriage, I would have moments of sobriety, but would fall headfirst back into a downward spiral. I began to wonder whether I could ever break the habit. Was it in me to let go of something that had such a strangle hold on my life?

KENTUCKY SPORTS HISTORY

"What's going on in the inside shows on the outside."
—Earl Nightingale

After failing miserably once again, I really had to think things through and figure out what I was going to do with my life. I still wanted to live a Godly life, but there was just one thing stopping me—me. I could make excuses and not take responsibility for my life, but that's not me, Momma didn't raise any fool, even though I was acting like one.

During this time of introspection, I had already been working for Kentucky Sports History. Even while at Kentucky State, I had met Mr. Ferguson, who lived in Georgetown, Kentucky, he and a man named John Likens had started a program called Kentucky Sports History. Mr. Ferguson had been a successful dentist in town, and John Likens had been a successful basketball coach. They were both retired and thought of a way to start a business that could capitalize on the powerful Kentucky Wildcat brand. Kentucky Sports History is what they founded.

Kentucky Sports History is a basketball magazine on Kentucky basketball. It is made of articles highlighting the basketball season produced yearly. Former Wildcat basketball players like Ed Davender, Kenny "Sky" Walker, Derrick Miller, and me were a part of the Kentucky Sports History umbrella. Each player would have areas or territories where they would go out and sell advertising for the sports publication. By selling the ads, we would get a percentage of the ad cost. It was a great idea because the state of Kentucky was crazy about their Wildcats.

FAITH

The scripture says:

> Now faith is being sure of what we hope for and certain of
> what we do not see.
>
> Hebrews 11:1 (NIV)

Selling advertising taught me a lot of valuable lessons about life. The first and most important was faith. Faith to me was just a simple belief that God would do what he said he would do. It took an unshakable faith to go and knock on the door of a business and ask for the owner, and hope that he would buy an ad; most of the time the owner did not buy, most of the time I could not get past the gatekeeper. You know the gatekeeper; it's the assistant that greets you at the door to tell you the owner is busy and cannot see you at this time. What do you do, do you turn around and give up, or do you keep trying? There were days were I gave up and went home with my tail between my legs, but there were also days were I just called on the name of Jesus and asked him insistently to make a way out of no way.

Peggy was my biggest supporter when I came home defeated, despondent, and dejected. She would tell me, "Tomorrow is a different day; get back out there, keep fighting, never give up or give in. You did not give up on the court when you played, so don't give up here, it's just a different court, go out there and take no prisoners. Keep moving; if they don't want what you have to sell, keep moving, someone will buy, keep moving don't get down; don't give up, just keep moving. God said He would be with you even until the end, He said you would be the head and not the tail, above and not beneath. All you have to do is believe as the scriptures have said, and out of your belly shall flow rivers of living water." She also said:

> Ask and it will be given to you; seek and you will find; knock and the door will be opened to you.
>
> Matthew 7:7 (NIV)

By the time she finished with all those powerful scriptures, I was ready to fight. No more staying on the ropes, letting the negative conversation beat me upside the head, fight; I had to put up a fight. I felt like Rocky going after Apollo Creed. I was ready for the knockout punch.

Regardless of how many scriptures you quote or affirmations you memorize, sales will still be one of the hardest businesses in life. But it will also teach you the most about life. I went from door to door, quoting scriptures,

> I can do everything through him who gives me strength.
>
> Philippians 4:13 (NIV)

Quoting scripture was just like positive affirmation only better; it was God's Word, it could not fail. Still, there were times when I was too scared to go to the next door. I felt as if I could not take another "no." There were many times when I let the negative conversation prevent me from moving forward.

We all at certain points in life have what I call "come to Jesus" meetings with ourselves. You know those meetings where you have to grab yourself by the collar and say, "Hey you either get it together or else." Whatever you dream you can do, you can do. Dreams have power they force us to get up and do something. Do not allow yourself to stagnate. Nike use to have a slogan, "Just do it." No matter what the outcome, if you are passionate about what you do, "Just do it." Author Susan Jeffers wrote a book called *Feel the Fear and Do It Anyway*. The only way to defeat fear is to fight it, and then the fear loses its power. Fear has been defined as false evidence appearing real. If it's not real, attack it, overtake it, and don't let it overtake you. You are the master of your own destiny.

PERSISTENCE

"Winning isn't everything, but wanting to win is."
—Vince Lombardi

Sales have also taught me the importance of persistence. As I knocked on doors receiving rejection after rejection, I had to believe that every rejection was bringing me closer to a yes. I had to be like the stonecutter who spends days and days just trying to break the stone in half, people are walking by laughing, saying you are not going to break the stone, it is too big and too powerful, you are just a little old insignificant man trying to cut away at the big powerful stone.

I think it was Shakespeare who said, *"The constant dripping wears away the marble."* So the stonecutter continues to chop away, even in the face of laughter and adversity, a hundred times, two hundred times, whatever it takes. Finally after about 500 times, the stonecutter finally splits the stone in half. Was it the final hit? No, it was the constant and never ending persistence. If we would succeed in life, we have to be persistent, no matter how many no's we receive, go back tomorrow and try, try, again.

There is nothing like the ability to keep going when all else says quit. I remember hearing a poem that said:

> *Life is queer with its twists and turns,*
> *As every one of us sometimes learns,*
> *And many a failure turns about,*
> *When he might have won had he stuck it out,*
> *Don't give up though the race seems slow,*
> *You may succeed with another blow,*
> *Success is failure turned inside out,*
> *The silver tint of the clouds of doubt,*
> *And you never can tell how close you are,*
> *It may be near when it seems so far.*
> *So stick to the fight when you're hardest hit,*
> *It's when things seem worse,*
> *That you must not quit.*
>
> *(Author unknown)*

Truer words have never been spoken. There have been many days were I wanted to just throw in the towel, quit, give up, stop trying. But every time I would try to quit, something deep inside would tell me don't quit, don't give up, keep trying.

Winston Churchill said, "Courage is the ability to move from failure to failure without losing enthusiasm." I would say that's a great definition of persistence as well. There was another poem that came to mind, that said,

> *It takes a little courage, and a little self-control, and some grim determination,*
> *If you want to reach your goal. It takes a deal of striving, and a firm and stern- set chin,*
> *No matter what the battle, if you really want to win. There's no easy path to glory,*
> *There's no rosy road to fame, Life, however we may view it, is no simple parlor game;*
> *But its prizes call for fighting, For endurance and for grit; For a rugged disposition And*
> *A don't -know-when-to-quit.*
>
> *(Author unknown)*

Don't quit, persist. If you are pursuing your dreams and your goals persist. Fight for whatever it is you want to achieve in life. This is not a fight against your competition it's the inter-fight to be all you can be. I will continue to fight no matter what losses I may encounter the fight rages on.

PLAN OF ACTION

"All you need is the plan, the road map, and the courage to press on to your destination."

—Earl Nightingale

The other lesson sells taught me was you have to have a plan of action. Every day, I had to have mapped out the area I would work, and how many doors I wanted to knock on. If I did not have this prepared, I would quit before meeting my goal. I knew if I knocked on enough doors, I would eventually get someone who would purchase an ad. A plan of action is vital to any plan of attack. I don't know of any war hero that would go to war without a plan of action. I don't know any architect that would build a skyscraper without the blueprints. Develop your plan of action and then fight.

GOALS

Would you tell me, please, which way I ought to go from here?'
'That depends a good deal on where you want to get to,'
Said the Cat,
'I don't much care where——'said Alice,
'Then it doesn't matter which way you go,'
Said the Cat.

(Lewis Carroll, Alice's Adventures in Wonderland)

The other lesson learned were the importance of goals. You must have a goal. You must know where you are going and the route you must take to get there. If I have achieved anything noteworthy, it's been because of my dedication to goal setting. I pride myself on not just being a goal setter, but being a goal getter. Being a goal setter is great, but it's passive, it's just the first phase; after the setting, then comes the action. I am all about action; faith without works is dead. I can believe all I want; if I don't get up and make something happen, nothing will.

What if Rick Pitino would bring his Louisville Cardinals to your town and Coach Calipari would bring his Kentucky Wildcats? Well, if you lived in Kentucky, this would be a big deal. The town would be in frenzy. Let's say they are coming to your local gym to play a game. Both coaches would be in the locker room giving their best motivational speech on how no one remembers the team who came in second, we are here to win. The players are so excited that they just about tear the doors off the hinges trying to get out of the locker room. Once on the court, the managers throw out the basketballs so the teams can warm up. Just as the teams began to shoot, they find that there are no goals on the backboard. There is no way to keep score; there is no way to tell who won or who lost, because there are no goals.

Our lives can be the same way if there are no goals for us to shoot at. You must have a target and an idea as to when you will hit the target. There is no failure in not hitting the shot; the failure is not taking any shots because you feel like you will miss, shoot anyway. It's like the old saying, "Winners never quit and quitters never win." The only difference between a big shot and a little shot is the big shot is just a little shot, who kept on shooting. Keep shooting; don't worry about the misses keep shooting.

My number one goal in life is to please God. It's the one goal that I constantly pursue. It's one I continue to work on, knowing that there will always be room for improvement. Are there days that I feel like quitting, you bet. But I have been through enough of life's growth process to know that true growth comes from struggles, adversities, pain, and anguish. No one gets stronger unless they apply more weights, you can't be a body builder if you don't build the body. There is only one true way to build the body, and that is to lift heavier weights. Our struggles, our pains, and our disappointments are the weights we use to build this body, this mind, and this spirit.

POWER OF PRAYER

Therefore confess your sins to each other and pray for each other so that you may be healed. The prayer of a righteous man is powerful and effective.

James 5:16 (NIV)

A couple of stories really stand out when I was a part of Kentucky Sports History. These stories really speak to the power of God and his faithfulness to his people. One day, I was going through my normal routine of building new clients, but also renewing old clients. I went into the office of Mike Cromwell, the owner of Cromwell Development. Mike builds hotels, houses, and commercial buildings. Mike had been my client for at least a year. When I first signed Mike as a client, I thought he was a nuisance. His assistant would call every day to make sure his ad would run in the magazine. And I would repeatedly tell her every day, "Yes, your ad will be run in this year's magazine, just as I told you before." What we do is place an ad in the Kentucky Basketball publication for each business with their logo. When I went in Mike's office to renew for another year, he told me his business had been on the decline, and he would not be able to renew this year. Of course this was not what I wanted to hear, but I accepted it. So I said, "Mike, let's have a word of prayer that your business would pick up." I am sure this took Mike by surprise. As he later told me, he thought this was a ploy to get him to change his mind about buying an ad, but it was not. I was just acting in faith and wanted to see his business prosper. So right then and there, I prayed that God would give Mike favor and increase. After the prayer, I went on to my other appointments and did not think any more about the prayer. Days later, Mike left a message on my phone. An hour after I left his office, a man walked into his office and asked if he would build him a $2 million hotel. Now that is the power of prayer and crazy faith.

You just never know how God will bless you if you will only believe. I am not here to tell you believing is always easy. When you are faced with foreclosure on your home and don't know where the next payment will come from, it's hard to believe, but that is the very time you need to have crazy faith. What is crazy faith? It's unusual belief that God will do the impossible, the unthinkable it's crazy.

Another time I was out meeting clients and ran into Jimmy Dan Connors, the former Kentucky Basketball great and former owner of Old Colony Insurance. I had told Jimmy Dan that my family and I were going through a rough time; I had just lost my job at Kentucky State and before that lost my job with the Boston Celtics. I had wanted to sell one of our major ads, which was the front and back cover of the magazine. It would take a major player to step up and do a sponsorship of this magnitude. As I began to lay out the benefits of being on the front and back cover of our sponsorship books, I could see his mind thinking of possible candidates. In a whirlwind of thought, he blurted out the name Jude Thompson of Anthem Blue Cross and Blue Shield. As a general rule, I try not to get too excited about potential new clients until after I have met with them. But with this information I broke out in tears, you know those alligator tears that splatter all over the place. The emotions were too much; I could not hold them, embarrassing yes, justified definitely. My family had gone through so much; I had made a lot of foolish choices, with two job losses, the constant infidelity, and now it looked like God was providing a ram in the bush.

Jimmy Dan immediately got on the phone with Jude and told him he had someone he wanted him to meet. So he sat up the meeting, and I was off to meet with Jude. My meeting with Jude was divinely orchestrated. Jude turned out to be more than just a client, but also a trusted friend. Jude went way beyond just buying an ad; he took me and my father to the Kentucky versus North Carolina game in Rupp area. We sat right on the floor.

It was something right out of a dream. I could hardly believe I used to play on this same floor, in this huge arena with 23,000 adoring fans. I began to wonder what it would be like to be a Jude Thompson, to be in a place where you can bring so much joy to people who have lost hope. I had really lost a lot of hope and faith after the two job losses, and now felt as if I was at the bottom of the totem pole. It's excruciatingly tough after having been on top to go all the way back down to nothing. It was the term "rock bottom" that I had heard so much about during my days of attending SAA groups. But my friendship with Jude gave me an array of hope. He showed me that God had not totally cast me aside as a sheep for the slaughter; he did care about me.

Jude also took me to the Louisville and Cincinnati game. This was a huge rival. My old boss, Rick Pitino, was the coach at Louisville, so it was great going to see him and the team after the game.

Bill White was another person I befriended while being a part of Kentucky Sports History. Bill was the founder of Independence Bank. I had met him through another client. One of the essential rules of sales is always ask the question, "Do you know of anyone else that can help me in this endeavor?" That's how I met over half of my new clients, through referrals. Bill and his bank also became a trusted client and a great friend. We even started a radio show together. We were both motivated by helping people, so we started a show that spoke an encouraging word to people who felt like there was no hope for their situation. We were both believers and wanted everyone to know, no matter what they may be facing, there was someone who would never give up on you, and His name is Jesus Christ. We tend to give up on ourselves, others will give up on us in a heartbeat, but He will never leave you nor forsake you.

I remember Bill telling me the story of how he had come from nothing to owning his own bank. He said when he was a teenager he use to clean banks, and every day he would do his best to make sure the banks he cleaned were spick and span, but in one of the banks he cleaned, there was a lady that worked in the bank that would always leave him nasty messages. "You didn't clean right, the waste basket was not in the right place, you touched my phone, I can see your fingerprints." He could never clean the bank to this woman's liking; he never forgot it.

Twenty years later, the same bank was interviewing the same Bill White to run its operation, he remembered walking into the bank and seeing someone that he recognized, as he walked up to the lady he said, "Hey I know you."

And she said, "No, I don't think we have met."

And he said, "Oh yes, you are that lady who use to leave me nasty messages when I was a teenager cleaning this bank. You need to start leaving friendlier messages."

Bill went on to become the owner of that bank, and the lady started leaving nice messages for the cleaning staff. No matter how big you get, treat people the way you want to be treated. My mother used to tell me, "You meet the same people going up as you will coming down, so treat people with dignity and respect."

In naming some, you inevitably alienate the many people who help you get to where you are today. There were so many people who helped me and my family in a desperate time of need. It's amazing how God will reposition you and give you favor that you do not deserve. These were people that seemingly came out of nowhere to help my family and I when we were in a hopeless situation. When things seem hopeless, that's when God will show up and show out. Usually when we figure we have it all together, we don't think about God much, but when things get crazy in your life, look for God. One of my spiritual fathers,

Bishop Michael E. Ford, would say, "Where there is an entrance to a problem, there has got to be an exit. I have found Jesus to be that way out, time and time again. He is that way of escape. He will not put on you more than you can bare, but with the temptation will make a way of escape.

SUBWAY

"You just keep pushing. You just keep pushing. I made every mistake that could be made. But I just kept pushing.
—Rene McPherson

Somewhere around 2005, we decided to apply for a Subway franchise. Yes, that's right; I have always wanted to be a business owner. I am a great fan of anyone who launches out on faith and starts a business or franchise. I love the story of Ray Kroc, one of the founders of McDonald's; Bill Gates, the founder of Microsoft; and Sam Walton, the founder of Wal-Mart.

These were people who found a need and filled it. There were also local athletes and coaches who had transitioned their life from athletics to business, like Junior Bridgeman, the owner of BF companies, and Wade Houston and Charlie Johnson, former owners of Active Transportation. I sought these people out on a continual basis, particularly Junior Bridgeman the restaurant magnate. I wanted to know how he became so successful in business.

Junior used to play basketball for the University of Louisville back in the 1970s. After his college days, he then went on to have a long and illustrious career in the NBA with the Milwaukee Bucks. I figured this could be someone I could really learn from and get some advice. But if you know Junior, you know he is a man of few words. He is like EF Hutton; when he speaks, people listen. I went to Junior on numerous occasions for advice on the restaurant business. His advice was always the same. You will have to work extremely hard, and you will have to have a second to none commitment. The same advice he gave me, he was given over twenty years ago by the man who mentored him in the restaurant business, Dave Thomas (founder of Wendy's fast food restaurants). After taking the advice of his mentor, Junior has over 150 restaurants; now that's the sweet smell of success.

I had read enough on my own, and talked to enough Subway franchisees to know this was where I wanted to be; at least, that's what I thought at the time. After praying about the opportunity and talking it over with Peggy, we decided to apply for a loan for the franchise fee and the building permits. We were not in the best of financial shape after having lost two jobs, but we acted on crazy faith. There is no substitute for faith that is so fervent that it causes you to march on in the face of doubt and adversity. I was crazy about having the opportunity to redeem myself. I felt like I had been a total failure with the lost opportunity in Boston and now the lost opportunity at Kentucky State. I felt the need to do something great, something substantial, something noteworthy, to bring us out of this financial albatross.

Sometimes God allows us to wander around the same mountain for a reason. Sometimes God will allow you to have your way, until you discover the only way to success is His way. I could not see this all-important lesson at the time. I was too blinded by the perceived lure of success.

TRAINING

It took about a year for us to get financing, read through the circular (the book given to all franchisees on the Subway business), and then do the training in Connecticut. The training was intense and it was tough, really tough. We went over everything relating to the operation of a Subway franchise; not only was there classroom training, but also in-store training. The classroom training was put through the ultimate test when we went to an actual Subway store.

The big test was going from classroom to actually working with a live customer. It was quite an experience, making the sandwiches, relating to the customer, and then working the register. One of the biggest problems I had was not learning the business, but putting on those plastic gloves. I have sweaty hands, so plastic and sweaty hands don't mix too well; it was like oil and water. So I had a devil of a time getting those gloves on. People would step to the line to order a sandwich, and I would be wrestling with those darn gloves holding up the line. Since the sandwiches were all made to order, you had to be fast. Needless to say, I was not the fastest sandwich maker in the business.

Subway has the business down to a science. There is a formula for everything, the amount of meat, the amount of vegetables; everything has been measured right down to the amount of mayonnaise and ketchup to put on a sandwich. All you had to do was follow the plan.

One of the biggest things you have to be aware of in the food service business is your food cost. If you let your food cost get out of line, it can decimate your business. What is food cost? It is the amount of money it takes for you to buy the food, what you sell the food for, and how much you use. If you put too many ingredients in one sandwich, you would have to reorder food faster than ordinary, which means you have to spend more money to buy more food, for resale. This is a formula for disaster.

The second major concern in any business is people. Running a food service business is like recruiting for a basketball team, you not only look for talent, but you better look for character. True enough, it's hard to test a person's character until you put them on the team and see how they react under fire. As hard as we tried to find good character people, inevitably we would get someone who would work well for a week maybe two weeks, and then they would start stealing the food or taking money from the cash register. I remember feeling so used and abused. Here we would give a person a job, which really needed a job, and then they would blow it by stealing or taking money that did not belong to them. It absolutely blew my mind. But in some respects I could relate to the lack of character issues, as I had been known to blow a few golden opportunities myself.

We had security cameras in the store, but it did not matter; if a person wanted to steal, they stole. You cannot make someone do right if they are intent on doing wrong. Everyone has to come to their own reality of what right and wrong is.

One of the biggest decisions we had to make about our new Subway restaurant was its location. We really did not have a choice in the matter. When a spot came available, you either accepted or waited until another spot came open.

Franchise corporate told us that a spot had come open in Wal-Mart. Well quite naturally, we thought this was fantastic. They did not tell us until later that it could either be in the front or the back of a Wal-Mart store. Well if you have walked in any Wal-Mart, you know the place to be is in the front of the store. That way, people see you when they come in, and when they leave. After going back and forth for weeks about the location, corporate finally told us we would be in the back of the store. I felt like Rosa Parks must have felt on December 1, 1955, when she was asked to give up her front seat on the bus she was riding in Montgomery, Alabama. The only problem was I didn't have the same conviction to fight for our right to be in the front of the store; I just rolled with the punches and took the back spot, something that neither Rosa Parks nor Martin Luther King, Jr., would have ever agreed to.

We felt like someone had just robbed us of our American dream. The difference in location could mean the difference between making it big and not making it at all. To add insult to injury, this was one of the oldest Wal-Marts in Louisville at the time.

While the news was dismal I wasn't about to get down and stay down, no. I am a rebounder. What is a rebounder? A rebounder is someone in the game of basketball that positions himself to grab the ball off the rim or backboard once that ball is shot. Rebounders are important; you cannot take a shot or make a pass until you get the rebound. No rebounds, no shots. No rebounds, no victories. It's the same in life; if you are not positioning yourself to rebound from every fall, there will be no shots at success. I love the book *Rebound Rules,* by my mentor Rick Pitino. If you are going to be successful in life you must position yourself to rebound. So we ultimately went with the back of the store decision. We were still upbeat and positive. Besides, corporate was telling us they had good numbers out of back of the store Subways. So we started the building process.

My good friend Mike Cromwell did the construction on the store and got it built in record time. We were off and running. In May of 2006, the doors were open and we were selling sandwiches. We were really excited about our little Subway business. After about two months, our excitement turned to horror as we began to see the back of the store location was a grave mistake. There just were not enough people coming in the back of Wal-Mart to buy Subway sandwiches. It didn't take long to realize, I could not just work in the Subway store, and expect the Subway bills and our own personal bills to get paid. So I went back to selling ads for Kentucky Sports History, which meant Peggy had to take over operation of the store.

While Peggy's leadership qualities are undeniable, her working in the store from open to close was taking a tremendous toll on our family and our already damaged marriage. We were both burning the candle at both ends of the stick. I was working Kentucky Sports History during the day and working on a Master's Degree at night. There was no extra time for marital bliss or family strengthening.

INDIANA WESLEYAN UNIVERSITY

"Great men are little men expanded; great lives are ordinary lives intensified."
—Wilfred A. Peterson

For many years, I had wanted to go back to school and get my master's in business administration. Indiana Wesleyan University gave me that opportunity with its flexible time schedule of attending classes one day a week for two years. While the work was tough, the teachers were all very willing to help any way they could. They also understood that everyone in the class had a real job. I started the classes in August of 2004 and graduated in December 2006. This was a major accomplishment because I had been out of school since 1988.

The thing I liked most about Wesleyan was not only that the professors were very understandable about our work commitments, but also they were all Christian people trying to live for God. We started each class with prayer requests. What a powerful way to start class. I had never been to a Christian school before, although most of my life had been spent in the church.

I was most proud in December 2006, to receive my MBA from Indiana Wesleyan University.

No excuses. We have no excuses for living our dreams. You may be saying I will wait until the kids get out of the house to start dreaming again. No, start now. I hear you say I will wait until I get a better job or my husband gets his promotion. No, start now. All we have is the right now. There is no promise that things will get better, yes I hope and pray and believe they will, but if they don't I still have to pursue, I still have to strive for perfection. So what is stopping you from getting that degree, what is stopping you from starting your own business? Nothing but you.

VACATION

> "The miracle, or the power, that elevates the few is to be found in their industry, application, and perseverance under the promptings of a brave, determined spirit."
> —Mark Twain

After suffering through many trials and tribulations, we decided to close the Subway restaurant. We had to concede that it was probably not God's will, but my will that opened the store. We lost a lot of money, a lot of time, and could have lost our marriage and family. We later had to declare bankruptcy and start over. Even with the losses, there are lessons to be learned, I always try to find the silver lining in any experience, positive or negative.

One of the positives that came out of closing the restaurant was that I had started to send out resumes for coaching jobs. Peggy had pushed me not to give up on my dream of getting back into coaching, no matter how many times I told her no one wanted me. I had sent out hundreds of resumes, all with the same outcome: "Thanks, but no thanks." For years, I had been sending out resumes only to be rejected, so I had stopped trying to send them out. I was tired of the rejection. I knew that I should never give up, but after a while life begins to grind you into pulp; you start to question everything that you ever believed. But in the back of my mind, I knew that God could do anything he wanted to do, if I could only believe. It just seemed like He didn't want to grant my request to get back into coaching. Maybe I had disgraced His name enough; maybe *He* was saying enough is enough.

After closing the store, we decided to leave the past behind and go to Destin, Florida, for a vacation. This was one of the few times we were able to take a vacation with our whole family. My parents played a major role in Peggy and me sticking together, so they made the trip with us.

The trip was fabulous; being near the ocean was absolutely Heavenly. There was only one problem: it rained the whole time we were there. My kids were so frustrated. When you think of going to Florida, you do not think of rain, but sunshine, sand, and the beach. The day before we were suppose to leave to head back to Kentucky, the sun came out. It was like Noah's Ark, when after forty days and nights of rain, the dove flew out of the Ark and found the fig leaf and brought it back to Noah, so Noah knew then the water was subsiding. When the people saw the sun poke its head through the clouds, they came rushing out of their hotel and condos like they had never seen the sand and beach before in there life. Just before going down to the beach to reserve a spot with umbrellas and chairs, I called back home to check our messages. What I heard on the answer machine shocked me into disbelief. The voice on the other end said, "This call is for Winston Bennett. I am Joe Zakowics, athletic director at Mid-Continent University in Mayfield, Kentucky. We would like to talk to you about our men's basketball coaching vacancy." What is this a joke, who is playing around on the recorder? I was astounded and in a state of bewilderment; was this real, after four years of waiting for an opportunity to do what I love, could this be true? I immediately returned the call; the athletic director said they would like to interview me once we returned from vacation. I was so excited and yet paralyzed with fear all at the same time. I didn't know what to do, so I just started praising God, even though I had never heard of the school and did not know where Mayfield, Kentucky, was. I was so happy that anyone wanted me to come and coach their team; it didn't matter where Mayfield was. It could have been on the moon as far as I was concerned.

Certainly all the rejection notices had nothing to do with my coaching resume; my pedigree was as strong as it could be. I spent three years as an assistant at the University of Kentucky, and then went on to become an assistant with the Boston Celtics. Those were the positives. As in life, most people dwell on the negatives. Because of the negatives, I had been passed over hundreds of times in my quest to coach again. I was treated as if I had leprosy.

After my conversation with Coach Zakowics, the athletic director, I explained everything to my family. Everyone was overjoyed that my opportunity to coach again had finally come; not only that, the sun was shining and the kids were antsy to get to the ocean to swim. So I ran feverishly down to the ocean side to reserve a spot with the attendant. The attendant was a joyful fellow, not only pointing me in the direction, but also actually assisting me in setting up the umbrella and chairs. After we had traversed through the hot sand, a little lady appeared from out of nowhere it seemed; actually she surfaced from under the umbrella that was next to ours. She said, "Hello there, my aren't you a big fellow, you look like a Kentucky ball player I use to follow."

Then she said, "You look like Winston Bennett." I was so caught off guard; my words were a little slurred. Why yes, I am he. While amazed at her newfound celebrity, she went on to say her name, but what really blew my mind was when she said, "I am from a small town called Mayfield, Kentucky." I was floored, all the blood rushed out of my body. I couldn't believe it; out of all the places to meet someone from, Mayfield, Kentucky. I mentioned to her, that I had just spoken to an athletic director from Mayfield, Kentucky, from a school called Mid-Continent University. She said, "Oh yes, that's a great school, my daughter went there."

I knew then, this was more than happenstance; this had to be divine intervention. Nothing just happens; everything is divinely filtered, good or bad. What are the odds that my family and I could be thousands of miles away from home and meet a lady who is from the very place that called me about a job. What an awesome God, He does extraordinary things, things that boggle the mind.

The rest of the day was like a blur, all I could think about was the little lady from Mayfield, Kentucky. I went up to the condo and told the rest of the family what happened, and all they could say was it had to be a God thing.

Needless to say, our vacation served its purpose, Peggy and I were able to start the mending process, and the parents and kids had a great time.

Have you ever felt like your greatest opportunity keeps passing you by? Do you feel like your past has stolen your future? Do not despair, I have been there; four years I tried and tried to get back into coaching, but it seemed that everywhere I turned there was only rejection. I had to realize God was not going to allow me to get back into coaching until he felt like I was ready. I want you to keep the faith and keep trying, keep sending out resumes no matter how many rejection notices you receive, keep applying for the loan, and keep looking at the house that you pictured. You have to be completely convinced that eventually that "no" will turn into a "yes", just as it did for me.

COACHING AT MID-CONTINENT

Once back in Kentucky, I went and met with the executive board at Mid-Continent University. I was very impressed with the President, Dr. Robert Imhoff, and the athletic director at the time, Joe Zakowics. I thought this could be a great opportunity, but I did have some major concerns. When I arrived on campus for my meeting, I could not believe what I was seeing. On my first visit, I went right past the microscopic campus, I saw Mid-Continent on the sign, but there wasn't much there. It was not like the large expansive entrance to the University of Kentucky or the Boston Celtics complex. It was just a bleep on the monitor. The school was out in the middle of nowhere. Once on campus I notice there were not many buildings; it was all in a very small area. There was a soccer field, the Mid-Continent Cougars had been known for their soccer team; they had won a couple of championships. There was a baseball diamond, and a softball field, but no basketball court. I looked all around the place, but could not find a basketball court except for the outside, blacktop court that reminded me of where I used to play.

In my meeting with the president, it was evident that as there was no on campus basketball facility; basketball had not meant much at the university. After all, the president was a former soccer player and coach. I noticed also there was not much office space, when I went into what was to be my office, I just about fainted; it was the size of a walk-in closet. I was indeed on the backside of the mountain, as my mother had proclaimed before passing away. With all the negatives, I always try to extract the positives. The first positive I could see was the opportunity to help put this Christian institution on the map for basketball. They were already there in soccer, but the hierarchy wanted to bring me in to change its basketball fortunes and also for my name recognition. I realize the name Winston Bennett means something in the state of Kentucky, even with all my hang-ups and problems; I was still a part of the winningest college basketball program in history, the Kentucky Wildcats. Even though I knew the school wanted me for my name attraction, the biggest thing I could offer was Jesus. There were plenty of great coaches to choose from, but hopefully once they looked beyond all the problems, they could see in me a deep love for Christ. Besides, I felt like I needed Mid-Continent more than it needed me. It was truly a blessing to have this opportunity to do what I loved at an institution that proclaimed the name of Jesus Christ. I was also thankful for my illustrious past of having been associated with the most storied team in NBA history, the Boston Celtics. But I was most grateful for my connection to the winningest program in collegiate history, the Kentucky Wildcats.

Being a part of Kentucky basketball was like being a part of Queen Elizabeth's royal court. There were exclusive privileges given only to the chosen few. One of the privileges was once a Kentucky ball player, always a Kentucky ball player; they never forget you. Most fans can quote your point-per-game average, your rebounding average, and your win-loss record. Basketball is serious business in Kentucky. So it was more than a little tough coming from a place that worshipped basketball and its team, to a place with absolutely no basketball pedigree, no gym, and no plans to build one.

The athletic director did promise me that the inside soccer field would be changed, and a hardwood court would be laid to accommodate basketball. True enough, the athletic director did get a wood floor put over the soccer field, but I didn't know it would be a kitchen floor. When sweat hit the makeshift kitchen wood, the floor instantly turned into the local ice skating rink. We would have to stop practice whenever sweat hit the floor. If it rained, the lights in the gym would immediately go out; practice was halted for thirty minutes to an hour before they came back on, if they came back on at all (in August 2010, the president allowed us to get a real wood floor in our practice facility).

Even with some positives, and a lot of negatives, there were not a lot of schools knocking down my door asking me to coach their team. After much prayer and deliberation, I decided to take the job. This was not a tough decision, coaching the game of basketball was a labor of love. I had spent the majority of my life either playing or coaching the game. I did not have to reinvent the wheel; I was just passing on what had already been placed inside of me.

DEALING WITH SELF

I started the job in June of 2006. I was excited about my new position, yet I still had myself to deal with it. I hated being alone, I always yearned for female companionship. My first month on the job was spent in a hotel, and then eventually I moved into a little house not far from campus. Peggy and the kids would come down when they could. The days in the little two bedroom home reminded me of my childhood, growing up in the little house on Penway. There were days where it felt that the walls could talk, at that time there was no working television in the house so I was in complete solitude. Those times of total loneliness were the worse; those are the times that the silent movies play in my head. You never seem to forget those hot steamy scenes playing with vivid plasma screen clarity, and the surround sound moaning with Luther Vandross playing in the background.

Thank God it wasn't long before my family had moved down to rescue me.

I have a gorgeous wife who dresses to kill, and should be featured in Essence magazine. She is God fearing and the consummate wife. I love her dearly although my past attraction to other women may not substantiate that claim. There has been no excuse for my willful lack of restraint in the area of sex. My pastor in Louisville would tell me, "this ability to overcome your sexual urges must be an *All Consuming Passion*. You are no different from any other man, we all have urges and attractions, but the difference is, we don't give in to them, were you do. You don't fight the feeling. You have got to start fighting for your life."

After making a potentially career ending mistake, a mentor told me, "I don't trust you." I was thinking to myself what do you mean you don't trust me, I was really boiling over inside, I wanted to say something, but I didn't I just listened. He said, "While I don't trust you——I also don't trust myself." He would say, "We all have areas were we have to give the maximum effort in order to get better." He said, "You have to fight just as you did when you were trying to be a great basketball player. That same tenacity you used to defend and grab rebounds will be required to overcome your flaws and weaknesses. I am sure there were days when you did not want to practice and go the extra mile, but you did it because you knew it would make you better." As I thought about his statement, it made a lot of sense. I had given my all to be the best basketball player I could be. I had done whatever it took to make it. Now I would have to use the same strategy to save my life from the ravages of sex addiction.

TEAM TURMOIL

My first season at Mid-Continent was turbulent to say the least. I really did not get much of an opportunity to recruit, so I had to coach the players that were already there; I was playing the hand I had been dealt. We really weren't athletic enough to play the running, pressing style I had been accustomed to playing. We ended up going 4–15 in the conference and 7–25 overall. It was not the type of season I had expected. It was deplorable in my book, and a major disappointment. I didn't come to Mid-Continent to rack up 7–25 seasons; I was hoping to take the cougars to the winner's circle.

After such a trying and turbulent year I really began to question my resolve as a coach. I remember our president, Dr. Robert Imhoff, called me into his office for a meeting. I thought the meeting was going to be one of those highly disappointed meetings over such a lackluster season, but he really called me into his office to make sure I knew why I was at Mid-Continent. He said, "Winston I know you love coaching and I know you love winning, but the real reason you are here is to win souls not games. Yes I want you to do your very best in representing the school on and off the court, but your biggest and most important representation is to Christ. Win these young men to Christ. Let your testimony save those who have the same challenges. Shine the light on darkness so that we all can walk in the light." When I left that meeting I felt totally free of the constraints that winning and losing can place on the psyche. I still wanted to win, that would not change, but I would start to focus on winning souls starting with my own.

DEATH

While our first season was over, there were still trials and tribulations to face. The most difficult was the sickness of my mother. My mother, Shirley Ann Bennett, had been the rock of the family forever. She had contracted rheumatoid arthritis in her forties and had never been the same person. Her mobility to preach and teach had been taken away by the disease. She was the one who told me if I did not get a handle on this sex thing, it would take everything I have, and it has, just as she predicted. But now, she was in the hospital, bleeding to death. The doctors wanted to take her leg, because there was no blood flow to her feet, but after further discussion with the family, we unanimously decided against that option. The doctors then tried a procedure that would cause blood to flow to her feet and ankles, but it didn't work. Along with trying to find ways to save moms leg, now the doctors found that mother was actually losing blood profusely, and there was no hope. She was put on a breathing tube just to keep her alive. This was no way for my mother to live. She had been in pain for so long. One day when I went up to see her, she was singing, "Winston, Winston, Winston, I love you so much," and she would keep singing it. She was talking about my father; they had been married for forty-five years. Through many ups and downs, they had stayed the course. My mother never wanted my father to leave the hospital. He would stay in her room by her side day after day without a break. This went on nonstop for three grueling months.

In the meantime, I was on the road recruiting when I got the call, the day of reckoning had occurred, my mother had passed from this life into glory. I was as far away as I could be and still be in the States; I was in California. When the call came in, it felt like I was frozen in time, motionless, the world stopped.

After an apparent bout with disillusionment, I cried like a baby. It was my mother, the one who brought me life, the one who reared me in the church. The one that never gave up hope that I would one day beat my sexual urges and not let it rule my life. She was my hope; she would never miss a birthday or anniversary without sending a card. She would never let an opportunity go by without saying I love you. Wow, she was the woman that Proverbs 31 talks about a virtuous woman.

On May 12, 2008, my mother Shirley Ann Bennett passed from this life into glory.

I had plenty of time to think about this great woman of God as I flew from California to Louisville, Kentucky. The impression she left on my life and the lives of others are indelibly engraved upon my heart. Her whole life was one of sacrifice, commitment, and perseverance. She was a slave of Jesus Christ. She loved people like Jesus loves the church. She was not moved by money, nice cars, or big houses; she wanted to see Jesus. She would often say, "To be like Jesus, Oh to be like Jesus, all I want, is to be like Him." She would say, "Weeping may endure for a night, but joy comes in the morning."

The gathering at the watch service and the funeral spoke to the life that mother lived. Hundreds of people came to admonish this child of God. I could see by her influence, by watching the crowd, what life was all about. Sometimes my wife and I would sit at the kitchen table having a cup of coffee and one of us would pose the question, "What is life really all about?" We had been around people with more money than they could spend, and yet didn't seem happy, we had been around people with beautiful homes, but didn't seem happy; we had been around people who had the most beautiful cars, but still did not seem happy or content. I think it was Paul who said, "Godliness with contentment hath great gain." Again the question popped into my mind, *what is life all about?* That day, the answer appeared as clear as day. It's all about pleasing God, and how do we please God? By obeying His word. We are supposed to be little replicas of Him. We are to be reflections of his glory. I understand the significance of the WWJD (stands for "What Would Jesus Do?") insignia you sometimes see on peoples' wrists. If I would ask myself what would Jesus do in any situation, I would be a better me, I would make better choices and decisions. That's my goal is to be like Him.

THE 2008–2009 SEASON

The 2008–2009 season would prove to be a bittersweet season. Bitter just remembering I had lost one of the most important people in my life, my mother; sweet because the team showed a remarkable improvement from one year to the next.

The astronomical improvement really started at the end of last season with the recruitment of some top-notch student-athletes. Kenny Thomas, the 6'8" forward/center from Essex, New Jersey, led us in scoring and rebounding; he was a force in the paint. He also made first team All-Trans South Conference.

His teammate at Essex was Donovan Willis, a 6'2" leaper that could handle and shoot. He probably would have led the team in steals if he had not gotten injured on a dunk in the game against Missouri S&T.

Aaron Pearson proved to be the leader of the team. Not only was he a great player but also he was over a 3.0 student. Aaron was a very aggressive point guard that would steal you blind if you did not handle the ball carefully. He had most opposing guards afraid to death to dribble the ball around him; they knew with a blink of an eye Aaron would take their ball and score on the other end.

At the shooting guard spot, we had Josh Woodley, probably the best three-point shooter on the team. If he had his feet set forget it, it was going down for three points. Josh was also over a 3.0 student.

His sidekick David Gratton was probably the most talented player on the team, but he was so undisciplined. He wants to play the girls and have a good time. He had a tough year as a student and as a player. It remains to be seen whether he will discipline himself for this level of play.

TiRon Peoples was our other two guard. Ti has come a long way, he has always been a great athlete who could hit the stand still three point shot, but he has to work on the other parts of his game, like defense and rebounding. He is also a much-improved student.

Keiran Nunley played the small forward position for us. He is very athletic, a great slasher who gets to the rim off the dribble. He needs to work diligently on improving his medium-range jump shot. He also struggled in the classroom. Keiran is an interesting person. He always wears a smile. I find this very encouraging because Keiran comes from a rough background. At times, he is not able to speak to his mother because he does not know where she is. Sometimes she is with relatives; other times she is struggling to find a place to stay, just the other day I called Keiran after hearing that his twenty-six year old brother had died of a brain aneurism.

This is why I must press on, I must continue to fight, I lead young men who are going through a lot more than I. Often times, all I can tell them is to trust God. I can't tell Keiran I understand how he feels to lose his brother, because I am an only child, I can tell him what it means to lose a mother because I have lost mines.

Jerry Follot is another one of those talented players that has just not come into his own yet. Jerry is about 6'6" and can shoot the three-point shot; he will look like an all-star in practice and then disappear in the games. He has got to learn to just play. His number one comment has been, "I am scared of messing up." You cannot go through life being scared of messing up. Guess what? You are going to mess up in this game we call life, but you have to keep on playing, make note of the mistakes, learn from them, and just keep on playing.

At the power forward spot was Sinsa Korkut. Sinsa was one of those guys that just does whatever it takes to win. He rebounds but does not jump very high; he posts up and always finds a way to get his shot off. He was just a winner. He was over a 3.0 student.

Ansil Williams plays the center position for us. Ansil has come a long way. He still must get better at making free throws, but he works hard. He is a tremendous young man, as is all our players.

Kazim Ahouno also plays the center and the four spot for us. I am so impressed with this young man because of his demeanor. Kazim did not get much playing time this year but never complained, he just kept on working. Kazim is also over a 3.0 student, he had all A's.

As you can see, I have been blessed with a great group of young men. All of these guys are young men you would not mind your daughter bringing home. It is my job not only to be a good coach but also to let them see Jesus Christ in me. That is my ultimate job, to win souls for Christ. I am not talking about ramming it down their throat, but just being an example of Jesus Christ. Follow me as I follow Christ. Will I make mistakes? Absolutely, but my heart is to follow Christ and to strive for perfection in Him.

With this group of young men, we went 10–6 in the conference and 15- 15 overall. This is the best record the school has had
in basketball and the first winning season in the conference. The
LORD truly is doing a great work in us.

I would be remiss if I did not mention the glue guys that
make our team a success. Besides the players themselves, the
managers and coaching staff are the real glue. These are the guys
that get very little glory, but do all the grunt work that has to be
done in order for any team to be successful.

David Smith was one of the assistants that I kept on board
when I first got the job here at Mid-Continent. Coach Smith is
probably ten to fifteen years my senior, and is a very wise man.
He was more than just a coach; he is my friend and accountability partner. He was the one instrumental in recruiting this great
talent of young student athletes. Shortly after our season, Coach
Smith came to me and told me that the Lord was leading him
in a different direction. He was leading him into advancement
or fundraising. Mid-Continent is a small school that has experienced explosive growth of about 2000 students. This includes
the Advantage program, which is a program for working adults
who want to get their degree; they can get it at night one day a
week for two years. Mid-Continent also brings the classroom
to you, as they are in partnership with many businesses in Kentucky and Illinois. They will actually have their professors come
to your place of business and teach class.

Mid-Continent University does not have its own arena, yet.
We play our basketball games at Mayfield High School, which
seats about 5,000 people. While we thank the people at Mayfield
High School, we still need our own facility. So this is one of the
endeavors that Coach Smith is working on by being a part of the
advancement program.

I envision Mid-Continent having its own multi-purpose facility seating three thousand students for games and graduations. The facility will have three basketball courts. One court will be the main court for men's and women's basketball games, the other two will be used as practice courts for men's and women's basketball and volleyball, can you see it? It sounds crazy right a school that presently utilizes a High School for graduation and to play its games, I just happen to serve a crazy God who can do anything. I have no idea where the money for this endeavor will come from, but I serve a God who is rich in houses and land, He holds the palm of the world in his hand. Our campus has experienced phenomenal growth; we need a new chapel, new residence halls, etc. I believe God has the person out there right now who can bring the vision into reality.

Great accomplishments don't happen on their own it takes people who are willing to buy into the vision of the leader. My top assistant was newly hired Howard Dillard. Coach Dillard's dad used to coach at Mid-Continent, and Coach Dillard use to play at Mid-Continent, so he was a natural fit. He is not only my top assistant, but he also coaches our junior varsity program, along with working at the Calloway Sheriff's Department. So he wears a lot of different hats.

My final assistant is Ryan Smith. Ryan is a young man with a lot of energy. He was a graduate assistant for us this past season and will be a full-time assistant this year. He absolutely loves his job. He will be a great head coach one day.

2009–2010 SEASON

This was truly a banner year. We knew going into the season we had a chance to do something special, with all the guys we had coming back from last year's team. Our seniors didn't disappoint. We ended up going 24–13 overall, 12 -4 in the conference. It was the most successful year to date in Mid-Continent basketball history. We finished second in the Trans South conference a first for the school in basketball. We went on to the national Christian tournament (NCCA tournament made up of Christian colleges and universities) and finished third, again a first for the school in basketball. I was also able to win Coach of the Year honors in the Trans South Conference, a very humbling honor of which I am grateful.

The accomplishment I am most proud of is the graduation of four of our seniors, Donavon Willis, Josh Woodley, TiRon Peoples, and Kazim Ahouno. The rest of the senior class is coming back for a fifth year to complete their degree (Kenny Thomas, David Gratton, Sinsa Korkut, and Aaron Pearson).

Mid-Continent is one of the few schools that will scholarship their student athletes to come back to finish their degree. Our president is such a stickler for education that he does not let our students leave the school without a degree. His only requirement is the student athlete must have shown progressive acceleration towards their degree for their full tenure at the University. Student-athletes are expected to work in the athletic department, sweeping, cleaning, or anything else that might need to be done around the school. What a small price to pay for a fifth year scholarship.

This has been a wonderful year not only for us on the court, but for me personally. It's been the best year spiritually in a long time. God is blessing me and my family in a supernatural way. We believe as our pastor declared it's the year of the supernatural, this is the year of overflow, of more than enough. I know you think I am crazy since we are in a recession, and the big three automakers have all declared bankruptcy, many top businesses has either totally collapsed or needed government intervention, like AIG, Fannie Mae and Freddie Mac. Bernie Madoff swindled over $50 billion of taxpayer money and was sentenced to 150 years in prison and on and on and on. I still believe it's the year of overflow, countless blessings in the midst of mass layoffs and foreclosures. This is crazy you say. You are right; it's crazy faith. If you are going to make it in today's turbulent society, you need crazy faith. When all Hell is breaking lose, it takes crazy faith to know that God's got you covered. He knows the end from the beginning. Why worry when He's got everything in his hands? When I worry, it's because I think that I am in control. Well guess what, we are not in control; yes, there are choices that we are responsible for making, but God is in control.

GREAT EXPECTATIONS

The greater the struggle, the greater the blessings. How can I forget the story of Job? Job was a wealthy man in Biblical times. If he were living today, his wealth would compare to Warren Buffett or Bill Gates. Job had astronomical wealth.

The Lord asked Satan, "Have you considered my servant, Job?" Satan had been to and fro on the face of the earth.

The Lord told Satan, "There is none like him on the earth; he is a blameless and upright man, one who fears God and shuns evil."

Satan replied, "Does Job fear God for nothing? You have placed a hedge around him, no wonder he serves you. If you will take that hedge from around him, he will curse you to your face." So God told Satan, "You can do anything you want to him, except mess with his soul and spirit." So Satan went and destroyed all of Job's cattle, he destroyed his servants, and he destroyed his sons and daughters. As if that wasn't enough, Satan went back and asked God to afflict his skin and his bones, but Job still didn't curse God or lose his integrity. He came back after his wife told him to curse God and die, and said, "Woman are you crazy? Naked I came into the world, naked I will return, the Lord giveth and the Lord taketh away, blessed be the name of the Lord."

No matter what Job encountered, he was determined to stick with the Lord and hold fast to his integrity. Because he was sold out, committed, and dedicated to Christ, in the end the Lord gave him double for his trouble. Now that's great expectations. There have been days where I felt like Job; it seemed like everything was going wrong, but the Lord would bring this story back to my remembrance, double for your trouble. You may be facing an addiction, loss of a marriage, children are acting up, just remember, double for your trouble. You may have loss your house; you may have loss your job, but remember, double for your trouble.

One of the reasons I have crazy faith is due to my Pastor Anthony Walton. He is the epitome of great expectations and crazy faith. He is a prime example of someone who *Fights For His Life*. Pastor Walton has not always been a pastor; in his book *Under the Shadow*, he tells how at one point in his life he was facing a twelve-year prison sentence for armed robbery. He had spotted a lady at a car wash and decided to rob her; for whatever reason, he was not picked up until five years later, after he had changed his life around and had decided to do what was right. He had gotten married and was working in a grocery store. And then one day, his lawyer called with the news that he had to turn himself in after five years of being a free man. He had been married for two years already. As he went into prison facing twelve years, he wondered what would become of his marriage and what would become of him. He knew he could not do twelve years. He began to wonder why, after five years of doing the right thing, would he be picked up now. He was a burgeoning comedian that could have been the next Richard Pryor, or Steve Harvey; he had it all going for him and now this.

The only thing that gave him hope was an old Bible in the corner of his cell; he was just at the point of taking his life, and committing suicide when his eyes spotted the Bible. When he spotted the Bible, he picked it up, but when he picked it up, he dropped it. When he picked it up for the second time, it had opened to Isaiah who said:

> Surely the arm of the Lord is not too short to save, nor his ear too dull to hear. But your iniquities have separated you from

your God; your sins have hidden his face from you, so that he
will not hear.

Isaiah 59:1–2 (NIV)

After reading these words, a peace came over him. He began to
remember his Sunday school teacher and how she told him Jesus
cares about you. As he began to think about those moments,
he kneeled by his bed and began to cry out to God for help.
To make a long story short the Lord did help, he remorsefully
repented of his sins, and he found Christ in his cell. The twelve-
year sentence was changed to a little over three years. After
coming out of prison with a committed love for Christ, he went
back to work at the little grocery store were he first began. After
working a while at the grocery store, his pastor Bishop Sherman
Merritt from Nashville, Tennessee, had summoned one of his
ministers to start a work in Paducah, Kentucky. The minister
that was working in that area gave up the work after a few trips
to the small town; he could not see that his effort was producing
the results of a vibrant ministry. Brother Walton was eventually
asked to take over the ministry in the little storefront church.
Sunday after Sunday, he would act in faith and go from Nashville to Paducah to minister to as few as a handful of people.
The location of the small church was in a noted drug-infested
area, with prostitution and gambling; it was public enemy number one. No one in their right mind would start a ministry in
such a dilapidated area. But neither the area nor the sparse numbers deterred Brother Walton from acting in faith and obedi-
ence. Little by little five people, became ten, and then fifteen,
it wasn't long before the small storefront became a full-fledged
congregation.

While it didn't happen overnight, it did happen, the once
full-fledged armed robber became the minister of Jesus Christ.

Pastor Walton's congregation has grown so much that now the people have out grown the church. He told the people a while back, that "God will have to build us another church; we have out grown this storefront." Just after he made the proclamation, the church went on a fast. On the first day of the fast, the mayor of the city of Paducah called, and told Pastor Walton that he knew a builder that had a building that he was looking to get rid of. So the mayor sat up a meeting for the builder and Pastor Walton. In the meeting, the builder told Pastor Walton that he was praying for someone who needed his building, and the Lord sent you. He said, "You know what; I may just give you this building." So just like the pastor had prayed and proclaimed days before, that the Lord would make a way out of no way, He did. Now, Pastor Walton believes in faith, that God will bless the church with the finances it needs to build and furnish the new church. Now that is great expectation.

We have no excuses, no matter what you are facing twelve years in prison, or twelve days, God can deliver with a mighty and outstretched hand.

DECIDING THAT
I WANTED TO WIN

My team at Mid-Continent University started winning when they got tired of losing and discovered that their way wasn't working. As a result, they began to find ways to improve themselves individually and as a team.

That proved to be my answer for victory as well. When I had gotten tired enough of being defeated, tired of constantly being embarrassed and of embarrassing others, tired of feeling like a failure, I decided to do whatever it took to win—and my efforts began to show results.

This was war. I had an enemy called sexual addiction, and I had to learn to fight him—and win. I had been a loser too long.

Aside from the things all of us do to grow and be strengthened spiritually—reading the Bible, regular church attendance, fellowship with other believers, and fasting and prayer—there are some specific and very practical things that I discovered I could do to help myself, and I began to put them into action.

First, I stopped trying to do everything myself, and became part of a team. Until that moment, I had struggled alone—and in vain—to overcome. From that moment on, I never tried to work at it alone. One person couldn't do it, but a whole team could.

On my team I recruited, my wife, my children, my parents, my pastor, my fellow coaches, my players, and my counselor.

Peggy was the first and most important member on my team. As my wife, she holds me accountable. When I leave home, I first tell her where I'm going, and then I call her after I have arrived at my destination. When preparing to return home, I call her again and let her know that I'm leaving, and she knows about what time to expect me home. If I ever fail to follow this agreed-upon routine, she will know that something is wrong.

If I have to go out of town, I invite my wife, my father, or a fellow coach to go along. I try to never go alone. If I need to stay overnight, I always try to take someone with me. There are times where it's not always feasible for someone to be with me; during those times I rely heavily on calling and texting Peggy for accountability. It's not that I need a babysitter. It's just that I don't want to take any unnecessary chances with my soul.

Pastor Anthony Walton, along with Bishop Michael E. Ford, provides the spiritual oversight for my life. Their spiritual insight has proven invaluable to my continued success.

I also see a Christian counselor who holds me accountable. I will admit, I don't always want to follow this routine, but in order for me to be the best me I can be, I have to stick to the game plan. There have been those times when I decided I could handle my problem myself without sticking to the game plan, when those times occurred I suffered devastating and humiliating defeat. No matter how often your conscience tells you you can make it on your own, denounce that persuasive voice and know this is not a walk that can be conquered on your own. You cannot be the Lone Ranger in this battle; it will take the whole cavalry to win.

Through counseling and Christian teaching, I have learned that the battle starts in my mind. It was there that negative thoughts began, and I had to learn to dismiss them quickly, and never linger on them, and give them room to grow. When the thought came to me to speak to a lady and get her phone number, I had to fight it. I could no longer just give in. This was a fight for my life; it was an all-consuming passion.

This war was not with a magazine publisher, an Internet provider, or a woman. The enemy was in me. I was the problem, and I had to take control. If the power to do these acts was in me, then the power *not* to do them was in me too. I could make a decision not to date any woman other than my wife. This did not rid me of temptation, but it did give me the power I needed to fight. Drug addicts, alcoholics, and smokers don't just quit what they are doing cold turkey, they have to distance themselves, change their attitude, change their environment, and get counseling. The next step is the biggest and then they have to put into practice everything that they have learned, the easiest thing to do would be to go back to the addictive behavior, the hardest thing to do will be to fight. It's a great thing to educate yourself as much as possible about the enemy you face, but education is nothing without application. We have to determine in our minds to fight. Women don't just disappear, they are not going to stop being attractive. I remember a young man who was having women problems decided to go to the church and see a wise old priest in his eighties, and asked him what he should do about his endless attraction to women. The young man was excited to finally meet someone who could give him the key to defeating his problem, this was a patriarch a man of God someone who prayed daily and fasted often. So with courage and conviction he said, "old man of God when will this uncontrollable attraction to women go away." The old Priest scratched his head, looked up to heaven, as if to say Lord forgive me for what I am about to say, and said, young man you have to ask someone older than me.

Wow!!! What a revelation, here is a Priest eighty years old and he still found women attractive. The moral of the story is if the problem is not going away then we have to work on ourselves and discipline ourselves to do the right thing and make the right decisions. The same can be said for any life controlling issue, the issues don't all of a sudden just walk out of our lives, we have to fight to keep our self-clean and do the right thing. Life is a fight; no one goes through life without fighting. In fights you take some hits and give some hits. We get knocked down but we find our way up. There is no disgrace in getting knocked down; the disgrace is not trying to get up once you get knocked down. After being knocked down over and over again, I found the secret. The secret was in my will to do the right thing; it was in my will to fight. It hurt my flesh when there was something I really wanted to do and couldn't, but when I understood that eternal damnation awaited me if I did those things, the decision became easier. I had to understand that a lot of us have the same fight, I am not the only man that is attracted to women, you are not the only women attracted to men, and so what is the answer? The answer is in the discipline and in the desire to do what's right. We all can chose to go our own way with no rules and no values, but sooner or later we would destroy ourselves. Rules and regulations are put in place to keep us from annihilating ourselves. My first order of business is to obey the rules and regulations that God has set forth in His word. The word of God is my road map for success.

So a big key for my victory has been understanding my limitations, knowing what I can and cannot do. There are some things I will never be able to do, at least not alone, and there are some places I will never be able to go without a team member

FIGHT FOR YOUR LIFE

accompanying me. There are movies that I cannot watch because watching them might cause me to think about an old girlfriend, and relapse back into my old way of thinking. Guilt and shame are my enemies, and I avoid them like a plague. They often lead me to seek isolation and to feel that God was going to punish me. I try to keep my line of communication open with God and with the people who are important to my success at all times.

Deception and lying are such a big part of the sexual addiction cycle that I avoid any form of lying and work to keep my life soundly in the light. I have had to learn to become brutally honest. And no matter how ugly the circumstances, I insist on shining the light into it. Where light is, darkness has to go.

Many times, when I was less than honest with Peggy and she later found out about it, I was somehow relieved. Now I try to live in truth daily, so as not to leave any room for surprises.

I once heard the story of a wise old man who lived in the foothills of Venice, Italy. It was said that the old man, who, incidentally, was blind, could answer any question that was posed to him.

One day two youngsters thought they would fool the old man. So they proceeded up the mountain to confront him.

When they found the old man, one of them said, "Old man, we hear that you can answer any question posed to you. In my hand is a bird. Is the bird dead, or is the bird alive? What do you say?" And he smiled; sure that he had at last fooled the blind man.

The old man scratched his head and looked bewildered. Then, after only a moment of hesitation, he answered, "If I were to tell you that the bird was alive, you would close your hand and crush it to death. But if I were to tell you that the bird is dead, then you would open your hand and let the bird fly away. The answer to your question is in your hands."

Whatever question you are facing today, the answer is in your hands. If you want to overcome your addiction, it's in your hands. If you want a better job, it's in your hands. If you want more money, guess what, it's in your hands. Everything you want and need is in your hands.

This is a great truth. The Scriptures teach us:

> "Furthermore, tell the people, This is what the Lord says: See, I am setting before you the way of life and the way of death."
>
> Jeremiah 21:8 (NIV)

So, it's up to me. God has set life and death before me, and it is up to me to walk in Him, and make the right decisions.

And this message is for you, too. No matter what you are facing in life, the solution to the problem is in your hands.

Jesus confirmed this truth when He said:

> From the days of John the Baptist until now, the kingdom of heaven has been forcefully advancing, and forceful men lay hold of it.
>
> Matthew 11:12 (NIV)

Take it, my friend. Victory is yours, but you must fight. Nothing just happens. You have to forcefully and violently take it. In other words, fight for it. Fight for a better you; fight to lose the unwanted pounds, fight to get your education, fight. Nothing happens without a knock down drag out fight.

FROM TRAGEDY TO TRIUMPH

As I said at the start, my life has been crazy, but what I meant was my life has been led by crazy faith, through ups and through downs; crazy faith in God has brought us safe thus far. It's not enough to just have crazy faith; you also must have a crazy will to fight. The greatest fighter I have ever known was Muhammad Ali; Cassius Marcellus Clay was his name before his conversion. Ali use to say, "I am the Greatest, I am the Greatest." He said this statement so much that he started to believe it, and then he went out and proved it. When you are fighting for your life, it's not enough just to say it; you have to go out and prove it. We are all in a fight of some kind; I could not battle the strangle hold sex had on me until I understood I was in a fight for my life. I could no longer play around with old girlfriends and collect phone numbers; I was in a fight. I was in a fight for my family, my career, and for my life. When you determine that nothing will take your family, your career, or your spirit, you will fight for your life.

So what is tragedy to triumph? The tragedy has been the Hell that my life has been through because of a willful disobedience of God's word. I knew what His word said but I didn't always do it. I had allowed sex to be my God instead of the one true God, Jesus Christ. That's true tragedy when something other than God rules and controls your life.

The triumph has been my wife and family sticking with me through this gruesome process. Marriages today don't last; fifty percent of all marriages end in divorce, and the stat is even higher for Christians. Most marriages would have been in divorce court after the first infidelity. I have countless infidelities to my record. So the triumph continues to be my wife, Peggy Bennett, the lady who most exhibits God's love and faithfulness to me. God loved us when we were not fit to be loved. Peggy has continued to love me through unspeakable hardship, I have not been fit to be loved yet this woman has shown me the agape love that only God can give.

I said publicly on ESPN's program Outside the Lines that if the tables were turned and Peggy was the one who was sleeping around, I don't think I could do what she has done, and be a person of unconditional forgiveness. In truth, I know I couldn't. After having said that, I received an email from a gentleman who saw the interview and wanted to tell me how nauseous my statement made him. He said, "How could you say you wouldn't forgive your wife as much as she has forgiven you, if she happens to lay with a man. You make me sick." The reason I said I couldn't do it is the same reason that Peggy says she didn't do it, but God did. God has done a special work in her heart. If I was to be put in the same circumstances, God would have to do a special work in my heart as well.

We all know its God's will for us to forgive and turn the other cheek, but for most of us, it would take an act of Congress to forgive countless infidelities. Why has my wife stayed with me when most marriages would have disintegrated? I believe that she has an unquestionable belief that God can do anything. When I say anything, I mean anything. We have seen people miraculously get healed of cancer, we have seen dead people get raised to life, and we have seen other marriages revived from divorce. So we believe that the same God who performed miracles of healing, brought the dead back to life, can also deliver our marriage. While we wholeheartedly believe that God can instantly deliver anyone from anything, most problems are solved through God's divine process. I can't overemphasize that total deliverance is usually a process. I think when God says you are healed you are healed instantly, but it takes us a long process to believe in the healing. No one wakes up cured of any extreme weakness or addiction overnight, it's usually a process.

Sex has ruled my life since I was a teenager. I can't expect to wake up and expect the attraction to women to just be a thing of the past. I wish it was that easy. I can expect with every stand I take, with every "no" I make, that the battle will get easier. The key is in my will to fight. No matter how many times I fall, I have to get up and fight again. I have to realize, too, that a person can only take so much, so I could lose my wife and my family on the road to recovery, but I still have to keep fighting. When you see a boxing match and a truly ferocious fighter who wants to win gets hit with a surprising blow, which drops him to the canvas, does he just stay there?

No. He is grabbing for the ropes, stumbling, tripping, and maybe even falling again but all the while trying to get up. There have been many times where I thought I had it licked and got hit with an upper cut that took me to the canvas, if you would be honest with yourself life has thrown you some upper cuts as well. So what are we going to do, lay here and wallow in self-pity or get up and keep fighting? I chose to fight, what about you. Fighting is an action word, you have to do something, throw some punches, rope a dope, but do something. We are fighting for our lives here; don't look at me I am fighting too.

As you continue to fight for your life, remember this poem, called the *Man in the Mirror*:

When you get what you want in your struggle for success and life makes you King for a day, go to the mirror and look at yourself and see what that man has to say, for it isn't your father or mother or wife, whose judgment upon you must pass, but the fellow whose verdict counts most in life is the one stirring back from the glass, you may be like Jack Horner and chisel a plum and think that you are a wonderful guy, but the man in the mirror says you only a bum if you can't look him straight in the eye, for he is the fellow to please; never mind all the rest, for he's with you clear and until the end and you've passed your most dangerous and difficult test if the man in the mirror is your friend, You may fool the whole world down the pathway of years and get pats on the back as you pass, but your final reward will be heartache and tears if you've cheated the man in the glass.

(Author unknown)

Life, with all its distractions, can cause us to lose focus on the things that are really most important. There's nothing that's more important than my family, my soul, and my spirit. For a long time, I have put success before my family; I have put sexual stimulation before my family; but now the game is over, and the fight is on. I have decided to fight for my life. My soul and my spirit want to be with Jesus one day, and hear him say, "Well done my good and faithful servant." There is nothing more important than to make my savior happy.

So fight my friends. Fight for your life.

EPILOGUE

My life is still a fight, and I believe it always will be. Occasionally, I am challenged, when an old girlfriend comes into town and calls to ask how I'm doing, or when my mind reflects on one of those steamy scenes of the past. I cannot say that I'm no longer tempted when this occurs. But each time, I must reach deep within, find the strength God has given me, and fight. Now, more than ever, I love my wife, my family, and my Lord. But the fight still rages on. I am not out of the woods yet. Every day brings a new challenge. Some days are easier than others, but I still have to keep my guard up. Whenever I rest or think that I have this fight won, I get hit with an upper cut that floors me.

The relationship between Peggy and I has suffered so many blows that it seemed to be all but destroyed, but through prayer and continued counseling the two of us have decided to keep fighting together. My relationship with my children is also greatly improved since I have more time at home with them. Professionally, I'm enjoying my time as head coach at Mid-Continent University, but I'm also preparing for a very different future. God has been so good to me that I must share my experiences with others, and I plan to do that more and more.

My plan to share my story is one that has been further ingratiated with the life of one of my distance mentors, Tyler Perry. Now Mr. Perry doesn't know he's my mentor, but often times we never know who is looking at our lives, we never fully realize the lives we touch when we decide to be transparent with our story. My story is not one that I wanted to give to the world, willingly. But again, I felt like my life could help those who have the same struggle. On October 20, 2010 I sat mesmerized by Tyler Perry's story, as he sat tearfully explaining to Oprah Winfrey how as a youngster he had been molested on countless occasions. Each time he was molested he said the perpetrators left him with baggage he did not want. After all the years of molestation Mr. Perry said he really did not start to find himself and regain his life until he understood that the baggage that had been left with him was not his. He didn't have to be afraid of people who had stolen his childhood innocence. He no longer had to fear his father, who had victimized him on several occasions. While my story is not one of molestation, it is one of fear, the fear of never being good enough, and running to something that I thought was my saving grace: sex. It has taken me thirty years to understand that, like Terry Perry said, I am not my past, I am not what has happened to me or what I have done, I am what God says I am, I am a child of the King.

My grandmother's prediction that I would become a nationally known speaker has come to pass. I've been giving motivational and inspirational programs all over the country. As for the book she predicted that I would write...well, you're reading it.

May all the glory be unto our Lord and Savior Jesus Christ.

HAVE WINSTON BENNETT SPEAK AT YOUR NEXT EVENT OR CONFERENCE!

Winston Bennett is available for keynote presentations and full-day seminars. He is a frequent speaker at associations, business meetings, churches and conferences of all types.

Winston knows that what we need is not another motivational speech with a lack of action, knowledge without application is wasted time. His Fight for Your Life program will move you to action. Having the game plan to fight for your company, your family, and your relationships is the key to success in every area of life. Winston will not only motivate and inspire you, but he will also give you the steps to get in the ring and fight, and defeat the enemy that has defeated you. What we need today is leadership that will take the bull by the horns and fight. Usually the fight is not against your competition, the fight is in you. It's the inner fight against fear, procrastination, and those negative thoughts that wreak your date with success.

Winston's raving fans include: Cleveland Schools, Fidelity Investments, Detroit Diesel, Glenmoor Country Club, Internal Revenue Service, Kentucky Procurement Association, Kentucky Schools, Kentucky Propane Gas Association, KCJEA-KMCA Joint Summer Convention, Kentucky State University, Kentucky Tennis Hall of Fame, Kentucky Society of Certified Public Managers, Inc., Michigan Schools, Mid-Continent University, Purchase Area Development District, TC Enterprises (Quixtar), University of Kentucky, just to name of few.

Winston's presentations are a combination of innovation, motivation, and inspiration. Contact him today to elevate the minds, the thoughts, and the attitudes of your association, your business, or your organization.

Also send Winston your name, address, and, email and get the 5 Secrets to Fight for Your Life. For more information visit him on the web.

Winston Bennett MBA
Motivational/Inspirational Speaker/Author
www.winstonbennett.net
www.fite4yourlife.com (twitter)
www. facebook.com

RECOMMENDED READING

As a Man Thinketh, by James Allen. This edition published by Barnes & Noble, Inc. 1992

Bounce Back, by John Calipari with David Scott. New York, NY: Division of Simon & Schuster, Inc. 2009

Failing Forward, by John Maxwell. Nashville, Tennessee: Thomas Nelson, Inc. 2000

False Intimacy, by Dr. Harry W. Schaumburg. Colorado Springs, Colorado: Nav Press, 1997

Flagrant Foul, by Barry Jones. Mustang, Oklahoma: Tate Publishing, LLC. 2008

Out Of The Shadows, by Patrick Carnes, Ph.D. Center City, Minnesota: Hazelden, 1994

Quiet Strength, by Tony Dungy with Nathan Whitaker. Cold Stream, Illinois: published By Tyndale House Publishers, Inc. 2007

Rebound Rules, by Rick Pitino with Pat Forde. New York, NY: HarperCollins Publishers, 2008

Swim Upstream, by Dave Myers. Mustang, Oklahoma: Tate Publishing, LLC. 2010

The Magic of Thinking Big, by David J. Schwartz, Ph.D. New York, NY: Simon & Schuster, Inc. 1987

Think and Grow Rich, by Napoleon Hill. New York, NY: Ballantine Books, 1960

Under The Shadow, by Anthony E. Walton. Clarksville, Tennessee: I.T.N.O.J. Publishing Consultants (IPC), 2004

Who Knew It Was Broken, by John Gibbs. Hyattsville, Maryland: Capricorn Publishing, 2008

Winston Bennett MBA
Motivational/Inspirational Speaker/Author
www.winstonbennett.net
www.fite4yourlife.com (twitter)
www. facebook.com